WHAT DOES
A WOMAN WANT?

THE LACANIAN CLINICAL FIELD

A series of books edited by
Judith Feher Gurewich, Ph.D.
in collaboration with Susan Fairfield

WHAT DOES
A WOMAN WANT?

SERGE ANDRÉ

FOREWORD BY FRANCES L. RESTUCCIA
TRANSLATED BY SUSAN FAIRFIELD

OTHER

Other Press
New York

Production Editor: Robert D. Hack

This book was set in 11 pt. Berkeley by Alpha Graphics of Pittsfield, New Hampshire.

Library of Congress Cataloging-in-Publication Data

André, Serge.
    ⌐Que veut une femme? English]
    What does a woman want? / Serge André ; foreword by Frances L. Restuccia : translated by Susan Fairfield.
        p.   cm.
    Translation of: Que veut une femme?
    Includes bibliographical references (p. 329) and index.
    ISBN 1-892746-28-X (pbk. : alk. paper)
    1. Women and psychoanalysis.   2. Women—Psychology.
3. Femininity.   I. Title.
BF175.A69613   1999
155.3'33—dc21   98-50494

To the woman who knows how to lie to me . . .

Contents

The Lacanian Clinical Field:
Series Overview

Lacanian psychoanalysis exists, and the new series, The Lacanian Clinical Field, is here to prove it. The clinical expertise of French practitioners deeply influenced by the thought of Jacques Lacan has finally found a publishing home in the United States. Books that have been acclaimed in France, Italy, Spain, Greece, South America, and Japan for their clarity, didactic power, and clinical relevance will now be at the disposal of the American psychotherapeutic and academic communities. These books cover a range of topics, including theoretical introductions; clinical approaches to neurosis, perversion, and psychosis; child psychoanalysis; conceptualizations of femininity; psychoanalytic readings of American literature; and more. Thus far nine books are in preparation.

Though all these works are clinically relevant, they will also be of great interest to those American scholars who have taught and used Lacan's theories for over a decade. What better opportunity for the academic world of literary criticism, philosophy, human sciences, women's studies, film studies, and multicultural studies finally to have access to the clinical insights of a theorist known primarily for his revolutionary vision of the formation of the human subject. Thus The Lacanian Clinical Field goes beyond introducing the American clinician to a different psychoanalytic outlook. It brings together two communities that have grown progressively estranged from each other. For indeed, the time when the Frankfurt School, Lionel Trilling, Erich Fromm, Herbert Marcuse, Philip Rieff, and others were fostering exchanges between the academic and the psychoanalytic communities is gone, and in the process psychoanalysis has lost some of its vibrancy.

The very limited success of ego psychology in bringing psychoanalysis into the domain of science has left psychoanalysis in need of a metapsychology that is able not only to withstand the pernicious challenges of psychopharmacology and psychiatry but also to accommodate the findings of cognitive and developmental psychology. Infant research has put many of Freud's insights into question, and the attempts to replace a one-body psychology with a more interpersonal or intersubjective approach have led to dissension within the psychoanalytic community. Many theorists are of the opinion that the road toward scientific legitimacy requires a certain allegiance with Freud's detractors, who are convinced that the unconscious and its sexual underpinnings are merely an aberration. Psychoanalysis continues to be practiced, however, and according to both patients and analysts the uncovering of unconscious motivations continues to provide a sense of relief. But while there has been a burgeoning of different psychoanalytic schools of thought since the desacralization of Freud, no theoretical agreement has been reached as to why such relief occurs.

Nowadays it can sometimes seem that Freud is read much more scrupulously by literary critics and social scientists than by psychoanalysts. This is not entirely a coincidence. While the psychoanalytic community is searching for a new meta-psychology, the human sciences have acquired a level of theoretical sophistication and complexity that has enabled them to read Freud under a new lens. Structural linguistics and structural anthropology have transformed conventional appraisals of human subjectivity and have given Freud's un-conscious a new status. Lacan's teachings, along with the works of Foucault and Derrida, have been largely responsible for the explosion of new ideas that have enhanced the inter-disciplinary movement pervasive in academia today.

The downside of this remarkable intellectual revolution, as far as psychoanalysis is concerned, is the fact that Lacan's contribution has been derailed from its original trajectory. No longer perceived as a theory meant to enlighten the prac-tice of psychoanalysis, his brilliant formulations have been both adapted and criticized so as to conform to the needs of purely intellectual endeavors far removed from clinical re-ality. This state of affairs is certainly in part responsible for Lacan's dismissal by the psychoanalytic community. More-over, Lacan's "impossible" style has been seen as yet another proof of the culture of obscurantism that French intellectu-als seem so fond of.

In this context the works included in The Lacanian Clini-cal Field should serve as an eye-opener at both ends of the spectrum. The authors in the series are primarily clinicans eager to offer to professionals in psychoanalysis, psychiatry, psychology, and other mental health disciplines a clear and succinct didactic view of Lacan's work. Their goal is not so much to emphasize the radically new insights of the Lacanian theory of subjectivity and its place in the history of human sciences as it is to show how this difficult and complex body of ideas can enhance clinical work. Therefore, while the American clinician will be made aware that Lacanian psychoanalysis is not primarily a staple of literary criticism or philosophy but a praxis meant to cure patients of their psychic distress, the academic community will be exposed for the first time to a reading of Lacan that is in sharp contrast with the literature that has thus far informed them about his theory. In that sense Lacan's teachings return to the clinical reality to which they primarily belong.

Moreover, the clinical approach of the books in this series will shed a new light on the critical amendments that literary scholars and feminist theoreticians have brought to Lacan's conceptualization of subjectivity. While Lacan has been applauded for having offered an alternative to Freud's biological determinism, he has also been accused of nevertheless remaining phallocentric in his formulation of sexual difference. Yet this criticism, one that may be valid outside of the clinical reality—psychoanalysis is both an ingredient and an effect of culture—may not have the same relevance in the clinical context. For psychoanalysis as a praxis has a radically different function from the one it currently serves in academic discourse. In the latter, psychoanalysis is perceived both as an ideology fostering patriarchal beliefs and as a theoretical tool for constructing a vision of the subject no longer dependent on a phallocratic system. In the former, however, the issue of phallocracy loses its political impact. Psychoanalytic practice can only retroactively unravel the ways in which the patient's psychic life has been constituted, and in that sense it can only reveal the function the phallus plays in the psychic elaboration of sexual difference.

The Lacanian Clinical Field, therefore, aims to undo certain prejudices that have affected Lacan's reputation up to now in both the academic and the psychoanalytic communities. While these prejudices stem from rather different causes—Lacan is perceived as too patriarchal and reactionary in the one and too far removed from clinical reality in the other—they both seem to overlook the fact that the fifty years that cover the period of Lacan's teachings were mainly devoted to working and reworking the meaning and function of psychoanalysis, not necessarily as a science or even as a human science, but as a practice that can nonetheless rely on a solid and coherent metapsychology. This double debunking of received notions may not only enlarge the respective frames of reference of both the therapeutic and the academic communities; it may also allow them to find a common denominator in a metapsychology that has derived its "scientific" status from the unexpected realm of the humanities.

I would like to end this overview to the series as a whole with a word of warning and a word of reassurance. One of the great difficulties for an American analyst trying to figure out the Lacanian "genre" is the way these clinical theorists explain their theoretical point of view as if it were coming straight from Freud. Yet Lacan's Freud and the American Freud are far from being transparent to each other. Lacan dismantled the Freudian corpus and rebuilt it on entirely new foundations, so that the new edifice no longer resembled the old. At the same time he always downplayed, with a certain *coquetterie*, his position as a theory builder, because he was intent on proving that he had remained, despite all odds, true to Freud's deepest insights. Since Lacan was very insistent on keeping Freudian concepts as the raw material of his theory, Lacanian analysts of the second generation have followed in their master's footsteps and have continued to read Freud scrupulously in order to expand, with new insights, this large structure that had been laid out. Moreover, complicated historical circumstances have fostered their isolation, so that their acquaintance with recent psychoanalytic developments outside of France has been limited. Lacan's critical views on ego psychology and selected aspects of object relations theory have continued to inform their vision of American psychoanalysis and have left them unaware that certain of their misgivings about these schools of thought are shared by some of their colleagues in the United States. This apparently undying allegiance to Freud, therefore, does not necessarily mean that Lacanians have not moved beyond him, but rather that their approach is different from that of their American counterparts. While the latter often tend to situate their work as a reaction to Freud, the Lacanian strategy always consists in rescuing Freud's insights and resituating them in a context free of biological determinism.

Second, I want to repeat that the expository style of the books of this series bears no resemblance to Lacan's own writings. Lacan felt that Freud's clarity and didactic talent had ultimately led to distortions and oversimplifications, so that his own notoriously "impossible" style was meant to serve as a metaphor for the difficulty of listening to the unconscious. Cracking his difficult writings involves not only the intellectual effort of readers but also their unconscious processes; comprehension will dawn as reader-analysts recognize in their own work what was expressed in sibylline fashion in the text. Some of Lacan's followers continued this tradition, fearing that

clear exposition would leave no room for the active partici-
pation of the reader. Others felt strongly that although Lacan's
point was well taken it was not necessary to prolong indefinitely an ideology of obscurantism liable to fall into the same
traps as the ones Lacan was denouncing in the first place. Such
a conviction was precisely what made this series, The Lacanian
Clinical Field, possible.

—Judith Feher Gurewich, Ph.D.

Foreword
Retroactive Determination:
Discovering Late Lacan in Early Freud

FRANCES L. RESTUCCIA

From reading and teaching Jacques Lacan, I have come to realize that all commentaries on his work are necessarily interpretations, and therefore distortions. One could of course by now make such a clichéd point about the relation of "primary" and "secondary" texts in general. But in the particular case of Lacanian theory, because of its constitutive obscurity, anything written about it seems unignorably to be the product of a choice among interpretive possibilities, to have an angle, if not an axe to grind. At the same time, some Lacanian critics are more faithful than others to Lacan's opacity; I certainly have my preferences among them.

One of the many brilliant aspects of Serge André's *What Does a Woman Want?* is that he manages to preserve the richness of Lacan even as he necessarily gives you something more. In other words, *What Does a Woman Want?* is like the woman to whom André dedicates his book—"the woman who knows how to lie to [him]"—insofar as the Lacan it presents seems to be Lacan, the real thing. A woman, writes André, "pretends to be the Other who doesn't exist, and allows the man to misconstrue the object of his fantasy." Just as she offers the pretense of a sexual relation, André's study offers the pretense of available, albeit complex, Lacanian theory. I do trust André's work, despite of course my sense of its seductive power, in a way that is for me unrivaled.

Although *What Does a Woman Want?* is a written version of a seminar given by Serge André in 1982–1983, the thinking it embodies maintains the highest level of psychoanalytic theory (does not seem at all dated), even as it addresses the clinical scene, tying it together with Lacan's concept of femininity. (In fact, the publication of André's translated text dovetails in a timely fashion with Bruce Fink's recent translation into English of *Encore*.)

André's cohesive, beautifully shaped study commences, as it concludes, with the enticing idea that psychoanalytic intervention arrives at a certainty about what is impossible to say or, in other words, at the truth of a missed encounter with the real. This impossibility, this "not-all," is of course femininity, to which the response of the unconscious (unable to articulate femininity) is castration. To Serge André, psychoanalysis from Freud to Lacan designates femininity as the primary form of this "not-all" and locates "in the theory of castration the response that the unconscious elaborates when faced with the impossibility of saying what the feminine embodies." In turn, the analytic process enables the subject to confront this lack in his/her knowledge of "femininity."

André is able to arrive at this climactic point in his text via Freud, since in André's reading of Freud the anatomical is beside the point. Implicit in Freud's approach, according to André, is the notion that, surpassing anatomy, the meaning of the terms "male" and "female" is unclear. We are left only with approximations. Freud, melting into Lacan, works out a difference between the sexes by focusing on "the organ as caught up in the dialectic of desire and hence 'interpreted' by the signifier." André offers a striking explanation of how the notion of the phallus as lack evolves in Freud. The little boy's sense of castration comes to be understood in terms of the presence or absence of his penis, having no relation to the female genital, which consequently is foreclosed. The vagina goes unsignified from the start, both in Freud and in the little boy's and girl's experience. Hence, too, from the start, the question is posed of how, from the position of castration or defective knowledge, that is, from the position of the subject, the truth of a being—"the female being"—who incarnates that "defect" can be revealed.

In any case, instead of the female genital, the boy apprehends castration. Instead of "masculine or feminine," unconscious knowledge prefers the dichotomy "castrated or not castrated." Anatomy is beside the point from the start. The phallus is the penis potentially missing. As early as Freud, then, sexual difference may be sought not between two sexes but between two subject positions. Moreover, it is because Freud regards sex as determined by the subject's relation to castration—"men" and "women" being situated differently in relation to it—that Lacan locates the roots of his (in)famous idea that there is no sexual relation in Freud as well. Early Freud underlies late Lacan; Lacan makes such groundwork visible.

But Freud and Lacan also part ways over the topic of castration, for Lacan conceptualizes castration as the condition of any possible femininity, rather than (as Freud conceptualizes castration) an obstacle to femininity. André traces in

Freud's work the gradual cloaking of femininity and the real by the symbolic, setting them aside. Lacan, however, insists on the real *in* the symbolic system, and this difference reflects their difference on femininity. Freud, that is, stops up the gap of the real, camouflaging it with the phallus. It can therefore be said that Lacan, in bringing out the nonanatomical meaning of castration in Freud, its imbrication with the signifier, restores an initial truth of Freudian doctrine, but a truth eventually eclipsed by Freud's theory of castration. André's aim is twofold: to show both how Lacan's teaching allows us to account for the trajectory of Freud's work as well as how Lacanian theory surpasses Freud's impasses. Lacan takes up the Freudian project "the wrong way round," starting with the later emphases (the castration complex, the primacy of the phallus, the splitting of the ego) and then lapsing back to Freud's early encounter with the real.

Approaching this Freudian real, André proceeds to discover the *jouissance* in Freud by explicating Freud's seduction theory in terms of a child's initial role as object of the *jouissance* of the m/Other. The child gives to the m/Other who first takes care of him/her "a *jouissance* that it would not be wrong to call sexual," writes André. And it is, furthermore, variables within this original experience of passivity that determine the choice of neurosis. André offers extremely useful, clarifying accounts of how the hysteric's and the obsessional's psychic structures pertain to this initial passive position as object of the m/Other's *jouissance*: "The way in which this original experience of passivity is taken up and reworked in fantasy, and recalled in repression and the return of the repressed, determines the choice of neurosis." André explains the transforming role of repression as it works to signify, and thereby sexualize, the real, and he explains how the process can go wrong. He intertwines Freud and Lacan to consider the question of the metamorphosis of the organism into the body, or, in other words, sexualization.

What André is exquisitely zeroing in on with all this is the paradoxical interdiction through sexualization of a non-sexual *jouissance*, the *jouissance* of the Other. The underlying question is the cause of Other *jouissance*. Is it the repressed signifier itself or a preexisting lacuna delimited as trauma and elevated to the level of sexual trauma? André leads us to believe that only in its retroactive symbolic determination is the real "already there." Repression produces trauma, just as symbolic organization/sexualization produces the real, a point that may be *derived*, claims André, from Freud. Yet especially because André had earlier established a major difference between Freud and Lacan by pointing out Freud's conception of castration as an obstacle to femininity, rather than femininity's condition for being, I am tempted to propose that André's early, Lacanian Freud, like Lacan's real, would seem to be "already there" in André's retroactive symbolic determination.

It is the case, of course, that between 1919 and 1925 Freud's thinking on femininity radically changed. He began to look into the prehistory of the feminine Oedipus complex. He began to realize that a daughter's relation to the father does not preclude her primary relation to the mother. (And, as a result, Freud posited that a natural homosexuality, or something akin to it, exists in women.) Yet once Freud faced the asymmetry between the girl and the boy—that for the boy the castration complex resolves the Oedipus complex, while for the girl they overlap—he arrived at an impasse. How does a masculinity complex, or penis envy, lead the girl to become feminine? Like the boy, the girl turns toward the father, bearer of the penis, in order to pull away from the mother as love object, which raises the question of how the girl avoids homosexuality. The feminine Oedipus complex would seem to allow, at this point of alignment with the father, nothing but a regression to the preoedipal relation to the mother. To separate from the mother, the girl must give up passivity; yet that is precisely what she much achieve, vis-à-vis the father, upon separating.

It is here, André shows, that Lacan comes to Freud's rescue by pointing out that the girl is not completely subject to the paternal metaphor, by, in other words, opening up a "beyond" of phallic sexuality. André offers an intricate, step-by-step explanation of why, and how, the girl is both inside and outside the law, basically because the signifier of the phallus fails to signify femininity. The girl must attempt to identify with the maternal figure whom she must also abandon as a love object, so the feminine Oedipus is inherently difficult: How does identification with the mother make it possible not to love her? This is "a total paradox." Likewise, the girl must favor vaginal *jouissance* (bound up with the relation to the father) and give up clitoral *jouissance* (bound up with the relation to the mother). But in a sense (and this Freud apparently misses), she retains it all. The mother is preserved through the achievement of maternal identification; the clitoris continues to play its role in the vaginal sex life of a woman. Instead of one *jouissance* supplanting the other, there is a doubling. As Lacan points out, the girl merely divides, rather than substitutes, never really relinquishing the preoedipal (passivity), while at the same time by no means regressing entirely to it.

Lacan's focus, especially in *Encore*, becomes feminine *jouissance* or femininity as "the problematic of a being who cannot entirely subject herself to the Oedipus complex and the law of castration." Lacan accents the division that the primacy of the phallus effects in the girl. André clarifies that femininity, to Lacan, is a product not of castration alone but of a twofold division of *jouissance*. It is, in fact, as André elaborates, phallic *jouissance*'s interdiction of the *jouissance* of the Other that allows Lacan to resituate feminine *jouissance* in its appropriate place relative to castration. This is a radical move. Lacan reverses the relation between being and the signifier and therefore the relation between the two forms of *jouissance*. Nothing exists without the signifier, even being. The *jouissance* of the Other, and in turn femininity, are evoked by the phallic function; they are unsignifiable, even as they rely on signification to be born. Feminine *jouissance*, similarly, would appear to be not-all within the phallic function yet dependent upon the phallic function for its very existence. Lacan responds to Freud's impasse with a paradox. The phallic signifier serves as a veil and consequently points to a beyond of the veil, a beyond beyond the phallic function. In a way it's simple, and André is brilliant not only in conveying this idea but in offering it as a way out of Freud's quagmire.

Perhaps most readers of *What Does a Woman Want?* will have already read André's previously translated and published chapter "Otherness of the Body." Here André enlightens us on the two ways in which the sexual relation fails, this "failure" being a result of the aforementioned twofold division of *jouissance*. The man cannot have as a partner a sexed Other, but only an *objet a*, a fantasy. The woman remains out of reach. But while fantasy compensates the man, the woman makes up for the lack of a sexual relation with, Lacan proposes, God, or the Other, or what is incapable of signification. Here then is a reply to André's title's question: what does a woman want? She wants as her partner a being beyond the law of the phal-

lus, for through such a supreme Being, a woman can become
all Woman. There is no sexual relation in a way, then, because
there exist "man" and "woman," whose *jouissances* are incom-
mensurable, unassimilable to each other, irreducibly heterogeneous. Woman, or woman's body, metaphorizes the Other,
and there is no signifiable relation to the Other. And this
aporia, the result of the phallus as signifier, inscribed on the
body from without and therefore unable to signify the sexual
relation, or relation to the Other, while at the same time pointing to it as an impossibility, and so providing (merely) a phallic *jouissance* that intervenes between the subject and the
Other, is instituted by Lacan's law of castration speaking in
response to Freud's impasse. Penis envy in Freud is somehow
meant to lead to femininity, but this goes nowhere. So, instead, Lacan shows that the woman exceeds the phallic function and, moreover, that the phallus enables this achievement.
Whereas Freud at this juncture wants to subject the female
sex to law and reason, Lacan, progressing beyond Freud, explains what makes woman an enigma and calls for the preservation of her mystery, in order to sustain desire through the
question of the desire of a woman. In other words, woman
no longer founders in the face of castration; castration leads
the way to its own transcendence.

Luckily, the woman is willing to play the role of the Other
who does not exist. She masquerades, André explains, "so that
[the] man will remain 'a' man and not be 'The Man'" for one
thing, so that she may "avoid the slippery slope of desubjectivation," subjective catastrophe. In this the woman seems
realistic (my common-sense term): well aware of the inad-
equacy of the sexual relation and the failure of the *jouissance*
of the Other's body, she knows that things would only be
worse were the sexual relation to be established (could it be).

In Chapter 14, "Love and the Woman," André proposes that what a woman wants is to subjectivize her body or to obtain a supplementary unconscious, "a supplement that will allow her to exist as a subject in the place where she is just a body in *jouissance*." What is intriguing to me is the apparent contradiction in André's response to his book's title question: What does a woman want? Earlier she wanted God; now she doesn't. She wants a man, not a Man. Which is it? Or is this split itself in André's text a clever, though accurate, reflection of the split in woman, divided between what she is as a subject and her unsubjectivizability? Indeed, André defines femininity as an oscillation between castration and the hole in which no subject can be inscribed as a subject.

In the end we return, briefly, to the clinical scene. If a woman is not-all, not fully determined by the unconscious, then she is not-all analyzable. At first, André presents as the dilemma of psychoanalysis that it can at best allow a woman to speak as a "man." But at the end of his final chapter, "From the Masquerade to Poetry," he reminds us that the examination of what a woman wants "marks the origin of psychoanalysis as a clinical practice." André initially entertains the idea that a woman wants an unconscious and that psychoanalysis can install it for her. But André also suggests that femininity, being beyond the repressed or sexualized, and therefore entailing the uninterpretable, links up with the analyst's knowledge that he does not know. His task consequently becomes not to grasp, or try to enable the analysand to grasp, femininity but to comprehend that to do so only fortifies the deception of the "signifier's major utopia." The gap must be left unplugged; meaning must be *made* inscrutably absent.

I found André's concluding passages riveting from both theoretical and clinical standpoints. The analyst, he remarks, should avoid attempting to give substance to femininity, through either phallic or extra-phallic means. Instead, "he must respond from the place where meaning has a chance to slip away." Rather than filling the hole with a new signifier, a new meaning, the analyst might offer a "hole-effect." And this idea leads André to tease out a suggestion Lacan makes: that through poetry meaning might be made absent, which is an accomplishment since something is never so present as it is when it is absent. Since meaning has no meaning, the aim of psychoanalysis should be "not to follow the movement of the unconscious, but to find a way out of that movement, that is, to cause 'it' to change." Whether the goal is reached through analysis or creativity, it would seem to be to spawn a new signifier that irradiates and lets operate the unsignifiable, unsubjectivizable hole in the Other.

Newton, MA/Paris
October 1998

Preface

This is an abbreviated version of a seminar I held at the Fondation Universitaire in Brussels during the year 1982–1983.

Since the time of its initial publication in 1986, several authors have attempted to treat the same subject. None of them, however, has taken up the challenge I posed in the final chapter of this book when I offered what seems to me to be the obvious answer to the question: What does a woman want?

This answer, enigmatic though it may be, is simply the assertion of the eternal virginity of woman. This virginity, which has nothing to do with the existence of the anatomical membrane of the hymen, concerns a veil that is immaterial and yet in no way unreal, a veil placed between the woman and herself, between her identity and her body, between the speech that gives rise to her desire and the silence that preserves her *jouissance*.

I want to pay tribute here to the woman who knew, better than the psychoanalysts, how to make that silence resound: Giulia Sissa, whose *Greek Virginity* (1990) indirectly reminds psychoanalysis of its duty to speak eloquently and, taking the Delphic Sybil as its model, illustrates the striking difference—indeed, the opposition—between two ways of proclaiming the truth: the oracle and the verdict.

Serge André
June 1994

What Can I Know About It?

What makes a psychoanalyst's intervention pertinent? It is, Lacan tells us, a knowledge placed in the position of truth. The apparent abstraction of this formula should not conceal from us its radically new message, its promise of a new relation to knowledge—knowledge as it is decoded from the unconscious—that is usually characterized by the absence of a truth effect. Perhaps we can observe this especially well nowadays: with the accumulation of knowledge that is available, overflowing, accessible to all, such knowledge no longer has an effect on anyone. The methodology of psychoanalysis, on the other hand, involves the discovery and actualization of a knowledge that affects us, that engages our subjectivity.

But it is important to make clear that the term *truth*, as used here, should not be taken to imply accuracy, nor should it be limited to what leads to the persuasion or the belief of the subject (and of the psychoanalyst). As Freud (1905c) showed in his study of the parapraxis, truth is best acknowledged through error. Besides, although truth can be uttered only within the structure of fiction (as is self-evident in the myth of Oedipus), it is not this fiction that constitutes the end of the analytic process, although it might well confirm its effectiveness. The point is to attain a certainty, not a belief; and this certainty is associated not with what the fiction says, but with what the fiction defines as impossible to say. Here we may recall the reconstructions to which Freud (1918b) devoted his attention in the case of the Wolf Man, and the recourse he had to take to the notion of a "pre-historic" reality of the subject.[1] Truth, in the end, is the always missed encounter with a real that can be indicated, in discourse, only as umbilical point, lacuna, missing representation.

Psychoanalytic knowledge, then, does not function from a position of truth, except to the extent that it operates as knowledge with a hole in it, affected by a central flaw, and this determines the status of truth as half-saying [*mi-dire*]. Psychoanalysis does not allow for *knowing all*, since the unconscious *does not say all*. Lacan invites us to understand that this flaw is not some kind of imperfection that the progress of research might allow us to overcome, but that it is the key to the very structure of knowledge. It is appropriate, therefore, to give an affirmative form to our proposition: psychoanalysis allows us to know "not-all" because the unconscious says "not-all."

In what follows I shall attempt to show how, from Freud to Lacan, psychoanalysis has come to designate femininity as the major, and no doubt original, form of this "not-all," and

---

1. We see the "prehistoric" emerge—or emerge anew—in connection with femininity, when Freud emphasizes the importance for women of the primal relation to the mother.

the theory of castration as the response that the unconscious elaborates when faced with the impossibility of saying what the feminine sex embodies—a response that, functional though it may be, remains nonetheless a fiction. Castration is the construction by means of which the human being seeks to speak of lack, but, by this very fact, it reveals the impossibility of speaking of lack as such. To speak of a lack is already, in one way or another, to fill in the gap. How could it be otherwise, given that we, as speaking beings, are dependent on the signifier, that, as Lacan puts it, the unconscious is structured like a language? For the analyst there can be no question of rallying behind Wittgenstein's statement to the effect that we must be silent about that of which we cannot speak. The primary operative discovery of psychoanalysis, after all, is that the human being never stops wanting to speak of what he cannot say (woman, death, the father, etc.). From this standpoint, our path of inquiry is defined by an impossible maxim: what we cannot speak of must be spoken!

What does "being a woman" mean? That is certainly the Question par excellence, since we have no supporting evidence as we do when it comes to knowing what a man is. As for what a woman wants: as age-old wisdom has it, one never knows for sure. Hence the inevitable oscillation between the cult of woman as mystery (enigma) and the hatred of woman as mystification (falsehood). But these two positions merely sustain the misrecognition of what constitutes the true question of femininity, because they both postulate that woman is like a hiding-place, concealing something (cf. Granoff and Perrier 1979).

It is Freud's genius to have noted that anatomical factors are of no help on this point. Whatever we may legitimately ascertain through observation of the exterior or the interior of the human body remains without effect for us, since what must be grasped is not a difference of organs or chromosomes determining our configuration, but a difference of *sexes*, this word referring, beyond the materiality of flesh, to the organ as caught up in the dialectic of desire and hence "interpreted" by the signifier. Any dictionary of slang will provide examples of the many names given in current usage to the genital ("pecker," "pussy," etc.), an inventory showing to what point the speaking being will go to indicate that the genital is a metaphor.

We'll set off, then, from this point: the reality of sex is something other than the real of the anatomical organ. Now this reality, as Freud asserted beginning with his paper on infantile sexual theories (1908a), recognizes only one organ, which at this point in his work he designated by the term "penis." There is, initially, an ignorance, an unknowing (*eine Unwissenheit*) that nothing can mitigate, he writes, in which the first infantile sexual theories will be lodged. Freud says that these theories "go astray in grotesque fashion," but that they nonetheless contain "a fragment of real truth" and are, in this respect, "analogous to the attempts of adults, which are looked at as strokes of genius, at solving the problems of the universe which are too hard for human comprehension" (p. 215). Here we are at the heart of the question of the relation between knowledge and truth. For Freud, these infantile sexual theories have implications above and beyond error, falsehood, or dissembling. In fact, we must note that perception itself is subject to them.[2] In other words, the signifier is introduced into the real, bringing along with it a sort of hallucinatory

---

2. It is important to note that for Freud (1895) perception is organized by representations.

operation of thought: when he sees a little girl's genitals, the boy's pre-existing prejudice distorts his perception, so that he apprehends not a missing member but something that is still very small and will grow bigger.

And when, in 1923, Freud returns to this initial approach to the problem, far from questioning the existence of a fundamental ignorance of the female genital, he stresses this even more and shows the theory to be even more misleading. For, with the discovery of the primacy of the phallus, it is castration itself—the very center of the knowledge from which the analyst awaits truth effects—that comes to replace the elaboration of infantile sexual theories. Speaking of little boys who discover the female genitalia, he writes:

> They disavow the fact and believe that they *do* see a penis, all the same. they gloss over (*beschönigen*) the contradiction between observation and preconception by telling themselves that the penis is still small and will grow bigger presently; and they then slowly come to the emotionally significant conclusion that after all the penis had at least been there before and been taken away afterwards. The lack of a penis is regarded a result of castration, and so now the child is faced with the task of coming to terms with castration in relation to himself. [pp. 143–144]

And a little further on he adds: "In all this, the female genitals never seem to be discovered" (p. 145).

Let us measure this sliding that takes place between 1908 and 1923. The thesis of 1908 proposed that there is only one genital, the penis, always present but not necessarily prominent, developed in boys and in the process of development in girls. In 1923, the thesis of a single genital is maintained, but in a nuanced way. Whereas earlier the little boy did not at all notice the lack, as if perception were not functioning, in 1923 he observes it (because he denies it and feels a contradiction), but he veils it by making lack a mode of existence of the phallus. In other words, there is only one genital, the phallus, but it manifests itself in two ways: presence or absence. This means that the lack of a penis, if it is acknowledged, is acknowledged as a (missing) phallus and not as a female genital. Castration is thus that which excludes—or, to use a Lacanian term, that which *forecloses*—the female genital[3] as such. Castration makes absence into a vestige of presence; it is an embellishment (the literal meaning of *beschönigen*), or, even better, a euphemism.

The little girl is just as caught up as the boy in this logic of euphemism: she too, says Freud, becomes aware of her genital with the help of the phallic signifier, she too sees in it a diminished or castrated phallus. And, as a result, the female genital remains undiscovered for her as well. If this idea seems shocking, this is because we have not appreciated its subtlety. When Freud concludes that the female genital is never discovered, when he tersely ends the paper on "The infantile genital organization" by stating that this ignorance lasts into adulthood in the form of the signifying equivalence of the vagina and the womb,[4] he does not understand by this that the little boy and the little girl are unaware of the *materiality* of the vagina. All one has to do is observe children to realize that, very early on, they engage in explorations that leave no doubt as to their knowledge of anatomy. But Freud's discov-

---

3. Translator's note: in French, *le sexe* means both "sex" and "genital organ."

4. "The vagina is now valued as a place of shelter for the penis; it enters into the heritage of the womb" (p. 145).

ery implies that the facts thus ascertained are not *signified* in the unconscious as an opposition of two complementary genitals. The vagina is well known as an organ, a body part, but it is not acknowledged, on the level of the signifier, as a female *genital*.

Now, the theory of castration is more than the belief that the neurotic installs in the place of something he can't bear; it is also the anchoring point of the myth of Oedipus, on which Freud intended to base his practice. No wonder, therefore, that he comes up against "analysis interminable": while the theory of castration provides an explanation of how neurosis is constructed, it turns out to be unable to provide the key to getting out of it. So it is understandable that Freud had to confront difficulties and contradictions in the two great papers of 1931 and 1933 on "Feminine Sexuality" and "Femininity." For the question that arises, and that becomes especially acute when Freudian clinical practice is addressed to women, presents a paradox. Briefly, what is at issue is knowing whether, with defective knowledge (that of castration), we can reveal the truth of a being who is herself the incarnation of this defect: the female being. The question of the truth of analytic knowledge is thus directly linked to the way in which this knowledge accounts for femininity.

THE HYSTERIC AS THE
PSYCHOANALYST'S PARTNER

Isn't this, after all, the very question that the hysteric asks the psychoanalyst? In questioning, after her ironic fashion, the father's potency and his capacity to desire, and in refusing the role of sexual object assigned to her in male fantasy, the hysteric sustains an interrogation that goes beyond the intersubjective relations of her family romance. She takes aim at the limits of the oedipal myth and the power of the phallus. The purpose of her discourse is to show that the oedipal myth and phallic logic misconstrue the existence of woman as such. Hence the touch of challenge, between hope and resentment, that often marks her transferential relation to the analyst. That is what she requires him to understand: Is he really the dupe of the Father? And what can he know about what a woman is and wants? We recall how Freud (1905b) failed with Dora, going all out to get her to accept her position as sexual object for a man (Mr. K.), when all along Dora's question is aimed at the enigma that is represented for her by the other woman (Mrs. K., wife of Mr. K. and mistress of Dora's father). Dora's position is based on the worship of a mysterious femininity actualized in the body of Mrs. K.; this body is her question. If Mrs. K. is in danger of being unveiled, deprived of her aura of mystery, Dora feels that she herself is being cast down, reduced to the level of a mere object of exchange between her father and Mr. K. It is against this disparagement that she rebels; but Freud, in 1899, does not understand this and, shoving her at Mr. K., just repeats Dora's fantasy: Haven't her father and Mr. K. made a pact of which she is the object?[5]

This interrogation, by means of which the hysteric seeks to grasp her being over and above what she may be *for a man*, goes far beyond the domain of the clinical theory of neurosis. As Lacan emphasized, following Freud, the analytic process actually entails the hysterization of the subject. The subject of psychoanalysis is hysterical, or, more precisely, subject to

---

5. Recall that it was at her father's instigation that the young Dora had consulted Freud.

hysteria. For analysis inevitably leads the subject, through the defile of his demands—"Who am I?" "What is the object of my desire?"—to confront the lack in his knowledge concerning femininity. In this sense, hysteria is indeed the basic neurosis; the others are just variants or dialects of it. And it is the only one, moreover, that Lacan elevates to the rank of structure of discourse.

If this question involves a challenge, it is because the hysteric utters it as a *protest*. She protests, in the name of Woman, against the subjective division imposed on her by the inability of knowledge to name the feminine as such. This protest can be an obstacle in the analysis if the analyst plays the master, if he tries to impose on the hysteric the sentence pronounced by the unconscious. For, beyond the phallic logic of castration, the analytic process reveals to the subject that the object causing desire—the object of the sexual drive—is fundamentally asexual, which means that the sexuality of the human being is not originally linked to a differentiation of sexes on which the unconscious remains silent. It is in fantasy that the subject seeks to give female form to this object, but the skeleton of this representation is a gaze or a turd. Here the hysterical fantasy is especially demonstrative. Faced with the lack of a signifier of the feminine, the subject is prompted to fantasize an imaginary division in which he is located simultaneously in the place of both partners in a sexual relation.

This function of fantasy as doing duty for a sexual relation impossible to signify as such constitutes one thread in the reading of Freud's and Lacan's thought. It begins in Freud's paper on "Hysterical Phantasies and their Relation to Bisexuality" (1908b), where Freud establishes that, behind every hysterical symptom, there are always two sexual fantasies, one masculine and one feminine in nature. He returns to this thesis the following year, in "Some General Remarks on Hysterical Attacks."

There is good reason to inquire about the implications, here, of this term *bisexuality* that Freud presents as the essence of the hysterical fantasy and that, as we shall see, plays a central role throughout all of his work. It appears clearly at the end of the first paper mentioned above, and in the middle of the second, that, for the hysteric, bisexuality actually signifies a bi-*jouissance*. Thus Freud compares the case of a woman who, miming a rape scene in a hysterical fit, tears at her garment with one hand (as a man) and holds it tight against herself with the other hand (as a woman), to the case of a male masturbator who tries to feel what both the man and the woman experience in the situation he imagines.

It is, then, the place and the role of the Other as Other sex that is at issue in the hysterical symptom. As is shown by rape fantasies, so common in the discourse and the dreams of the hysteric, the hysterical subject presents as divided, torn between two representations that he seeks to identify as the one and the other sex. The hysteric is literally the site of a battle of the sexes whose scenario is always the same: a male *jouissance* is forcibly imposed on the femininity that, thereafter, sinks into the abstracted or hypnoid state described by Breuer. We shall return later on to this problematic of hysteria and of the bisexual fantasy underlying it. The brief allusion to it in these opening remarks serves only to draw the reader's attention to the links between Freud's early works and what appears only at the end of Lacan's teachings, namely this division of the subject in sexuation as formulated in the Seminars . . . *ou pire* (1971–1972) and *Encore* (1972–1973) as well as in *L'étourdit* (1973). Lacan's thesis, in these texts, is that the division of the subject in the face of the sexual is a division not between two sexes but between two *jouissances*, the one all-phallic, the other not-all, the first giving rise to the other as its beyond. I shall try to explain how this approach illuminates and renews the Freudian experience, and how it enables us to reconsider the question of femininity.

FROM FREUD TO LACAN: A CONTINUITY AND A DEBATE

In taking up again the question of what a woman wants, we must interrogate the foundations and the resources of the knowledge that the psychoanalyst draws from his experience. It is the analyst's touchstone, since femininity finds there its status as metaphor of truth. We know that Freud formulated the question as *Was will das Weib?*—"What does woman want?" In taking up this statement again with a modification: "What does *a* woman want?" I plan first to look at how the most recent developments in Lacan's teaching enable us to readjust the angle from which this question may be approached. Two terms should be highlighted in the formula: it is a matter of what a woman (not Woman) wants, and not what she desires. And so we have to determine whether psychoanalysis allows us to discern a wish that is specifically feminine. Might there be a wish whose object would be unshakably fixed for every woman?[6]

Freud saw "penis envy" as the bedrock that poses an obstacle to concluding the analyses of women; the idea to which

---

6. Since the publication of this text (originally distributed in the form of seminar notes), P.-L. Assoun's remarkable work *Freud et la femme* (Assoun 1983) has appeared. Assoun emphasizes the nuance of meaning between wish and desire, to the point where he makes it the foundation of a thesis concerning the radical opposition, in woman, between the register of wishing and that of desire. I shall not be following him on this terrain.

the theory of castration had led him by 1937 was that of an
impasse. As far as men were concerned, the analysis, in the
last resort, would come up against a fear (the threat of castration), and, in the case of women, against a wish (to have a
penis). Does Lacan's teaching enable us to find a way out of
this impasse? Answering this question entails putting in abeyance the equation of wish and fear through which Freud attempted to distinguish the class of men and that of women.
The problematic of the woman's penis envy should be identified, in his work, as an attempt to find the key to a unique
desire that would allow women to be gathered into a set. It is
precisely this notion of a "set of women" that Lacan radically
calls into question, and this is why I shall be emphasizing the
term *a* woman. In this way I shall try to explain how Lacan is
actually able to draw from his reading of Freud the conclusion that has become a well-known slogan, "The woman does
not exist," a formula that is bound up with another, equally
provocative one, "There is no sexual relation."

For we must note the profound commonality and continuity linking Freud's work with that of Lacan, to the point
where it could be said that both are undertaking the same task.
In any case, this is the impression one gets from taking these
works for what they are: elaborations, works in progress, in
no way finished treatises. Freud's discourse, like Lacan's, cannot be reduced to a series of pronouncements to be considered "true," if only provisionally so. Their true teaching consists in the movement from one place to another, the *dérive*,[7]

---

7. Lacan uses the term *dérive* to translate Freud's term *Trieb*, usually rendered in French by *pulsion*. (Translator's note: Lacan (1960, p. 301)
explains that, for him, *dérive*, like English "drive," is closer to Freud's
meaning than the common English translation "instinct" and supplies the

that characterizes their elaborations throughout the course of what, eventually, becomes the sum of their work. It is, then, this movement, or what this movement is trying to get round or to get a grip on, that we need to account for in order to understand the full import of the statements that mark its course. In this way, rereading Freud's works from the first letters to Fliess all the way to the incomplete texts of his final days, we can see the emerging outlines of a journey, one whose aim was to define the question of femininity through a variety of successive approaches.

Although it is difficult to make sharp distinctions among them, I shall single out four major themes that seem to guide Freud in the course of this development. These three paths, as we shall see, constitute four interrogations regarding a key signifier whose meaning remained for Freud to clarify.

THE NOTION OF BISEXUALITY

The term *bisexuality* is an original signifier in the work of Freud. Around it was formed—and, several years later, un-formed—the relationship between Freud and his friend Wilhelm Fliess, which was in a way the foundation on which the edifice of psychoanalysis was built (cf. Mannoni 1969). This

---

connotation of forcefulness that may be lacking in *"pulsion."* In addition to being a punning equivalent of "drive," *dérive*, in itself, means "drift" and is related to words meaning "deflect" or "divert" (from a course), "derive" or "issue forth" (from an origin), and "unrivet"—all of these having the connotation of shifting away from an original direction or state of being. The word occurring shortly before this in the text, which I have translated by "movement from one place to another," is *déplacement*, which also means "displacement" in the psychoanalytic sense.)

signifier not only marks the origin of psychoanalysis but also recurs again and again throughout Freud's work up to the 1937 paper on "Analysis terminable and interminable." Indeed, although Freud's conception of sexuality led to a break with the idea of bisexuality advocated by Fliess—and their exchange of letters shows that Freud was quite soon in fundamental disagreement with Fliess on this point[8]—it is worthy of note that, once the break was expressed and achieved, Freud remained saddled with this signifier that would reappear in very different contexts in the course of his career.[9] Now, each time he uses this term he does so to say exactly the opposite of what he seems to mean. The word complicates his reflections instead of illuminating them, and one has the impression that it inevitably recurs under his pen because it sustains a remnant, absurd and inescapable, of his transference to Fliess.

We shall be looking at Fliess' notion of bisexuality and at what Freud objected to. But for the moment, in the context of this general presentation of Freud's approach, we may just briefly note that very early, from the time of the *Three Essays* (1905a), the concept of bisexuality begins to evolve in the direction of a contrast between activity and passivity. In fact, from this time on, Freud uses the term "bisexuality" in support of the thesis that there is a only a single libido, the male one. In reality, then, this term designates a strict monosexuality from the outset, and the question of bisexuality is hereafter located on the side of women—being women with a male libido, how will they manage?—and, in the case of men, on the side of homosexuals. In the *Three Essays*, Freud indi-

---

8. See Freud 1887–1902, Letters 80, 81, 85, 145, and 146.
9. See, for example, Freud 1905a, 1908b, 1919a, 1925, 1931, 1937.

cates that there are grounds for being more precise about the concepts of male and female. These are explained only in a note added in 1915, but we can find a basis for them as early as the 1896 paper "Further Remarks on the Neuro-Psychoses of Defence," where the contrast between activity and passivity is posited as the dualism encompassed by the term "bisexuality." When Freud uses this word, he does not have in mind a division of the sexes, a masculine/feminine opposition; he is designating a polarity that *takes the place of the difference between the sexes.* The note of 1915, moreover, is contemporaneous with the theory of the sexual drive elaborated in "Instincts and their vicissitudes" (1915a), where he shows that the sex drive in the human being is organized not on the basis of the male/female couple but instead around the inherently asexual polarities active/passive and subject/object. Henceforth, for Freud, the notion of the sexual drive takes on its connotation of enigma: from the point of view of the unconscious, the mutual attraction between male and female is a question, not an original given. If we speak of a sexual drive, the problem will therefore be that of knowing how the drive can be integrated into sexual difference.

THE CONCEPT OF LIBIDO

The idea that there is only a single libido is determinative in the long evolution of Freud's views on femininity. As early as the *Three Essays* we see that this term does not allow us to posit a difference between the sexes.

The concept of libido appears first in 1894 in the course of the correspondence with Fliess (Freud 1887–1902, Draft E); in the following years his definition would constantly be revised in accordance with the difficulty he experienced in determining, with the help of this single term, where matters stood with regard to a masculine pole and a feminine pole. Although he begins, in the first edition of the *Three Essays*, by postulating that the sole libido is by nature male and appears as such in the autoerotism of early childhood, he immediately comes up against the question: What happens after that in the case of the little girl, and, later, of the woman? He is thus led to maintain that the little girl's sexuality is fundamentally male and localized in the clitoris (which is the equivalent of the male glans). This male sexuality must later be repressed so that the little girl may change into a woman and her dominant erogenous zone may shift from the clitoris to the vagina.

We shall see how problematic this first idea turns out to be when Freud, in 1931 and 1933, tries to establish a general theory of femininity and of a hypothetical "feminine sexuality." But the thesis of a male sexuality to be repressed by the girl allows him to develop the theory of repression and to produce an initial explanation of hysterical neurosis. If the symptom is, in fact, the return of the repressed, the hysterical symptom in a woman should be considered to be the return of the masculine sexuality of her childhood. This is what Freud sets forth in 1909, in "Some general remarks on hysterical attacks." However, the logic of the approach he undertakes gives rise to an objection. If the libido is only masculine and must thus be repressed in the woman, how could a woman possibly have a sex life apart from the substitute offered by the hysterical attack? Or, more generally, is there a path for women other than that of hysteria (and of frigidity)? It is no doubt to circumvent this objection that Freud modifies and even splits his concept of libido—all the while maintaining its unity in principle—by introducing two essential distinctions that allow him to locate two organizing poles of the libido, poles that, without being identical to the masculine/feminine opposition, nonetheless outline a way to conceptualize a more typically feminine sexuality.

The first of these distinctions stems from the primary contrast between activity and passivity. It involves assigning to the single libido two aims, two different modes of satisfaction, one of which corresponds more to the masculine, the other to the feminine nature. In sum, there is only one libido, but it knows of two modes of *jouissance*: active and passive. The question of feminine sexuality now turns out to be more complex than it appeared in the first approaches to hysteria, for it concerns not only the repression or non-repression of the libido, but also the conflict between two means of satisfaction. Although the postulate of the single libido remains intact in the development of Freud's work, the assertion of its primary masculinity undergoes considerable modification through the demonstration of a passive *jouissance* that affects the child in the first relation to the mother. As a result, the problem of femininity is reframed in the following terms: like the boy, the girl must repudiate this passive *jouissance* in order to enter the oedipal stage, but she must then return to it in order to assume her appropriate feminine destiny. In other words, it is as if a properly feminine sexuality depended on a failure of the repression that constitutes the oedipal process.

The second distinction that Freud introduces into the center of his concept of libido is intended to resolve two difficulties: explicating the mechanism of psychosis and shedding light on feminine sexuality. It concerns the dichotomy, introduced in the 1914 paper on narcissism, between ego libido and object libido. In this way, while remaining single, the libido is divided not only with regard to its mode of satis-faction but also with regard to the type of object on which that satisfaction depends. This is a complex distinction, and it is all the more necessary to go into it deeply because it underlies the problem Freud raises in 1933 at the end of his paper on femininity, the problem of the woman's object choice and of the woman's more pronounced narcissism as evidenced in this choice and in the greater need for love that results from it. And in any case it is impossible to account for the particu-lar nature of female homosexuality if we do not assess the implications of this bipolarity.

FROM SEXUAL DIFFERENCE TO THE DIVISION OF THE SUBJECT

Another fundamental shift in the approach to the enigma of femininity concerns the notion of sexual difference. Freud established that the difference in the organs present in human anatomy is not signified, on the level of the uncon-scious, as a division between two *sexes*. Thus, from the origi-nal rejection of Fliess' notion of bisexuality, he had come to the point where, instead of relying on a split between two sexes, he inscribed the division introduced by sexuality in the ego, the "I" itself. In order to arrive at this *Ichspaltung*, this splitting of the "I" (1938a)—at which time, as Lacan says, he put down his pen—Freud traversed a series of oppositions. We have looked at the dichotomies between active and pas-sive and between ego libido and object libido. But there is still another polarity, one that Freud had begun to formulate in his study of Jensen's *Gradiva* (1907). It concerns what hap-pens, first for the little boy and then for the little girl, when, having discovered the anatomical difference between the sexes, they have to *state* what the situation is regarding the feminine genital as such. Freud first discovers that, since this difference does not register on the level of the unconscious, there arises in place of a signifier of the female sex something like what Gradiva exemplifies: a foot, raised vertically in an odd position.

Freud explains this discovery in the paper "On the Sexual Theories of Children" (1908a). The little boy does not see the absence of the penis in the girl; on the contrary, he maintains that it is there. In 1922 and 1923 Freud reconsiders this original presentation: the little boy does indeed see the lack of a penis, but he imagines this absence to be the result of a castration. And, the following year (1924a), Freud adds this fundamental detail that hands us the key to the process of misrecognition, or, as I called it above, euphemism: in order for the little boy to see the female genital as castrated, he must first have had to deal with a threat of castration that he ascribes to the female genital. This is what Freud calls the phallus, that is, the penis as potentially missing. In other words, the little boy, confronted with the female genital, does see something, but what he sees is not a female genital but castration. Instead of the masculine/feminine division that sexual anatomy seems to offer as evidence, unconscious knowledge somehow prefers the dichotomy not castrated/castrated. This is not without consequences for the subject of this knowledge.

Then in 1927, with the paper on fetishism, Freud takes a further step. He discovers that, confronted with the female genital area, some subjects are not content with either the attitude he had described in 1908 (seeing a penis there) or the one he had substituted in 1922–1924 (seeing castration there). They adopt both attitudes at the same time. On the one hand, they ascertain the lack of a penis, and on the other hand they maintain that it is present. They simultaneously acknowledge and do not acknowledge castration (let us add: without ever acknowledging the female genital as such). For the fetishist, then, it is not the female genital that is the problem, but castration, and to accommodate to it he can, as subject, split himself, the opposition between castrated and not castrated thereby becoming installed within the subject himself. And Freud concludes his study with this enigmatic sentence: "In conclusion, we may say that the normal prototype . . . of inferior organs is the woman's real small penis, the clitoris" (p. 157).

Let us pause for a moment on this assertion that gives fetishism a meaning going far beyond the clinical treatment of perversion. For if penis and clitoris are, in essence, fetishes, it could well be the case that the subjective splitting used defensively by the fetishist is present in all subjects. This is what Freud is leading up to in his paper on "Splitting of the Ego in the Process of Defence"(1938a). He states here that the process of splitting between desire and the real, which he had, early on, seen as the structure of psychosis and had then discovered in fetishistic perversion, also extends to the domain of neurosis. This splitting, when all is said and done, is a general principle of the tricky handling of reality (*kniffige Behandlung der Realität*). Freud's approach thus culminates in the thesis that sexual difference is to be sought less between two sexes than between two positions of the subject. The division of the "I," the ego—the three versions of which are neurosis, psychosis, and perversion—takes the place of sexual difference and is added to the divisions between activity and passivity, ego and object.

BECOMING A WOMAN

A fourth major theme can be discerned in the development of Freud's views on the question of femininity: if there is no feminine genital that can be articulated as such, then femininity must be conceptualized not as a *being*, there from the start as a given, but as a *becoming*, and a becoming that, paradoxically, becomes available to the girl as a result of her masculinity complex.

A preliminary form of this theory can be found in the *Three Essays* (1905a) and in the paper on infantile sexual theories (1908a): the little girl at first has a clitoral sexuality of a masculine nature, and a wave of repression is necessary in the years of puberty so that the woman can emerge by eliminating this masculine sexuality. But it is primarily from 1925 on that Freud develops this idea systematically and attempts to show *how a woman comes into being.* It is, in fact, at this time that he presents what he calls the prehistory of the girl's Oedipus complex. In contrast to what he had believed at the time of the Dora case, Freud now acknowledges that the little girl does not love her father, from the outset, in the same way as the boy loves his mother; she comes gradually to love her father through her relation to her mother. There is thus a difference that is actualized in a kind of development: the child, whatever its anatomy, is first and always a boy vis-à-vis the mother, and only in a second phase does a feminization, separating out boys and girls, occur vis-à-vis the father.[10]

What tips the balance between these two phases is the differential impact on the boy and on the girl of the discov-

---

10. We know that Freud struggled with the question of the feminization of the son in the face of the father's love, as an effect of the castration complex.

ery of the mother's castration: "*Whereas in boys the Oedipus complex is destroyed by the castration complex, in girls it is made possible and led up to by the castration complex.* This contradiction is cleared up if we reflect that the castration complex always operates in the sense implied in its subject matter: it inhibits and limits masculinity and encourages femininity" (1925, p. 256; emphasis in original). In other words, *it is through the effect of the complex that the girl must become reconciled with her anatomy.* This goes to show how, in Freud's thinking, femininity is scarcely "natural." But how can the castration complex promote the emergence of the girl's femininity? Freud's reasoning here is intricate and paradoxical. The discovery of the mother's castration brings in its wake, for both boy and girl, a devaluation of the maternal figure; moreover, since the little girl holds her mother responsible for her own lack of a penis, in addition to contempt she feels resentment that is transformed into envy of the one who has the penis. The little girl is thus led to turn toward her father, the bearer of the penis, in the hope of getting from him what the mother is by nature incapable of giving. To put it another way, it is insofar as she wants to have what the mother lacks that she becomes a woman.

Becoming a woman, then, seems to be an impasse, and Freud resigns himself to making penis envy the point beyond which the analysis of a woman cannot proceed. And so the fate of femininity, in Freudian doctrine, remains problematical. For if, as Freud argues in his 1931 paper on female sexuality, the little girl, in order to become a woman, must simultaneously change both her sex[11] and her object, how can such

---

11. In the section on "Femininity" in the *New Introductory Lectures* (1933) Freud says straight out that the little girl is a little man.

a change be assured if it is based on the wish to be like a man? There remains, then, after Freud, something to be explained about this process of becoming a woman that, for him, involves a sort of transsexuality specific to the girl.

* * * * * * *

How does the teaching of Jacques Lacan enable us to account for the trajectory of Freud's work and perhaps also to resolve the impasses at which it ended?

To the expression, endlessly repeated in the course of the last ten years of his Seminar: "there is no sexual relation," it is well known that Lacan added that, on the other hand, "there is nothing but sexual relations." Thus it is neither the materiality of sexual union nor the sexual connotation of any relationship that is involved in this formula, but the fact that there is a relation of complementarity necessarily linking men and women. Sexuality, in the human being, is not the realization of a relation in the mathematical sense of the term. It is instead the impossibility of writing such a relation that characterizes the sexuality of the speaking being. This thesis, about which much more will be said in what follows, caused a scandal. And yet it seems to me that it is a Freudian statement; it is even, I would venture to say, the opening statement of the Freudian doctrine here restored in axiomatic form. Indeed, by repudiating the concept of bisexuality in the sense maintained by Fliess, that is, in rejecting the idea that there exists a relation of inverse symmetry, as in a mirror, between the two sexes, Freud was actually basing his approach on the suspension of belief in a "sexual relation." This initial orientation took on its full implications in the years 1920–1925, when he was able to show how sex is determined, not by an anatomical given, but by the subject's relation to castration, which reveals not a symmetry but an essential dissymmetry between men and women.

Furthermore, Lacan says that *there is no signifier of the female genital*. This claim, first made in the Seminar on the Psychoses,[12] merely expresses on the level of the signifier what Freud had already noted on the imaginary level as "the ignorance of the vagina." Here again Lacan enables us to understand Freud: the vagina is unknown as *female genital* strictly speaking, but as hidden phallus, even as a new version of the womb (Freud 1923), it is known all too well. The ignorance of the vagina means that it is not recognized as radically Other in relation to the phallus. If there is no signifier of the female genital as such, this is because any signifier is in some way excessive with regard to the absence that is to be spoken of. Even words such as "hole" or "nothing" can only evoke the walls bordering the void that they try in vain to name.

The assertion that there is no specifically female libido leads Freud to reframe the problem from the point of view of a division: to be sure, the same libido animates men and women, but it splits according to its mode of satisfaction (active or passive) and its object (ego libido or object libido). Lacan, in turn, reopens the question of female libido but is determined to see it in terms of *jouissance*: Is there a *jouissance* specific to women? This issue, which he confronts head-on in his seminar *Encore* (1972–1973), has its basis in a division he had introduced twelve years earlier (1960), one that takes up again, and at the same time replaces, Freud's distinction between active and passive modes of satisfaction: the distinc-

---

12. Lacan 1955–1956a, p. 176. (Translator's note: again, it should be kept in mind that *le sexe* means both "sex" and "genital organ.")

tion between two types of *jouissance*, one forbidden by the signifier and linked to being itself, the other permitted by the signifier and linked to phallic signification. In so doing, Lacan undertakes a process of displacing the question of femininity from the realm of sex to that of *jouissance*. Bisexuality becomes bi-*jouissance*, and the problem now is knowing whether there is a *jouissance* in excess of male *jouissance*.

Similarly, the shift in Freud's work from the question of sexual difference to that of the splitting of the "I" is taken up and extended by Lacan. In fact, his aim in *Encore* and in his article "*L'étourdit*" (1973) is to show how the bi-*jouissance* that divides the libido simultaneously implies a twofold division of the subject, one part being all phallic, the other not-all. Thus, like Freud, he rejects the idea of a synthesis of the subject in its relation to *jouissance*.

Finally, when Lacan states that "The woman does not exist," isn't this a way of taking up Freud's notion that femininity is not being but becoming? Yet what we have here is no mere repetition of the Freudian impasse, but rather a genuine solution. To open the way to becoming a woman, Freud had based his argument on the differential impact of the castration complex on the boy and the girl. By introducing the logic of the signifier in the unconscious, Lacan is able to bring this process of becoming back from the far (and, to say the least, hypothetical) horizon of development and to derive it instead from the effects of the signifier.

But he does not accord the same importance to castration as does Freud, for whom the hole of the female genital is completely covered over, completely "euphemized" by castration. The girl, according to Freud, has at her disposal only the reference to castration in order to become a woman. But clearly, using this guideline is not enough, since it condemns the subject to fixation at the level of penis envy. For Lacan, the relation between hole and castration is not one of mere concealment. The logic of the signifier explains why this is so, for the hole must not be considered prior to the signifier that comes to name it (and to fail it). The hole becomes apparent as such only through the signifier that carves out its borders and produces it as its exterior. The signifier, in other words, does not only signify—it also rejects. The phallus does not camouflage the hole but rather causes it to emerge as its beyond. This paradigm provides a new key to the reading of the castration complex. Lacan expresses it very well at the beginning of Seminar XI: "Where is the background? Is it absence? Not at all. The rupture, the split, the stroke that makes an opening causes absence to emerge—as the cry does not stand out against a background of silence, but on the contrary makes it emerge as silence" (1964, p. 26, translation modified). In accordance with what Lacan is pointing out here—defining the *creative* function of the signifier—the phallus and castration do not represent obstacles to femininity; on the contrary, they are the conditions of any possible femininity.

2

The Paranoid Science of the Sexual Relation

At the very beginning of Freud's work on femininity there occurs, as we have seen, the signifier *bisexuality*. But this term takes on its true import—a simultaneous fascination and rejection—only in the context in which Freud came to grips with it, namely that initial drama of psychoanalysis played out in the relationship of Freud and his friend Fliess (Freud 1887–1902). This relationship bears the marks of an authentic transference. The bond between the two men was based not so much on their respective attributes as on a certain relation to knowledge that, taking sexuality as its objective, was transformed into a love relationship: each man became enamored of what he supposed the other to be like.

When they met in the fall of 1887, neither had produced a definitive work, but they had in common a strong interest in sexuality that led them to the conviction that it was there that lay the cause of the illnesses they were treating. This meeting was due to chance. Fliess, a rhinolaryngologist from Berlin, had come to Vienna for a period of study, and Breuer had recommended that he take Freud's course in neurology. Their relationship began with mutual referrals of patients, gradually became very friendly, and turned into an idyll around 1895. Freud had truly found in Fliess someone to speak to; he confessed that if he rarely wrote to Fliess, this was because he was writing a great deal *for* him (Letter of September 23, 1895), and he confided that it was in trying to tell Fliess about the theses he was developing in his "Project for a Scientific Psychology" that matters became clear to him (Draft B of February 8, 1893).

Fliess, then, played the role of the one who made Freud speak and the one who could know what Freud was trying to formulate in his works, and certain passages of the correspondence mention the universal knowledge Freud attributed to him. The disappointment was all the greater when, some years later, Freud realized that Fliess hadn't at all understood his concerns, especially when it came to his discovery of the Oedipus complex. The supposed knowledge placed Fliess in the position of the Other, which led to lovers' misunderstandings and to illusions of narcissism, since what Freud got, or believed he got, was never anything more than his own message in an inverted form.

In addition, we may note that this relationship was marked by a peculiar exclusion of women, beginning with their own wives. Entrusting Fliess with his Draft B, Freud urged him to hide it from his new wife (Letter of February 8, 1893). Their meetings—which they called their "congresses" —always took place without their wives. And, thanks to the curiosity of Max Schur (1972), we know that if the wives were thus kept apart from the friendship, this was because they were or had been the source of serious problems between the men.

This exclusive relationship reached its peak in 1895. But the culmination of the idyll was also the period of the greatest misunderstanding between Freud and Fliess. Freud, caught up in transference love, was completely blind to a series of conflicts whose emergence over the following years would gradually pull the two men apart. During the years 1895–1898 the disagreements arose and became frequent; Freud attempted to deny or to suppress them, but from 1900 on he could no longer conceal them, and, after the meeting at Achensee in the summer of that year, it became clear that a break was inevitable.

What was the basis for the alliance between Freud and Fliess, and how was it entered into? In order to understand this, we have to take a closer look at Fliess and at the ideas that, at least for awhile, made him seem to Freud to be a universal genius, even "Messiah" (Letter of July 10, 1893), entrusted with the task of resolving the difficulties in his first essays. As I mentioned, it was the conviction that the cause of mental illness was to be found in sexuality that brought them together. But we still have to assess the meaning each man ascribed to the term "sexuality," and in particular to the idea, held in common, of a primary bisexuality.

It is striking that Fliess' study, *The Relation Between the Nose and the Female Sex Organs, Presented in their Biological Significance* (1897) reveals, well hidden beneath the appearance of a pseudo-scientific discourse, the structure of a paranoid delusion. It is still more astonishing that Freud, who in early 1896 was the first reader of this manuscript, had virtually no objections to this "nose-genital," as he called it. On the contrary, he sang its praises, extolling its brilliance and originality and finding nothing to emend (Letter of February 13, 1896). He allowed himself to be thoroughly seduced by

Fliess' organic theories, since, in the same letter, he suddenly seems to accept an account of neurosis that conflicted with the theory of repression that he had begun to work out two years earlier.

This book, with the advantage of Freud's *imprimatur*, was published in 1897. It establishes the foundations of a system that, on the basis of very little clinical experience, soars to the heights of constructing a universal theory of nature and deciphering the great mysteries of life and death. Fliess' point of departure is the nose: it is here that he grounds his fundamental certainty.[1] In his view, the nose is nothing less than the mirror of the female genital. He ascertained that certain parts of the nose change for the worse during menstruation, this being manifested in the form of nasal congestion, increased sensitivity to touch, or a tendency to bleed. He therefore sees these parts as equivalent to genitals, and, since they swell up during menstruation, he even refers to them as genuine erectile bodies.

Evidence for this relation between the nose and the female genital is, according to Fliess, to be found in nosebleeds that substitute for menstrual periods. His medical practice is to treat the nose, especially by anesthesia with cocaine and by cauterization, in order to alleviate menstrual problems, calling this the nasal form of dysmenorrhea. He sees an analogous inverse symmetry during pregnancy, where a nasal effect of menstrual congestion is caused by the suppression of the uterine menstrual flow that cannot find its customary outlet.

---

1. In the sense in which Lacan (1955–1956a) defines certainty as a basic phenomenon of psychosis.

Thus menstruation is the process regulating the rhythm of life and death. And childbirth becomes a great menstrual period freeing in one flow the blood retained for nine months, the correspondence confirmed by what he calls the dysmenorrhea of childbirth, namely labor pains regarded as true menstrual cramps (which, like all dysmenorrhea, can be cured by administering cocaine to the nose). It is on the basis of this equivalence between pregnancy and menstruation that Fliess introduces his second fundamental idea, that of periodicity: the beginning of labor, in this view, is separated from the last menstrual period by an interval of x days, this being a multiple of the 28-day interval of menstruation, or x times 28.

Just as menstruation does not cease during pregnancy—being manifested not in uterine bleeding but in nosebleeds, nasal congestion, or labor pains—it also does not stop with menopause, where, according to Fliess, we see the first signs of a menopausal mechanism in the nose. Menstruation, he concludes, is a process that goes beyond the limits traditionally assigned to it, namely the time during which a woman is able to procreate. It is a process so widespread that Fliess soon discovers traces of it in men: he lists a number of cases of men who experience nosebleeds during intercourse.

At this point—about halfway through the book—Fliess' notions turn into a universal systematization. Having started out from the phenomenon of female menstruation, a nasal component of which he believed he had isolated (what Freud, later, would call a "displacement"), he now extends the scope of this phenomenon to the entire universe. He had already detached it from uterine menstrual bleeding by equating childbirth and menstruation; he pursues this by relating to menstruation a series of neuralgic pains and various maladies such as anxiety, asthma, migraines, urticaria, hemorrhoids, diabetes, apoplexy, teething, and, finally, the acquisition of language. At the same time, he detaches menstruation from the female sex by emphasizing the presence of analogous phenomena in men, which finally leads him to speak of male menstrual periods. Taking yet a further step, he concludes his work by inscribing menstruation beyond the limits of the human, announcing a complete monograph dealing with its manifestations throughout the whole of nature.

These multiple extensions are made possible by the idea of periodicity, which, at first simply a feature of menstruation, takes on such breadth that it become primary, completely overshadowing its original denotation. A kind of reversal occurs in Fliess' development, since at first menstruation is the principal idea and periodicity is secondary; in the end, menstruation is just a sign of periodicity. From the notion that everything menstrual is periodic, he comes to the point where he believes that everything that is periodic is menstrual. In this way he actually winds up with a grandiose conception of the universe as regulated by menstrual periods! Indeed, if the due date of childbirth is determined by these periods (of 28 or 23 days, the distinction of which will be explained below), the time of death must also be so determined, and the same with the rhythm of the development of tissues and functions (including speech), the occurrence of illnesses, and so forth. The author even devotes two pages of his work to maintaining that Napoleon lost the battles of Dresden and Borodino because he in effect had his period that day.

The law of periods thus appears to Fliess to be a natural law. But what object is it that is regulated by this law? It is, he says, the sexual toxin, the substance and sole principle of both life and death. On this foundation he constructs a theory

of anxiety that we may compare to the one that Freud is trying to establish at the same time: according to Fliess, anxiety
is just a discharge of accumulated sexual toxin not used up
in everyday life. We thus have the universal principle of "flowing," its periodic regulation, a listing of its normal or substitute pathways (the nose playing the role of a privileged valve
by reason of its mirror relation to the female genital); and the
substance, the fluid, that brings about these manifestations:
the sexual toxin, located beyond life and death because its
periodic discharge begins by constructing the organism and
ends by destroying it.[2] Fliess then has to discover the source
of this toxin and to explain how it moves through the body.
It is to this that he devotes the last chapter of his book—which
would not be unworthy of appearing in the *Memoirs* of President Schreber (cf. Schreber 1903). Although he locates the
production of the sexual toxin in the thyroid, Fliess lets it be
understood that his theory presupposes a kind of neurologi-
cal linkage between several organs as different as the sex
organs proper, the nose, the hypophysis, the tonsils and . . .
the ocular muscles of the nursing infant, all placed under the
control of what he calls "menstrual radiation."

But the most important aspect—and also the most obscure one—of this whole construction is the bipartition of the
periods into feminine series of 28 days and masculine series
of 23 days. A close reading of the book reveals no adequate
justification for this duality, a duality by means of which Fliess
believes he can demonstrate the human being's basic bisexual
nature. This is a postulate introduced empirically in order to
resolve certain difficulties that arise in clinical cases and that

2. This construction should be compared with Freud's theory of
libido and its role in the Eros-Thanatos conflict.

he later explains, when he turns to them, only by declaring in oracular fashion that numerical and sexual differences correspond on some deep level. Apparently this distinction between two types of periods—of 28 and 23 days—and their characterization as feminine and masculine are called for, in the logic of this work, by the need to secure the central thesis of Fliess' delusion: it is the mother who, transmitting her periods to the child, determines its sex. There exists a resonance between mother and child that depends on the very law of nature.

It is here that we can grasp the emergence of psychosis in Fliess' account. All of this sexual "science" has as its aim to prove that the periodic process—standing in for the law of the universe—is transferred from mother to child without the intervention of a third party. Now, at this same time, in 1896–1897, Freud, too, was wondering about what is transmitted from mother to child, but in very different terms, since his original idea was that of a transfer of sexual *jouissance* via the seduction enacted on the child by the mother or nurse.

Fliess finally establishes a theory in which, from the derivation to the determination of symptoms, everything is attributable to the mother, to whom the child remains bound, even beyond life in the womb, by a "co-vibration" animated by "menstrual radiation." In other words, one can do without the father; in order for the system to perpetuate itself, it is enough for there to have been at one time an original mother and the universal law of "flowing." As it happens, the name Fliess, in German, immediately evokes the verb *fliessen* ("to flow") or the noun *das Fliessen,* ("flowing"). It would not, therefore, be amiss to conclude that Wilhelm Fliess was merely seeking to make his own name into the very law governing the order of the universe, an attempt easily comparable to the delusional effort of President Schreber.[3] The periodic flux of a mysterious sexual substance traveling around in the body, passing between the nose and the genitals and a whole series of other organs that it causes to swell up and then diminish, is, after all, nothing other than a delusional metaphor of the phallus, that which can control the mother's all-powerful desire.

It is important to define the principles of this paranoid theory of the sexual relation, since it is only in opposition to it that Freud was able to formulate the structural rules of the unconscious. Indeed, it was only by tearing himself away from the seductiveness of the paranoid sexual science that he could undertake a psychoanalytic approach to the clinical treatment of hysteria, where the question of bisexuality appears in an entirely different perspective. And it was only by maintaining the central idea of the absence of a sexual relation that he could affirm psychoanalysis in the face of all the dissent in which paranoid science tended to reappear. For Fliess' concept of bisexuality is expressed in a sequence of fundamental arguments or postulates that can be found in whole or in part in each of the arguments raised against psychoanalysis. Let us review their main points:

1. For Fliess, sexual difference is a given from the outset: the biological distinction is sufficient to account for the phenomenon of sex.

---

3. Freud, moreover, at the time of his study of Schreber's paranoia, was aware of this parallel. He told Jung how much this study had helped him to understand Fliess' structure (Freud 1974, letters of February 1, 1908 and December 18, 1910), and to Abraham he declared even more frankly that it was in connection with Fliess that he had come to understand the mystery of paranoia (Freud 1965, letter of March 3, 1911).

2. The two sexes are linked by a relation of symmetry; each contains the other by way of repression. Fliess was to push this concept to its extreme consequences shortly after the appearance of his treatise on the nose; after 1897 he replaced the term *bisexuality* with *bilaterality*, assimilating the sexual difference to the opposition between right and left.

3. On the other hand, these two sexes are in reality mixed together by the unitary principle that traverses both of them. The universal law of periodic menstruation, transcending sex and the individual, integrates sex into nature, uniting it to the rhythm of the world.

4. Sexuality, therefore, is detached from the conditions imposed by the singularity of desire and reverts to the automatic realization of the eternal species. In this way sexuality and reproduction are reconciled.

5. The notion of bisexuality—whereby each sex is the carrier of the other and each person has received from his or her mother two periodicities, one dominant and the other repressed—signifies a principle of harmony instead of a dissonance. The subject is invited to the mirage of a totality based on a single vital substance. In the works that followed, moreover, Fliess would maintain the possibility of asexual reproduction, that is, the principle of self-generation.

6. Finally, this whole construction rests on the foreclosure of the paternal agency: everything depends on the mother, which whom the child maintains a lifelong relationship of natural harmonic resonance that nothing can disturb.

Freud argued against this "sexual science" point by point, even though he knew that he more than anyone had been open to the seductiveness of paranoia supported by scientific discourse. Surveying the development of Freud's thought from this single perspective reveals how he devoted himself to constructing a response to paranoid knowledge, and how he thereby dissolved his transference to Fliess. If we look again at the six items I have just enumerated, we can see that in fact Freud dealt with each of them:

1. As opposed to sexual difference as a biological given, Freud maintains the impossibility of inscribing this difference on the level of the unconscious. The unconscious asserts the primacy of the phallus over against sexual difference, a thesis that becomes explicit from 1923 on.

2. For the relation of symmetry posited by Fliess, Freud (1925, 1931, 1933) substitutes the notion of an essential dissymmetry between the boy's destiny and that of the girl.

3. As for the unity of the law of periodic menstruation, this principle could be compared to the concept of a single libido, were it not for the fact that the Freudian libido, being phallic, is the antithesis of a *natural* force; on the other hand, if the libido is divided, it is not divided between a masculine and a feminine pole, but rather between activity and passivity, or ego and object.

4. The primacy of the species over the individual, however, is an element that caused Freud some difficulty, as we can see in his reflections on the soma and the germ cells, or on Weisman's theories, in *Beyond the Pleasure Principle* (1920b).

5. Another radical difference of opinion: Freud's conception of bisexuality, vague though it may be, is quite the opposite of the idea of bisexual harmony. Bisexuality is never posited as the sign of a possible totality of the individual; on the contrary, it is the agent of a

))
, \   fundamental dissonance. Sexuality, for Freud, remains
traumatic, and, if we can speak of a psychic bisexuality,
it is in the sense of an irremediable division evidenced,
for example, in the conflict of fantasies that structures
the hysterical symptom.

6. Finally, is it necessary to point out that Freud's
principal effort was to highlight the importance, imaginary and symbolic, of the paternal function, thus break-
ing the illusion of a relation of natural resonance with the
mother?

Far from being immediate, this response was the fruit of
a long effort. It was the work of a lifetime, the result of an
unremitting will to decipher the enigma of sex. The secret of
this long struggle is outlined in the correspondence Freud exchanged with Jung and Abraham. He tells Jung how much his
explanation of the mechanisms of paranoia owed to his analysis of his relation with Fliess: it was Fliess' behavior toward
him that led him to the idea of repressed homosexuality in
paranoia (Freud 1974, Letter of February 17, 1908). Elsewhere he confides to him that Adler reminds him a lot of Fliess
(Letters of December 3 and 22, 1910). This memory was all
the more vivid because at this time Freud was immersed in
Schreber's *Memoirs* (1903), a task that, for him, amounted to
an analysis of his relationship with Fliess, to the point where
he felt unable to judge whether his study had any value beyond what it revealed of his own self-analysis (Freud 1974,
Letter of December 18, 1910).

Freud, then, had to renew time and again the struggle
against seduction by Fliess' paranoid science. The struggle
played itself out not only for Freud but also for each of his
pupils, and, in a general way, for every psychoanalyst who

undertakes to shed light on the enigma of sexuality. Indeed, although Freud could claim a victory with his 1911 study of Schreber's paranoia, the question remained unresolved, and it recurred in his relation with his pupils. I have already noted the passionate turn taken by his relation to Jung at exactly the time when he was finishing the work on Schreber. But the last straw was that, at this same time, Karl Abraham, the other great disciple, the other pillar on whom Freud had been sure he could rely, allowed himself to be seduced by Fliess in person! Thus Abraham (in Freud 1965, Letter of February 26, 1911) admitted to Freud that he was struck, in observing a case of cyclic psychosis, by the existence of masculine and feminine periodicity: he discussed this with a colleague, a friend of Fliess, and she informed him, a few days later, that Fliess wanted to meet him. This invitation put Abraham in a very awkward position in regard to Freud—he had been summoned by his analyst's analyst! Freud answered by return mail, indicating in no uncertain terms what his view of Fliess was and warning Abraham of the trap that awaited him (1965, Letter of February 13, 1911).

Abraham, of course, accepted Fliess' invitation, and after their meeting wrote Freud a letter that is a masterpiece of denial, a letter that reveals the nub of the problem. It emerges from what Abraham says that, clear-minded as he had been in recognizing the scientific weakness of Fliess' paranoiac system, he had nevertheless been seduced by it. Abraham at first tries to reassure Freud: he hadn't been spellbound as predicted. Yet he ends by declaring that he has made the most valuable acquaintance possible among the doctors of Berlin. In response, Freud once again issues a warning, referring to his own bad experience, his own transference to Fliess (1965, Letters of February 26 and March 3, 1911).

This confession seems to put an end to the conflict. From that time on, Fliess is no longer mentioned in the correspondence between Freud and Abraham, except incidentally and indifferently on the occasion of the publication of a work or his recognition by the Society in 1914. A silence, therefore, until September 1925, three months before Abraham's death, when Fliess suddenly reappears, and in a position regarding Abraham such that Freud can only cry out in despair. This exchange, one of the last between the two men, takes place just after the Congress of 1925, where, by an ironical twist of fate, Freud's paper on "Some Psychical Consequences of the Anatomical Distinction between the Sexes" had been read. Abraham, quite unwell at this time, tells Freud about his fatigue and his respiratory problems at the Congress and suddenly comes out with a confession: he is about to undertake a course of treatment with Fliess, whose ideas on periodicity are confirmed by Abraham's illness (Letter of September 8, 1925).

Freud responds at once: what he had feared has come true (Letter of September 11, 1925). What had he feared? Beyond the psychic enfeeblement of Abraham, who was worn down by tuberculosis, was doubtless his weakness where Fliess was concerned, and this, for Freud, seemed catastrophic. For here was Abraham, titular president of the Society in which Freud's pupils were gathered, placed in the same position vis-à-vis Fliess that Freud had been in twenty years earlier, when he had been ready to have the turbinate bones in his nose operated on by his friend.

The situation was all the more striking because the paper Freud had submitted to the Congress (Freud 1925) contained a number of arguments discrediting Fliess' theories. Freud had maintained the idea, fundamentally opposed to Fliess' organology, that it is through the complex that the human being has a relation to his anatomy, the complex being the condition of a person's sexed "nature." There was thus a kind of fate that pursued Freud and marked his lot with a touch of real tragedy. For he managed, by dint of effort and determination, to avoid the seductiveness of Fliess' sexual science and to give a different meaning to the primary notion of bisexuality, only to see his best pupils, those he treated like sons, succumbing one by one to the charm of paranoia. It was as if the vow he had made in days past, at the height of his transference to Fliess, kept coming true: he would name his expected child Wilhelm if it was a boy, Anna if a girl (1887–1902, Letter of October 20, 1895). It was Anna, but the ghost of this son Wilhelm, remaining in limbo, came back later to claim its due and each time seized the best of Freud's sons: Adler, Jung, Groddeck, Reich, Ferenczi, even Abraham. One after the other, each fell into step along the well-worn path of belief in the sexual relation, the path Freud had escaped in order to found psychoanalysis. And he remained absolutely alone, the only one to hold fast to the idea of a dissymmetry of the sexes, until Lacan became aware of him and took up the torch of the psychoanalytic discovery.

3

Encountering the Unnamable

It was to the extent that he was able to detach himself from the spell of Fliess' grandiose ideas that Freud was able to undertake the study of the dream process and the structure of hysteria, and to begin deciphering the function of what he at first called an "unconscious intelligence." A dream of Freud's marks this major new trend, the Dream of Irma's Injection (Freud 1900, pp. 106–120), the interpretation of which shows Freud first beginning to distance himself from Fliess' "science," and, perhaps as a result, having his first real encounter with the mystery of femininity. This dream, in effect, told Freud where the knowledge he attributed to Fliess ended and where his own could begin.

Irma had broken off her treatment with Freud, refusing the "solution" he had offered her. He does not hide from us the fact that he was strongly invested in this treatment, the young woman being a friend of his and close to his family. And so when his friend Otto, who had been to see Irma, told him that she was not doing at all well, Freud took this as a reproach. That same evening he wrote an account of the treatment in order to vindicate himself, and at night had this dream, the subject of a remarkable commentary by Lacan (1954–1955, pp. 147–160 passim). Irma appears, in pain. Freud is troubled, wondering to himself whether he had ignored some organic symptom, and wants to examine her throat. Irma, at first resistant, finally opens her mouth, and then Freud is faced with the dreadful sight of a large white patch and whitish gray scabs extending along some strange formations that resemble the turbinate bones of the nose. Three colleagues called upon for help play a rather comic role, one of them concluding his examination with the words: "There's no doubt it's an infection, but no matter; dysentery will supervene and the toxin will be eliminated" (p. 107). Now, the dream tells us, the origin of this infection is known: Otto, the friend, had recently injected Irma with a preparation of trimethylamine (the formula for which Freud sees clearly in heavy type), and it is likely that the syringe hadn't been clean.

An initial reading of this dream yields the following conclusion: Freud sees that he indeed overlooked an organic symptom, but this was the fault of Otto (Oskar Rie), who had used a dirty syringe. Freud is therefore exonerated by this dream: he isn't the guilty one; it is Otto, or then again it is Dr. M. (Breuer), who appears in the dream as an ignoramus, or it is Irma herself, because she refused the solution Freud proposed to her—all this according to the logic of the damaged-kettle story (pp. 119–120).

But Freud's associations take us further: over against the group of three friends there stands the figure, not present as such in the dream scenario but alluded to by the trimethylamine, of "the other friend," Wilhelm Fliess. Fliess had, as it happens, imparted to Freud a number of ideas about the chem-

istry of the sexual process, especially the idea that trimethylamine was a by-product of sexual metabolism. And Fliess is
also evoked by the odd twisting structures that Freud sees
deep in Irma's throat that remind him of the turbinate bones
of the nose—these, according to Fliess, being connected in
some strange way with the female sexual organs. And Freud
adds, without going into further detail, "I had had Irma examined by him to see whether her gastric pains might be of
nasal origin" (p. 117).

Now, we know today that this last allusion to Fliess really implies a condemnation, since we know how extensively
and how seriously Fliess was involved in this situation. We
owe to Max Schur the uncovering of the facts, which he found
described in the unpublished correspondence between Freud
and Fliess in March and April 1895.[1] The facts are as follows.
Freud had indeed asked Fliess' advice as to whether Irma
(whose real name was Emma) was suffering from some pa-
thology of the nose. Fliess made a special trip from Berlin,
examined the patient, suggested an operation, and, at Freud's
request, performed it himself in February 1895. Shortly thereafter, Irma began to suffer from constant pain and nosebleeds.
Freud grew alarmed and had her examined again, this time
by a Viennese ear, nose, and throat specialist, who discovered
that during the operation Fliess had left a fifty-centimeter-long
strip of gauze in the patient's nasal cavity! Irma had to undergo another operation so that this source of infection could

---

1. We may recall that this correspondence, far from being complete,
was copiously (or co-piously) censored by its American editors, who were
in charge of the Freud Archives in New York. Max Schur was one of the few
people allowed access to these secret archives, and he was of the opinion
that it was in the general interest of psychoanalysts to reveal the factors that
explained the dissention between Freud and Fliess. See Schur 1972.

be removed. In the course of this second procedure, she hemorrhaged severely and lost consciousness—and Freud, who was present, began to feel unwell and had to leave the room. In the following weeks, Irma had to have several further operations and experienced major hemorrhages that several times left her in critical condition.

Schur relates how Freud, in a letter to Fliess, expressed guilt at having had momentary doubts and affirmed that Fliess' medical judgment was irreproachable. Schur feels that the wish fulfilled by the dream of Irma's injection is not so much what Freud believed it to be—the wish to exonerate himself—as the wish to prove his friend innocent and so to maintain a positive relationship.

But can we rest content with seeing Freud's transference to Fliess as a positive relationship? Can we believe the protestations of good faith and friendship that Freud addresses to his friend? To do so would be to neglect the other, negative, aspect of the transference, clear in the dream although Freud may have wished to know nothing about them: "We were directly aware . . . of the origin of the infection. . . . [The] syringe had not been clean" (Freud 1900, p. 107). *We were aware*: doesn't this show that, in the dream, knowledge was located in Freud, and no longer in Fliess? As for the dirty syringe, it can mean only one thing. It is the knowledge that Freud, in the transference, ascribes to Fliess that turns out to be impure, whereas Freud, as he notes in his commentary on the dream, is always scrupulous about the cleanliness of the syringe, the purity of his therapeutic method. Therefore, even if the dream inculpates someone other than Fliess—which, after all, does not imply that the latter is exculpated—the guilt that is admitted is Freud's. And this guilt, when all is said and done, emphasizes his transference to Fliess, for by relying on

Fliess' knowledge, Freud did not "take [his] medical duties seriously enough" (p. 120), was not maintaining the high standard he had set when he undertook to treat Irma.

It is tempting, therefore, to compare the dream of Irma's injection with Freud's "Autodidasker" dream, which presents the same theme in reverse, since, as Freud tells us, it reveals the strange desire to be wrong, more specifically to be wrong in a case where Fliess is knowledgeable. This dream concerns another patient, whom Freud hesitated to diagnose as neurotic. He therefore consulted the man he calls "the physician whom I . . . respect more than any as a man and before whose authority I am readiest to bow"(p. 300), that is, Fliess. The latter, to Freud's great surprise, rejected the idea of an organic condition. Nevertheless, when he saw the patient a few days later, Freud told him that he could do nothing for him and advised him to see another doctor. To his astonishment, the patient then confessed the sexual origin of his symptoms, thereby confirming the diagnosis of a neurotic ailment. Freud tells us that he was relieved but at the same time ashamed: "I had to admit that my consultant . . . had seen more clearly than I had. And I proposed to tell him as much when I next met him—to tell him that *he* had been right and *I* wrong" (p. 301).

In outline, this dream analysis is like the earlier one. In both cases, Freud is in doubt about the correct diagnosis: neurosis or organic condition? And in both cases, although he relies on Fliess' knowledge to settle the matter, he is nevertheless skeptical about the reliability of the latter's contribution. Fliess is mistaken in the case of Irma,[2] and he is correct

---

2. Not only was he mistaken, but he wanted to deceive Freud; we can interpret his negligence (the forgetting of the gauze bandage) only as a wish to assure himself that the symptom would remain organic.

in the second case. Yet it seems that Freud feels just as guilty in both instances, and here is where his transference becomes shaky. What motivates both of these dreams is Freud's feeling of guilt—but what basis is there for this? Is it that he had dared to discredit the knowledge he attributed to his friend Fliess, or, more fundamentally, that he believed in this knowledge to the point of crediting it over his own insight, over his desire as an analyst? Freud decides on the interpretation favoring the first of these possibilities: these dreams were intended to maintain Fliess as the subject-presumed-to-know. We might call this the "official" version, but "unofficially" Freud is seriously questioning the knowledge he ascribed to Fliess, and this process would lead him, several years later, not only to see in Fliess nothing but a puppet from the point of view of knowledge, but also, as he would admit to Abraham, to consider him an irresistibly seductive object. When, in the "Autodidasker" dream, the patient finally vindicates Fliess at the very moment when Freud is about to discontinue the treatment, if shame is mingled with the relief he feels this is because the patient had vindicated Freud's desire even more than Fliess' knowledge.[3] The conclusion to be drawn from this dream is not so much that Fliess had seen matters correctly as that Freud had been right in his thesis about the etiology of the neuroses. The shame that then arose in him could only stem from having given in as far as his desire was concerned, from having had to receive from the Other (Fliess) the information he himself hadn't dared to impart to him.

---

3. Freud could also ascribe his disbelief in Fliess' diagnosis to the fact that the latter did not share his opinion concerning the etiology of the neuroses. Even if Fliess' science was exact, it could only be deceptive, in Freud's view, insofar as it rested on a false knowledge.

If, then, this dream reveals the odd desire to be wrong, it is—let us complete the formulation—the desire to be wrong in attributing to Fliess knowledge that he did not and could not have, knowledge that Freud already possessed though without daring to recognize and own it. If they are to assume their full import, these two dreams must therefore be placed in the context of Freud's transference to Fliess, that is to say, read in relation to the object of the transference. Seen in this light, they indicate that Freud's transference had reached a critical point at this time: the Other who was presumed to know was no longer an infallible Other, but one who could be mistaken and, above all, could deceive.

Now, what does this knowledge attributed to Fliess concern? The analysis of these two dreams provides a ready answer: the nature of femininity. It was, then, on this fundamental point that Freud stopped putting his trust in Fliess' responses. In the "Autodidasker" dream, his associations refer to a concatenation of signifiers linked by plays on words, substitution of syllables, or reversals, the aim of which, Freud says, can be summed up in the phrase *"cherchez la femme"* (1900, p. 300). Here we may note in passing a detail that Freud does not comment upon. A term that occupies a central position in the chain is the signifier "Breslau," this being the name of a city in which, he says, a lady who was a close friend of his family had gotten married; the marriage was unhappy, since the dream is based on the idea of ruination through women. But what he does not say is that Breslau is also the name of the city where, in 1897, he and Fliess had had a decisive "congress," in which Fliess had explained to Freud how his theory of bisexuality was tending in the direction of the notion of bilaterality, a development that Freud refused to endorse.

As for the dream of Irma's injection, it is entirely constructed around this enigma: what is a woman? To phrase this with the ambiguity that the dream itself employs, what is at issue, between Freud and Fliess, is to know what is discovered when Irma "opens her mouth." This opening—and we may take it on the anatomical level or on the level of the act of speaking—is already interpreted, indeed, theorized, in the dream. As Lacan says, "the dream Freud had is, as a dream, integrated in the progress of his discovery. That is how it acquires its double meaning" (1954–1955, p. 162). This is because what Freud's dream constructs, as a response to what is deep in Irma's throat, is in itself the beginning of an approach to femininity. For what Freud discovers when Irma opens her mouth, in a place where Fliess can see only infection, is the source of three themes that will recur in all his remaining work, three guidelines for understanding woman: the theme of the reality of the female genital organ and the horror it arouses; the theme of three women that culminates in the woman as a figure of death (and vice versa); and the theme of the umbilicus, of the non-recognizable, of womanhood as a hole.

Let us first consider this passage from the beginning of the dream: "She then opened her mouth properly, and on the right I found a big white patch; at another place I saw extensive whitish gray scabs upon some remarkable curly structures which were evidently modeled on the turbinal bones of the nose" (Freud 1900, p. 107). It was Lacan, in his second Seminar, who stressed the fact that this dream has two high points, the second being a kind of response to the first: the dreadful sight of the depths of Irma's throat, and, at the end, the emergence of the formula for trimethylamine. As for the first, Lacan says:

> There's a horrendous discovery here, that of the flesh one
> never sees, the foundation of things, the other side of the
> head, of the face, the secretory glands *par excellence*, the
> flesh from which everything emerges, at the utmost
> depths of the mystery the flesh inasmuch as it is suffer-
> ing, is formless, inasmuch as its form in itself is something
> that provokes anxiety. Spectre of anxiety, identification
> of anxiety, the final revelation of *you are this* . . . . [1954–
> 1955, pp. 154–155, translation modified]

This first part of the dream is thus the opening onto the horrible image of brute flesh, not dressed up by the erotized image
of the body. We find there, Lacan says further on, "the revelation of this something that properly speaking is unnamable,
. . . the abyss of the feminine organ from which all life emerges
. . . and also the image of death in which everything comes to
its end" (p. 164, translation modified).

For Lacan, the function of this dream is, first of all, to
indicate to Freud the true object of Irma's complaints, the
object that grounds the truth of her hysterical symptom
($\frac{\$}{a}$, in Lacanian notation). Irma, Freud tells us, complained of
feelings of nausea and disgust—in effect, of something unnamable arising in place of her body, something that made
her body appear desexualized, dephallicized, reduced to the
state of disfigured flesh, of thing—of object, Lacan will say at
a later time. For the hysteric's initial complaint refers to a state,
the state of a thing outside of sex to which she feels reduced
in the desire of the Other, and that provokes nausea and disgust. We shall have more to say about this.

Isn't it remarkable that Freud nevertheless does not stop
at this image without a name, this emergence of the real? The
dream continues; he finds the path that allows the dreamer
not to awaken. And what is this path? First of all, the subject

Freud disappears, and it is, obviously, this eclipse that ensures the continuation of the dream. He no longer has to pit himself against the real but is replaced by a merry trio composed of Otto, Leopold, and Dr. M. Thus, at the very heart of the dream, a response to the real begins to take form, one that will culminate in the formula for trimethylamine, an eminently symbolic writing. Lacan comments on the implications of this ending: "Like an oracle, the formula gives no reply whatsoever to anything. But the very manner in which it is set out . . . is in fact the answer to the question of the meaning of the dream. One can model it closely on the Islamic formula—*there is no other God but God*. There is no other word, no other solution to your problem, than the word" (p. 158, translation modified).

In short, Lacan's thesis is that the dream, in the very way it is worked out, is homogeneous with the psychoanalytic discovery and with the way in which the unconscious is constituted. The fact that we speak or dream is revealed, in the dream, to be caused by an unnamable real, a real that the unconscious attempts to define in the way one provides a border for a hole, by the system of the symbolic, by the signifying chain, in the same way as psychoanalytic knowledge attempts to designate this agency of the real with the help of formulas or mathemas. In this sense, the dream of Irma's injection is not only a formation decipherable by psychoanalysis but also a locus of the invention and implementation of psychoanalysis itself.

And, beyond the events of the Irma/Emma affair, this dream constitutes Freud's response to Fliess. Fliess, who is interested only in the material reality of the nasal infection, wants to account for it by the necessary flow of an equally material sexual toxin (the word *trimethylamine* alludes to this toxin). In so doing, he misses the point of both the real and the symbolic dimensions of femininity. What is more, in order to convince Freud of the correctness of this organologic approach, he goes as far as to "forget" a gauze bandage in the nose of a hysteric, in such a way that he maintains the infection he is supposed to be combating. Freud answers, in the very fact of his dream, by affirming the existence of the unconscious: from this perspective, the value of the trimethylamine is not that it is a chemical, but that it is a formula, a coding, a letter whose subject (Freud as well as Irma) is bearing up in the face of the traumatic real. Through this dream, Freud finds a way of telling Fliess that his nasal theories are themselves only a coding of the unconscious of a subject confronted with the horror evoked by the discovery of the female genital.

Another theme is broached in this dream, that of the three women, the end-point of which turns out to be death. The motif is introduced in a passage that alludes to both the falsity and the modesty of women: "I took her to the window and looked down her throat, and she showed signs of recalcitrance, like women with artificial dentures. I thought to myself that there was really no need for her to do that. She then opened her mouth properly . . . ." (1900, p. 107). Freud's associations to Irma lead to a close woman friend of hers, whom he had seen being examined by Doctor M; the latter had said that she had false diphtheritic membranes. Freud, for his part, thought that this girl was a hysteric, but that she did not want to consult him because, as he says, "she was of a very reserved nature. She was *recalcitrant*, as was shown in the dream" (p. 110). She too, in effect, resists opening her mouth.

From another point of view, the diphtheritic membranes evoke an association to Mathilde, Freud's daughter, who had been gravely ill two years earlier, and to another Mathilde, who had died, poisoned by the sulphonal Freud had prescribed for her. It is, he tells us, as if the substitution of the women in the dream were that of one Mathilde for another. Finally, the "false teeth," which he chooses to represent as "bad teeth," remind him of someone else. This other person, he says, was not a patient of his, nor would he want her to be: "she was bashful in my presence and I could not think she would make an amenable patient" (p. 110). Who was this person who was so bashful with Freud? A footnote explains that it was his own wife, but this time we understand that it was not a question of her opening her mouth: "the pains in the abdomen reminded me of one of the occasions on which I had noticed her bashfulness" (p. 110, note 1). Opening the legs and opening the mouth, then, are equated, the mouth and the female genital substituting for each other.

We have, then three women, accompanying Irma, who resisted Freud. They tell him nothing, they do not let him examine them, or they have returned to the silence of death. This theme of death and silence as representing one of the major figures of the feminine is found in other dreams of Freud's, and, later, in important papers whose central issue is the enigma of femininity—papers like "The theme of the three caskets" (1913) or "The uncanny" (1919b). And we cannot fail to be struck by the insistence of this association in many cases of hysteria; the case of Emmy von N., to be discussed further on, sheds light on daily clinical experience.

In this connection, two other dreams of Freud's should be compared with the dream of Irma's injection: the dream of the "Three Fates" and the first dream about Brücke, also known as the dream in which Freud dissects his own pelvis (pp. 204–208, 233). To the account of the former, Freud immediately associates the first novel he read, at age thirteen. At the end of this novel, the hero, who has gone mad, calls out the names of the three women who have caused the happiness and misfortune of his life. These three women bring to Freud's mind the three Fates who spin and undo human destiny. From this follows the interpretation of the dream, and especially of the mysterious hostess who receives the dreamer: "I went into a kitchen in search of some pudding. Three women were standing in it; one of them was the hostess of the inn and was twisting something about in her hand, as though she was making Knödel [dumplings]. She answered that I must wait till she was ready. (*These were not definite spoken words.*)" (p. 204).

This is one of the three Fates, but also someone who reminds Freud of a wet nurse and of his mother. He then recalls how, when he was six years old, his mother was teaching him that man was made of earth and must return to earth: she rubbed her palms together (as if making Knödel) and showed him the bits of blackish epidermis that came off them. The little boy had been astonished by this demonstration and reconciled himself to what he would later express in the adage, "you must give up your life to nature." In this way the major figure of femininity for Freud is brought onstage: it is the mother, but at the same time it is death, she from whom one comes and she to whom one returns, she who feeds us and who in the end absorbs us, nurse and cannibal at the same time. Let us pay special attention to the gesture by which the mother here initiates the young Freud into the mystery of death. It is from her body itself that something is detached, a small fragment that is presented as what is most real in the body (the earth of which the body is made), even as it incarnates the very realization of death. This remainder detached from the body beyond any image is a striking depiction of what Lacan calls the *objet a*, and we should compare it with the dreadful spot that appears deep in Irma's throat.

But, as in the Irma dream, there is also a second part, a response to the emergence of this dead part of the body. In the dream, Freud tries in effect to dress this mud that really comprises the body: he wants to slip on an overcoat (the sexual meaning of which he is well aware of), but he is prevented by a stranger with a long face. In other words, the dreamer seeks to re-wrap his body in a phallicized, sexualized veil. What is more, in the associations to the dream the overcoat that has a long strip with Turkish embroidery is directly connected with the female genital and what covers it (p. 206, with the reference to p. 186). The logic of the development of this dream therefore indicates that something prevents the dead part of the body from being camouflaged, clothed with the long tail, embroidered with Turkish patterns, in which we can see an amusing figuration of the phallus. And since it is from the body of the mother that this construing of the dream set out, what this means is that an objection is raised to the complete phallicization of the female body, and that this objection is none other than the female genital organ itself (in the dream, the stranger who wears a small pointed beard). We are getting close, here, to the formulation of an implicit theme that guided Freud as he worked out all of his initial ideas about femininity: there is something in the woman's body that resists phallic covering, something that detaches itself from her body like death itself: her genital.

Now—and this is the real point of the dream—just when he gets to the unnamable as such, the focal point of this elaboration, the whole concatenation ends up with a pun on Freud's own name. Freud observes that the development of the chain of associations to this dream, a chain that has led him to the female organ, has consisted entirely in playing on names: Knödel and Knödl, Pélagie and plagiarism, Brücke and Wortbrücke, Fleischl and Fleisch, Popovic and popo. And at the moment when, in connection with "Popovic," which contains "popo" (baby-talk for "behind"), he recalls a humorist saying, "He told me his name and blushingly pressed my hand" and notes that this sort of pun concerns him personally: "It could scarcely be denied that playing about with names like this was a kind of childish naughtiness. But if I indulged in it, it was as an act of retribution, for my own name had been the victim of feeble witticisms like these on countless occasions"(p. 206). In German, *Freude* means "joy," "rejoicing." So here, finally, is what escapes the construing of the dream, in the same way that something was detached from the mother's body inside the dream itself. It is, then, the link between joy and the female genital that gives meaning to the link between death and the mother's body. And so the final meaning of the dream is as follows: something escapes the name—that signifier par excellence that is the name—and escapes as well the embroidery of symbolic metonymy, and that something is *jouissance*. The symbolic/imaginary composition, in this regard, can only produce a remainder, a real remainder that falls as the fragments of epidermis fell from the mother's palms.

Another dream, one that I'll mention just briefly, also presents this close connection of the feminine and death; this is the dream in which Freud, "strangely enough" (p. 452), dissects his own pelvis at the request of Brücke (pp. 413, 452–455, 477–478). He discovers a sight that calls to mind the bottom of Irma's throat (and Lacan's commentaries on this topic). In the associations to the dream, the phrase "strangely enough" is linked to a book that Freud had offered to lend to a woman friend: *She*, by Rider Haggard, which Freud offers to her as "a *strange* book, but full of hidden meanings" referring to "the eternal feminine" (p. 453). We may note that this book serves as a substitute for a work that Freud himself had not yet written on the secret of femininity.

How, then, did Freud sense the relevance of this book in the construction of his dream? His pelvis first had to be gotten ready, then replaced on his body. Then, once again in possession of his legs, Freud undertakes an expedition accompanied by an Alpine guide who carried him for part of the way. After having encountered several kinds of danger, they come to the edge of an abyss, over which the guide sets two planks. "At that point I really became frightened about my legs," says Freud (p. 453). It is here that the dream comes up against an impasse, since, instead of crossing the chasm, Freud discovers two men stretched out next to two sleeping children. The analysis of the dream reveals a memory of seeing two skeletons in an Etruscan tomb near Orvieto: "It was as though what was going to make the crossing possible was not the boards but the children. I awoke in a mental fright" (p. 453). The Haggard novel also ends with death; the woman guide, instead of bringing back the secret of immortality for herself and the others, meets death in a mysterious fire. Once again death sets a limit to the development of Freud's thinking about woman, death that is here presented as an impassable abyss, a hole on whose border children are sleeping and on which the dream is silent.

This theme finds its ultimate expression in the 1913 paper on the three caskets. Starting with the scene in *The Merchant of Venice* in which Bassanio, seeking the hand of Portia, has to choose which of three caskets contains the girl's portrait, Freud discusses a well-known narrative motif found in *King Lear*, the story of the judgment of Paris, the Cinderella story, and Apuleius' fable of Psyche and her sisters. In each case a man must choose among three sisters, and in each case the one who should be chosen is mute. She is silent; one might say, evoking Irma, that she does not open her mouth.

Now, according to Freud, muteness in a dream is a common representation of death. The third sister, the one who is to be chosen by the hero, is thus Death herself, the goddess of Death. We can thus name these three sisters: they are the Moirae, the Fates, the third of whom was called Atropos, the Inexorable. And Freud ends his study with words that sum up one aspect of his approach to the Mother and Woman:

> We might argue that what is represented here are the three inevitable relations that a man has with a woman— the woman who bears him, the woman who is his mate, and the woman who destroys him; or that they are the three forms taken by the mother in the course of a man's life—the mother herself, the beloved one who is chosen after her pattern, and lastly the Mother Earth who receives him once more. But it is in vain that an old man yearns for the love of woman as he had it first from his mother; the third of the Fates alone, the silent Goddess of Death, will take him into her arms. [p. 301]

Thus death is the term Freud uses to signify, in a general way, what remains of the mother, of the mother as real, as forbidden. To the extent that one part of her remains outside the signifier, as a zone of silence in relation to what is said and named, the mother is equivalent to death. Hence, in "The uncanny" (1919b), Freud will say that the common fantasy of being buried alive is just the transformation of the fantasy of living in the mother's body. The only weakness in this reasoning lies in the confusion of death with the temporal end of life. The truth about death is not this material endpoint that is only a representation of death. Lacan (e.g., 1953) sheds light on this question when he finds in death one of the figures of the real. If death has such importance for us, speaking beings as we are, this is because it is what negates discourse, the muteness that breaks the sword of speech. Thus it is not surprising to find it, in the unconscious, as an equivalent of the mother, indeed of femininity, since the development of Freud's theory show us that something of femininity remains absolutely beyond the reach of language, interdicted (*interdit*) in the etymological sense of the term, that is, present in the muteness interpolated between spoken words (*entre les dits*). Nor will we be surprised to find that the theme of death is one of the primary markers of the discourse of the hysteric, appearing as anxiety about being dead or experiencing her body as dead. Something of the female body is left to death, to muteness—precisely the part that has to do with her genital, insofar as it could oppose the phallus, which is basically talkative.

But the dream of Irma's injection reveals a third theme that is essential to the problematics of femininity for Freud, and this is the umbilicus, the unknowable thing toward which the entire system of representations converges. This term appears in a note commenting on the part of the dream in which it is said that Irma "opened her mouth properly." Freud observes that "the interpretation of this part of the dream was not carried far enough to make it possible to follow the whole of its concealed meaning." He then adds: "There is at least one spot in every dream at which it is unplumbable—a navel, as it were, that is its point of contact with the unknown" (1900, p. 111). Confronted with the question of knowing what was in the depths of Irma's mouth, Freud came up against two obstacles that must be distinguished from one another: Irma's resistance to opening her mouth, to speaking, and the fact that this mouth, once open, proves unfathomable. Irma may begin to speak, but this does not imply that she will say everything, nor that Freud will know everything. Something unknowable will remain.

At this point we are, to be sure, quite close to the theme of muteness and death, but the idea of the navel complicates this muteness and duplicates it: there is a silence outside speech that opposes it, but there is also a silence at the very heart of speech. This is what Lacan will later illustrate with the topological figure of the torus, whose surface is defined not only in relation to an external emptiness, but also in relation to an internal emptiness that it encloses. Here, then, we have a third way to understand what it is about speech that expresses the reality of the female sex: it is what appears as a lacuna in discourse, a hole in the signifying fabric. We find this theme of the lacuna, immediately after the Dream of Irma's Injection, in Draft K, which Freud sent to Fliess on January 1, 1896. In the section on hysteria, Freud offers an opinion on the origin of hysteria very different from the one he had defended in his 1894 paper, "The neuro-psychoses of defence." There he had maintained that hysteria begins with a conflict between the ego and a representation that is incompatible with it; the ego defends itself by separating the representation from the affect, the excitation, that triggered it and locating this affect in the body (the mechanism of conversion). But in Draft K, two years later, he argues that the primary phenomenon in hysteria is "a manifestation of fright accompanied by a gap in the psyche" (1887–1902, p. 154), that is, an absence of representation!

These two successive theories, though contradictory, are not really irreconcilable. The phenomenon that Freud describes in Draft K has more to do with prehistory than with the origin of hysteria, since the gap and the psychic fright are prior to the hysterical symptom, strictly speaking. Hysteria as such is established as a result of repression and repetition, when the subject encounters a representation that recalls that gap and that fright and these take on their value retroactively. On the issue of repression and its role in hysteria, moreover, Draft K introduces a nuance that redefines the notion of an incompatible representation: "Repression does not take place by the construction of an excessively strong antithetic idea, but by the intensification of a 'boundary idea' that will henceforth stand for the repressed memory" (1887–1902, p. 154). In this new approach, therefore, the signifier that will constitute the incompatible representation is chosen because it is somehow on the edge of the hole and delimits it; the hole in itself cannot, of course, be repressed, because it is just a hole and because only the signifier (what Freud calls the representation) can be repressed.

It is extremely odd that neither of these two notions—the gap and the boundary representation—was taken up in Freud's later works on hysteria. Yet they clearly indicate what he will find it so hard to describe, some years later, in the Wolf Man: the presence of a real element—outside knowledge because it is outside the signifier—at the heart of the signifying repression that determines symptoms, that is, the insistence of the real behind the symbolic/imaginary problematics of castration. Such negligence is all the more astonishing because these notions would have explained many points left in abeyance in the *Studies on Hysteria* (Breuer and Freud 1893–1895) or in the paper on the etiology of hysteria (1896c).

Let us look at the cases of hysteria that Freud reports in the years 1895–1900, rereading them from the perspective of two major trends in Freud's approach to femininity:

—the line of the *real*, and hence of the non-recognizable, of muteness, and of death, in which is inscribed the phenomenon of *disgust*; and

—the line of *castration*, and hence of the primacy of the phallus, in which is located the phenomenon of *horror*.

Over the years, the second orientation will gradually overtake the first one, to the point where it absorbs and overlaps it completely. Did the castration theory serve, for Freud, to close up an open breach at the beginning of his theoretical development?

4

The First Lie

A careful rereading of Freud's early works thus reveals two successive approaches to the issue of femininity, the first that of something unnamable, that is, of a real that makes a hole in speech, and the second, in contrast, based on something that is named, the primacy of the phallus that names the lack that is castration. We have seen that Freud encounters the unnamable in three forms: that of the real of the flesh, in which the female sex organ appears as desexualized; that of death, insofar as the feminine resembles muteness; and that of the lacuna in the psyche, the navel around which representations revolve. The question, then, is to know whether this nucleus of the real at the center of hysterical symptoms (and of Freud's own dreams) must remain out of reach, a hole in knowledge, or whether psychoanalysis can reduce this gap and bring about something we can know. That is the aim of Freud's desire to see and to know, right from the moment Irma agreed to open her mouth to his investigations.

That mouth suddenly opening in Freud's dream inevitably recalls the window that opens of its own accord in the Wolf Man's dream that Freud would analyze almost twenty years later (1918b)—a critical point at which the dream turns out to be just the fantasy of the dreamer, who, as a subject, has only to disappear from the scene to exist as a mere offstage gaze. Freud, however, goes beyond the sight of Irma's throat; his dream goes on to articulate its own construal. In that sense, this founding dream outlines the program for Freud's discovery: what he has to do is give an account of what he saw at the bottom of Irma's throat, to systematize that unnamable spot into a formula for which the dream provides the model. The challenge issued by Freud's desire is nothing less than to conquer the third Fate, Atropos, incarnation of death, whose name means "without figure" (in the sense of a rhetorical trope).

This is what is at stake in his theory and in the practice he began, more or less in the dark, with hysterics. Look again at the preliminary remarks to the *Studies on Hysteria* (Breuer and Freud 1893–1895); in the brief synopsis Freud gives there of the concept of abreaction, it is clear that the effect of trauma in hysteria is to leave the subject *unable to respond*, mute. Thus the event, or the fantasy, is traumatic in that it evokes a blank that, we are told, *mortifies* the subject. Freud places abreaction, which alone can cover over the gap of trauma, in the context of the *act,* or of speech through which language becomes equivalent to the act. Isn't this just what Freud himself does in the dream of Irma's injection, where the formula for trimethylamine replicates the whitish formations in Irma's throat? This doubling seems to me to reveal the true desire that the dream fulfills—a desire that is already, at least in potential, the desire of the analyst that Freud is at that moment.

For the dream takes place at a particular time in the life of psychoanalysis and of Freud. If as Max Schur (1972) claims, its aim was simply to exculpate Fliess in the Irma/Emma matter, Freud could have done this as early as February/March 1895, when the patient was being operated on. But the dream comes to him only on the night of July 23–24, 1895: Why the long wait? The correspondence with Fliess suggests an answer to this question. For on July 23 there occurred a major event in the maturation of Freud's desire: he began, in a kind of fever of inspiration, to write his *Project for a Scientific Psychology* (Freud 1895). This project is, precisely, to reduce to a series of letters, formulas, and schemas the fundamental concepts of the psychic apparatus and of psychopathology. So we might say that the formula for trimethylamine serves as a symbol for the "solution" in which the *Project* was to culminate.

The undertaking that began on July 23 aims to discern the unnamable, to reintegrate it into the symbolic system, to insert it in a formalization. Freud was to encounter a number of difficulties over the years that would lead him to elaborate a complex and sophisticated signifying organization. And the result of the progress of this elaboration, the perfecting of the "solution," was that in the end there was no longer a place in the Freudian symbolic system for the unnamable real that had motivated its production. This is the gain—but also the loss— implied by the establishment of the theory of repression and of the castration complex. And so Freud would finally write, in his *Outline of Psychoanalysis* (1938b) that the real is always unrecognizable.[1]

---

1. We can trace Freud's itinerary schematically and mark out its boundaries. After having invented and almost immediately abandoned the

This movement in Freud's work, in which the real is gradually covered over by the symbolic until it completely disappears, is what we shall be tracing. We shall see how the movement can be located in connection with the question of femininity. We shall then compare it to the journey that Lacan's teaching offers us, a journey that goes in exactly the opposite direction, for the movement of Lacan's elaboration is one of progressive revelation of the insistence of the real through and in the symbolic system. We shall see, in Freud, the development of a theory that sets out from the real and ends in castration, making of castration a veritable screen for the real to the point where, in the later texts, trauma itself is attributed to the fear of castration instead of to the emergence of the unnamable. For Lacan, in contrast, the decoding sets out from castration and ends in the real, in such a way that the symbolic system is revealed to be not a cover but that which digs out the holes through which the gap of the real can be seen. This inversion of the meanings in the respective systems of Freud and Lacan explains the different results of their reflections on femininity.

By the 1930s Freud can explain the problematics of femininity only in terms of the castration complex and the result-

---

notion of a border representation in relation to a gap, Freud became interested in everything that could serve to plug this gap, this hole: first the false memory, *proton pseudos* of hysteria, then the screen memory (1899) and the dream (1900), in which, oddly, the unrecognizable can become the already seen; then infantile sexual theories (1908a), the phobic object (1909), and the taboo (1913); then primal fantasies, until the discovery of the primacy of the phallus provides the concept that will enable him to stop up the gap of the unnamable completely. The hole thus becomes the lack of something or a wound, which leads to the paper on fetishism (1927) and its extension in the kind of generalized fetishism described in Freud's final paper on the splitting of the ego (1938a).

ing penis envy in the woman. But Lacan, especially in his seminar *Encore* (1974–1975), concludes that femininity can be understood correctly only in terms of that emergence of the real that causes a woman, even as she is caught up in the castration complex, to be *not-all* settled there, to have one foot inside and one foot outside it, since part of her does not correspond to the phallic function.

What Lacan is doing here is merely restoring an initial truth of Freudian doctrine, a truth that, as the doctrine became progressively elaborated, was eclipsed by the development of the castration theory. Thus it would be false to say that on this point Lacan is in opposition to Freud. He is simply taking up the Freudian project, with the proviso, stated at the beginning of the second part of the *Écrits* (1966), that he is taking up this project the wrong way round. For indeed Lacan starts at the end of Freud's work (the notions of the castration complex, the primacy of the phallus, and the splitting of the ego) and finishes by bringing back up to the surface what Freud had shown at the very beginning of that work: the encounter, at the heart of trauma, with a real that appears as "the correlative . . . of the representation" (1964, p. 59). We may add to this formula a nuance the importance of which will become clear as we go on: the *desexualized* correlative of a *sexualized* representation.

Let us go back to Freud's initial steps and to the original encounter with the real of the woman. How will he respond to this gap? How will he give substance to the formal model that the dream suggested to him with the formula for trimethylamine?

It is immediately after this first encounter that Freud begins, both in his own analysis and in his experience with hysterics, to put in place the function of the paternal agency and the Oedipus complex on the one hand, and on the other hand the beginnings of the theory of repression.

We may recall that at this time Freud thinks of hysteria as a reaction to the father's seductive manipulation of his daughter. In short, he traces hysteria back to the perversion of the older generation. Thus he is still transmitting the manifest discourse of certain hysterics (for example in the case of Katharina [Breuer and Freud 1893–1895]); the father's perversion somehow constitutes the knowledge through which the hysteric explains to herself why sexuality is so traumatic for her. Nevertheless, a reading of *Studies on Hysteria* shows that the hysteric's relationship with her father cannot be reduced to this sole encounter with perversion. The cases of Miss Lucy and of Elisabeth von R., for instance, point to a much more complex and subtle relation to the father. They indicate that the hysteric is not in a purely passive position with regard to her father, that she participates in setting up a relation of ambiguous complicity with him, one that is evident in Lucy's love for her teacher and Elisabeth's support of her ailing father.

It is in the course of his own analysis, and at the very moment when he discovers that, like the hysteric, he too had been the object of seductive manipulation by the Other, that Freud comes to reformulate the relation to the father and to establish the father as a central function for the subject. For, if the hysteric complains that she was seduced (or raped) by her father, Freud, for his part, complains that he was prematurely initiated into sexuality by his nurse and his mother.[2] This evo-

---

2. See Letters 70 and 71 in Freud 1887–1902. Freud recalls memories, dating from early childhood, of his mother and his nurse. Of the latter, he says, among other things, that she was the one who first caused

cation of the maternal genital as traumatic immediately leads him to the legend of Oedipus and to the idea of repression. The Oedipus complex is no doubt the foundation of psychoanalysis, but its theoretical scope must not make us forget that, while he is making this discovery, Freud is also in the process of being a hysteric; in other words, this decoding, operative as it may be, constitutes, for Freud himself, an encoding.

Moreover, we have to situate this crucial moment of the Freudian elaboration in the context of the person to whom it was addressed, that is, in the transference to Fliess. To the centrally important letter in which Freud confides his discovery of the Oedipus, Fliess, for the only time in their correspondence, makes no response. This leads Freud to write again twelve days later (1887–1902, Letter 72), and, still without a reply, to make another attempt on November 5 (Letter 74) in the most urgent terms: he is concerned that his interpretation of *Oedipus Rex* and *Hamlet* might not be well received and is eager for Fliess' advice. As in the "Autodidasker" dream, the desire to be wrong is perceptible beneath Freud's demand, but this too is an entirely ambiguous demand that could be phrased as: "I'm asking you to prove me wrong so that I can know that I'm right."

But what could Fliess have replied, given that his was a system based exclusively on the maternal function? For the

---

neurosis in him, and he calls her his professor of sexuality; he dreams that she washed him in water reddened by her menstrual blood. As for his mother, he recalls that at the age of around two he saw her naked when on a trip with her; this leads him to to evoke the story of Oedipus and to recall a childhood scene in which the nurse and the mother exchange roles. It must surely be at the moment when the reality of his mother's genital makes its presence known in his analysis that Freud discovers the Oedipus complex.

crucial point of the Oedipus, as Freud's later work would show, is less the love for the mother than the disturbance introduced by the father in the mother–child relation. The mainspring of the Oedipal theory is the designation of the paternal function as the basis of subjectivity, a function that Fliess had totally ignored. To this correspondence without reply we may compare the poem that, two years later, Freud writes for the birth of Fliess' second son (in Schur 1972, p. 546). This poem, the existence of which Max Schur has revealed, bears on much more than the event it was supposed to mark. It is a striking summation of the way Freud, armed with his discovery of the Oedipus, replies to the paranoiac theory of Fliess.

These astonishing lines are clearly contrary to Fliess' system, with its implicit postulate of the transference of the mother to her child. Here Freud celebrates the father's transference to the son. The opposition between the two poles, paternal and maternal, is absolute: on the father's side are law and rationality, on the mother's, in contrast to calculation, is a secret glow (*heimlicher Schein*), a glow that is doubtless just a semblance, since this is also the meaning of the German word *Schein*. But even more than a contrast to Fliess' paranoia is Freud's emphasis on the fact that the basis of this paranoia, namely the calculation of periods, occupies precisely the place of the paternal function. This is why he can wish that it will be the calculation that will be transferred (*sich übertragen*) to the son.

And this poem also explains the mission Freud assigns to the paternal agency or to its substitute: to curb the power of the female sex, replacing it in obedience to the law. He thereby emphasizes less the abnormality of Fliess' madness than its value as restoration. We cannot fail to think of the case of President Schreber that will claim Freud's attention ten years later, where the delusional construction shows in a quite spectacular way the effort to restrain the power femininity exercises over him and to submit it to a universal law.

It is noteworthy that this celebration of the paternal function occurs at the very same time that Freud was writing up the case of Dora (Freud 1905), where the exclusive accent on the paternal pole is precisely what leads to the premature interruption of the treatment, a failure that surely demonstrated to Freud the harmful effects of his own hysteria on his clinical practice. But before we criticize the father-worship Freud got involved in with Dora—as it happens, he himself was the first to express such criticism, and with exemplary candor—we have to emphasize the profound changes in Freud's understanding of hysteria, and of the father's role in it, from the *Studies on Hysteria* to the Dora case, changes that accompanied his discovery of the Oedipus complex.

For, with Dora, Freud redefines the position of the hysteric as that of *the father's lover*. The father is no longer the seducer who imposes his perversion on his daughter, but instead the one whom she chooses. In this early period of the development of his Oedipal theory, Freud envisions the complex from two symmetrically opposed aspects, depending on whether the subject is a boy or a girl: the son loves his mother and is jealous of his father, the girl loves her father and is jealous of her mother. It is just this alleged symmetry that limits Freud's understanding of Dora. Later on he will come to question it in his papers of 1931 and 1933 on feminine sexuality, where he will set up a fundamental asymmetry between the female Oedipus and that of the male. Nevertheless, it is the establishment of the paternal function in the Oedipus that enables Freud to approach hysteria as a *structure* organizing the transference and no longer merely as a set of symptoms to be undone one by one, as in the cases described in *Studies on Hysteria*. There is now a system in place by which psychoanalytic treatment can determine its own path.

At the same time as Freud was setting forth the initial guidelines of the Oedipus complex, he was struggling with the notion of bisexuality, which, a few years earlier, had seemed to cement his agreement with Fliess. But in fact, behind the debate over the meaning to be given to the term *bisexuality*, the theory of repression is coming into being.

In late 1897 and early 1898, that is, right after their Breslau "congress," discord arises between Freud and Fliess with regard to bisexuality. Fliess had just transformed his theory of bisexuality into a theory of bilaterality, assimilating the difference between the sexes to the difference between left and right. Freud cannot conceal his skepticism about this theoretical development but wants nonetheless to maintain confidence in it.[3] Yet his declared intentions are belied by a dream in which the formula for saying good-bye (*auf Wiedersehen*) is replaced by the odd neologisms *auf Geseres, auf Ungeseres* (Freud 1900, pp. 441–443). In his associations, Freud relates this signifying pair to other oppositions, such as salted and unsalted (of caviar), or leavened and unleavened (of bread). From there, he comes to conversations he had with Fliess about the meaning of bilateral symmetry, concluding that *Geseres/Ungeseres* refers to Fliess' idea that the opposi-

---

3. Compare, in the Freud-Fliess correspondence (Freud 1887–1902), Letters 81 (January 4, 1898), 85 (March 15, 1898,) and 113 (August 1, 1899). In the first, Freud's irony reveals his profound disagreement, but in the next two he is less caustic, asking Fliess for new explanations and stating that in principle Fliess is right. Again, the desire to be wrong. . . .

tion male/female comes down to the pair left/right: "After the child [in the dream] had turned to *one side* to say farewell words, he turned to the *other side* to say the contrary, as though to restore the balance. *It was as though he was acting with due attention to bilateral symmetry!*" (1900, p. 444). The apparent absurdity of the dream can then be explained; as in all such dreams, it represents criticism, irony, sarcasm. The dream is, once again, a transference dream addressed to Fliess.

But the relationship of the two men will not remain on the level of this comical, amiable irony. During their Achensee "congress," their last, in the summer of 1900, Fliess attacks Freud violently, accusing him of reading his thoughts or of reading only his own thoughts into his patients' material. We do not have Freud's version of this exchange (only an account written by Fliess in 1906), but, at the time, the rupture was complete and Fliess was totally caught up in his paranoia regarding Freud. Freud's sole allusion to these accusations occurs in a letter of August 7, 1901 (Freud 1887–1902, Letter 145), where, despite everything, he renews his offer of trust in Fliess and accompanies it with a proposal that Fliess collaborate on a work to be entitled *Bisexuality in Man*. Freud writes:

> You remember my saying to you years ago, when you were still a nose specialist and surgeon, that the solution lay in sexuality. Years later you corrected me and said bisexuality, and I see that you are right. So perhaps I shall have to borrow still more from you, and perhaps I shall be compelled in honesty to ask you to add your signature to the book to mine; this would mean an expansion of the anatomical-biological part, which in my hands alone would be very meagre. I should make my aim the mental aspect of bisexuality and the explanation of the neurotic side. [p. 335]

He concludes by expressing the hope that they will once more find themselves in agreement, even regarding "scientific matters." Fliess refuses this offer, and in subsequent letters accuses Freud of wanting to steal his claim to original ideas about human bisexuality. This accusation will later take concrete form when Fliess condemns Otto Weininger's book on female sexuality, and publishes a lampoon against Freud (see Schur 1972). But, to return to the 1901 letter in which Freud describes plans for a work on human bisexuality, he specifies that he is interested in learning more about the crucial problem of repression, which he sees as involving two sexual currents. Thus all Freud's reflections on bisexuality during the years 1895–1900 must be placed in the context of a theory of repression that, along with the question of the lacuna and the unnamable real, and the question of the function of the father, constitute the three landmarks of his elucidation of hysteria.

And it is precisely in connection with an essay on repression that we find the first mention of bisexuality in the Freud/ Fliess correspondence. In the famous Letter 52 of December 6, 1896, Freud starts with the hypothesis that the psyche is established by a process of stratification: the material present in the psyche in the form of mnemic traces is periodically reworked as a function of the subject's history. These revisions imply a series of inscriptions of the traces in the different systems (perception, unconscious, preconscious, conscious), among which mechanisms of translation and transcription are at work. In this conception, repression is a *faulty translation* from one system into another, and this gives rise to anachronisms, that is, to the survival of traces of the past. Applied to the major categories of psychosexual neuroses, this theory yields the following conclusions: for hysteria, repressed memories pertain to events that took place between 1 ½ and 4 years of age; for obsessional neurosis to events that took place between ages 4 and 8; and for paranoia, which Freud considered to be a defense neurosis at this time, between ages 8 and 14. As for perversion, it is distinct from the defense neuroses in that the capacity for repression is either not achieved at all or is achieved only after the psychic apparatus is in place. Freud also notes—and this is an essential point for both the theory of hysterical trauma and for the differentiation between hysteria and obsessional neurosis—that before the age of 4 (the boundary point separating the origin of hysteria and that of obsession), repression does not occur.

Freud goes on to introduce the reference to bisexuality, which from then on is seen as something entirely other than a biological given:

> In order to explain why the outcome is sometimes perversion and sometimes neurosis, I avail myself of the universal bisexuality of human beings. In a purely male being there would be a surplus of masculine release at the two sexual boundaries [p. 38], consequently pleasure would be generated and at the same time perversion; in a purely female being there would be a surplus of *unpleasurable* substance at these two points of time. During the first phases the releases would run parallel (i.e., there would be a normal surplus of pleasure). This explains the preference of true females for the defensive neuroses. [p. 179]

This passage equates, on the one hand, male, pleasure, and perversion, and, on the other hand, female, unpleasure, and defense neurosis (or repression). We can assess the scope and significance of this equation only in the context of three ideas with which Freud was much preoccupied at this time. The first, that libido is a male principle and repression a female one, is taken directly from Fliess, though later renounced (see Freud 1887–1902, Draft M and Letters 71 and 75). The second is that hysteria is associated with femininity and sexual disgust, obsession with masculinity and sexual pleasure. Initially broached in Letters 29 and 30 in October 1895, this idea would be taken up again in Draft K of January 1896 and in two important papers Freud writes that same year, "Further Remarks on the Neuro-Psychoses of Defence" and "The Aetiology of Hysteria" (Freud 1896b, c). These two latter texts introduce the additional equation of female and passive, male and active. The following table shows the series of oppositions through which Freud gives meaning to the notion of bisexuality:

<u>Bisexuality</u>

<u>Male</u>	<u>Female</u>
libido	repression
perversion	neurosis
pleasure	unpleasure
(sensuality)	(disgust)
obsession	hysteria
activity	passivity

Before we take a closer look at these oppositions, we must understand their origin and their aim in Freud's thinking. To begin with, from very early on Freud states that it is impossible to define the nature of femininity solely by reference to anatomy. On the psychic—or, more precisely, the unconscious—level, the duality masculine/feminine has the status of a question mark, and femininity itself remains an enigma, an unnamable. In fact, right from these first steps in Freud's work an entire system of reasoning gets underway, one that is a metonymy for the psychoanalytic enterprise itself, as invented by Freud, and also a metonymy for the logic of the hysterical process. In establishing a theory of repression in place of Fliess' notion of bisexuality, Freud's logic is as follows: since the feminine as such is an unnamable lacuna, a muteness and even a resistance to discourse, we can apprehend it only from the perspective of repression, which produces a representation, a trace, where there is— literally—nothing, neither representation nor trace. By so doing, repression offers material for analysis, a something instead of nothing.

And that is the first lie, the first pretense, that comes to us from the Other insofar as the Other is the locus of language. But it is also the case that it is only through this lie that the real comes into its true value, for it is only through this failed representation that the idea of an "off to one side" can emerge. That is what is at issue in the theory of repression in relation to trauma, that is, the theory of the retrospective constitution of the trauma as such. Furthermore, on a second level, the level of psychoanalytic knowledge, it is what gives impact to the theory of castration in regard to the female genital: to say that this genital is castrated is a signifying lie, and it is only by passing through this lie that the ex-sistence of a real that is not castrated can emerge.[4]

---

4. The thesis that the real, even if it exists before the signifier, can be discerned only by means of the signifier illuminates Freud's much later reflections on traumatic neurosis and the process of repetition. See Freud 1920.

Thus the theory of repression becomes a necessity in the development of Freud's thought only if we mark it as that which gives analyzable meaning to the trauma constituted by the discovery of femininity. Let us return to the *Studies on Hysteria* (Breuer and Freud 1893–1895) and the papers from the period 1894–1896. In the introduction to the *Studies*, Freud relies on a comparison between hysteria and traumatic neurosis. It seems at first that there is a valid analogy, since, in traumatic neurosis, it is not only the bodily injury that determines the illness, but also the accompanying fear, that is, the psychic trauma. But this analogy will not hold if we note, as Freud invites us to, that in hysteria the trauma is far from an *agent provocateur* that triggers the symptom. It is not the trauma itself that gives rise to the hysterical symptom but instead the memory by which it is designated; hysterics, as Freud notes, suffer from reminiscences.

In the section on the psychotherapy of hysteria, Freud states that the structure of hysteria consists of three layers. First he identifies a nucleus of *memories* in which the traumatic factor dominates and that is, as it were, the archive of the hysteric; then he notes that the grouping of these memories is characterized by the *formation of one or more themes* concentrically arranged around the pathogenic nucleus; finally he observes that the layout of these memories in relation to the nucleus is that of a *logical chain* extending toward the nucleus by way of a twisting path that he compares to the zigzag movement of the knight on a chessboard. Here we can see, in another form, the structure that appeared in the dream of Irma's injection, and especially in the very writing of the formula for trimethylamine: an umbilical structure (the traumatic nucleus) toward which, progressing by logical association and grouping themselves together thematically, a series of memories converge. What is this central nucleus, this navel around which everything is constructed, and what motivates the formation of the associative chains that converge on it?

On the issue of what triggers the process—that is, the issue of the split between a traumatic nucleus and a chain of representations that keep on pointing to it—the 1894 paper "Further Remarks on the Neuro-Psychoses of Defence" provides an initial, and very general, answer. Here Freud isolates three forms of defense that are analyzed as three modalities of a split between the *Ich* and the sexual representation that he calls incompatible. The symptom seeks to resolve this dissonance, not through a reconciliation but through dissociating or splitting off the representation. In hysteria, for example, the *Ich* separates the representation from the accompanying affect (that is, the excitation), with the result that the strong representation becomes a weak or innocuous one and the excitation is transferred to the body; this is the defense of conversion. In obsession and phobia, the same split occurs, but this time the affect, instead of being transferred to the body, remains in the psychic system. There it becomes attached to other representations that, while not themselves incompatible, become obsessional by virtue of this false connection; this is the defense of displacement or transposition. Finally, in hallucinatory psychosis, the *Ich* defends itself by rejecting both the unbearable representation and the accompanying affect and behaving as though the representation had never reached it. But, in so doing, it becomes separated from the reality to which the representation was attached, and this produces a new kind of split, no longer one between the *Ich* and the representation but between the *Ich* and reality; the defense operates through disavowal (*Verwerfung*) and hallucination.

This formulation is spelled out in more detail the following year when, in his "Project for a Scientific Psychology" (in Freud 1887–1902) he finally sets out the thesis that made it possible to give trauma its rightful place in relation to the reminiscences of hysterics: it is only in retrospect that a repressed memory becomes a trauma. This means that the traumatic scene does not contain its own meaning. It becomes traumatic only when, as a memory, it is evoked by an analogous scene. (This is the same process that, in Letter 52, Freud formalizes as a reinscription in another system.) As we shall see in the example he cites in support of his argument, it is only in this repetition that there arises, in the form of anxiety, a sexual excitation that could not appear on the original occasion. The signifying repetition enables us to see that in the original scene—which has now become traumatic—there was a real that could not be assimilated by the signifier, a real involving a *jouissance*.

Thus Emma, in the example, is afraid to go into a store alone. She explains this symptom by reference to a memory that goes back to her thirteenth year. At that time she had gone into a clothing store, but, when she saw the two salesmen laughing, she suddenly became panicky and ran out. She thought the two men were making fun of her appearance, and she confides to Freud that she believes she felt attracted to one of them. But the analysis gives rise to another memory, an earlier one, that had not occurred to her at the time she was in the store. At the age of 8, it turned out, she had gone into a grocery store to buy some sweets, and the grocer had placed his hand, through her clothing, on her genitals. Emma had not been at all shaken by this attempt, since she returned to this grocer later on. It was only with the second scene, five years later, that the grocer's act assumed a traumatic value and gave rise to the excitation—here, her panic.

This second scene is a perfect signifying repetition of the first in two respects: the laughter of the salesmen unconsciously evoked the distorted smile of the grocer, and the element "clothing" is common to both anecdotes. Hence it is as a memory that the first scene triggers excitation in the course of the second, excitation that is transformed into anxiety. Freud provides a remarkable diagram of this process (p. 412):

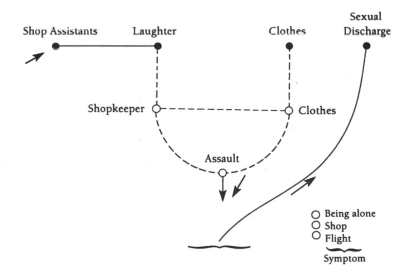

The black dots in this diagram represent the elements consciously recalled by the patient, the white dots those of the repressed scene.[5] But this diagram goes further than the commentary Freud supplies. For he does not explain the lower part of the diagram, where we find the nucleus or navel of this associative chain. The diagram shows that from the attack, the seduction, that is the focal point of the sequence, there extends an arrow at the end of which no signifier is provided: there is just a blank, but it is from this blank, this lacuna, that another arrow departs, ending in the sexual discharge at the time of the repetition.

What does this mean? First, that the real is present only retroactively, insofar as, on the unconscious level, the signifying repetition literally produces the real in its causal function. But beyond this, the double arrow shows that the effect of repression, going through repetition and the return of the repressed, is the sexualization of that which was not originally sexualized by the subject. *In short, repression serves to make the real a sexual reality.* And, of course (more will be said about this later on), if there is sexualization, there is by the same token the determination of something non-sexualized. This is the secret of the mechanism of disgust in hysteria.

This clinical example shows how the unconscious operates with the real—that is, not just how it treats the real, but how it produces it, how it determines it within the process of repression. For the real is not simply external to signifying

---

5. A Lacanian reading of this diagram would be as follows. The signifying repetition S1—S2 (here, the two occurrrences of the laughter and the clothing) is literally what retroactively produces the trauma of the emergence of the real left untouched by the signifier: $S1 \rightarrow \frac{S2}{a}$. But, at the same time, the repetition has the effect of situating this real in its place, the place of *jouissance*.

repetition; it is caught up in it. Even if it is not represented as such there, it is nonetheless present and makes itself known by anxiety effects in the very midst of sexual *jouissance*. What can this model teach us about the question of femininity in the logic of Freud's approach? Would we have to say that the same structure determines the relation between femininity (as real) and the phallus (as signifier)? This would imply that, for Freud, "becoming a woman" must be considered a retroactive effect to be situated as a lacuna in and through the primacy of the phallus and castration. Let us leave this issue in abeyance for the moment.

Draft K, dated January 1, 1896 (in Freud 1887–1902, pp. 146–156), provides some fundamental clarifications of these early theories of defense and trauma. For there to be a defense, Freud says, there must have been an incident of a sexual nature occurring before sexual maturity. But why does this sexual representation appear to the *Ich* to be incompatible, disagreeable? This question is all the more important because in a different domain from the psychoneuroses of defense, namely the domain of the perversions, the sexual representation does not seem to be marked by this connotation of unpleasure, indeed of intolerableness. At this point in the text, Freud introduces the concept of repression, linking it to *modesty*. This is an interesting juxtaposition, one that we can decipher retroactively by reference to the notion of the phallus which is far from Freud's mind at this point in his work. In his paper on "The signification of the phallus" (1958a), Lacan mentions the demon of modesty as essential to the function of the phallus. Modesty is phallic insofar as it indicates that something cannot be—or rather does not have to be—unveiled, because it is the veil itself, the phallus as veil, that is the point.

Now, in Draft K, what appears to be struck by repression or by the demon of modesty is the body in its organic function, that is, the body that has not fallen under the sway of the phallus, the body outside sexuality. And it is this distinction that enables us to resolve the false opposition that Freud sets up here between neurosis and perversion. If, in the perversions, certain bodily zones or certain organic functions give pleasure, whereas they are sources of unpleasure in the neuroses, this is not because the pervert is an immoral, shameless person, but because, for him, these zones and functions are completely phallicized. Freud himself observes that, beyond any perversion, everyday experience shows that morality is silent and disgust absent when libido reaches a certain level. It is clear, then, that disgust and modesty are not attached to any given anatomical zone but to the body insofar as it is not totally subverted by libido, to the body insofar as it remains an organic body.[6] This division of the body in the experience of disgust is the basis of the primary phenomena of hysteria and is a key to the process of conversion.

A third clarification provided by Draft K is that, if there is repression, there is also *the return of the repressed*. And it is this return that, in a second phase, gives rise to the symptom. Repressed ideas return of their own accord, slipping unhindered into the most rational associations. This thesis makes a bridge between the theory of repression and the notion of trauma; in both cases we are dealing with a retroactive effect,

---

6. This theme will reappear throughout Freud's work, especially in *Civilization and its Discontents* (1930), where it is the subject of two long notes in Chapter 4. There Freud speaks of organic repression, which, it seems to me, is to be understood as a repression of the organic in favor of the phallic. But this does not make matters easier, since we may wonder whether the term *repression* is appropriate in this case.

repression revealing itself in the return of the repressed, and trauma when it is evoked by a second memory.

Finally, and this is the fourth contribution of Draft K, Freud comes back to the triad hysteria/obsession/psychoses that he had established in "Further remarks on the neuro-psychoses of defence" (1896b). He brings it into relation with the rudiments of the theory of repression and tries to explain what, in each case, triggers repression. In obsessional neurosis, the basis of repression is an excess of pleasure; in hysteria, by way of contrast, it is an experience of fear, of unpleasure. But Freud immediately slips into an association of pleasure, activity, and masculinity on the one hand and unpleasure, passivity, and femininity on the other. The natural sexual passivity of women, he says, predisposes them to hysteria, and, in the case of male hysterics, an underlying sexual passivity is always to be found.

What is the meaning of this transition from male/female to pleasure/unpleasure and active/passive, the opposition obsession/hysteria coming to the aid of this displacement? The question is especially difficult to pin down in view of the fact that the successive pairs do not precisely correspond to one another; there is a certain divergence, with each new equivalence in fact calling into question the relevance of the preceding one. Thus the pair activity/passivity casts doubt on the pair pleasure/unpleasure ascribed to the pair obsession/hysteria. If the primary phenomenon of obsession is an experience of sexual pleasure, how can there be repression? How does this experience of pleasure return in memory accompanied by a reaction of unpleasure? Isn't there, at the basis of obsessional neurosis, something other than the active incident through which the subject prematurely obtained sexual pleasure?

Far from expressing the opposition pleasure/unpleasure, the distinction activity/passivity actually shows how precarious it is. Then Freud goes further, noting that in all cases of obsessional neurosis there is to be found a very early experience of passivity that later on combines with a pleasurable incident in such a way as to give it a distressing character; this is what leads to repression. Here we have the germ of another fundamental idea, one that Freud would set out in more detain several months later in "Further remarks on the neuropsychoses of defence" (1896b): obsessional neurosis is always constructed on a hysterical substrate. This idea is implicit in Lacan's problematic of the four discourses; if he formulates a hysterical discourse and not an obsessional one, this is because there is one, and only one, neurotic structure, and that is hysteria, of which obsession, as Freud says, is just a dialect.

In short, at this stage of Freud's elaboration, neurosis goes back to a primary experience characterized as one of sexual passivity. The notion of trauma and the seduction theory find their meaning here: the subject was caught up in a real experience but did not have the signifier that would have enabled him to respond (to abreact, as is said in *Studies on Hysteria*), that is, to transform this passive scene into one in which he was actively present. Without the signifier that would open up the possibility of action for him, the subject was confronted with a lacuna, which the hysteric expresses in manifestations of fear. We can therefore understand the role that repression plays in this process: the second phase chronologically but first logically (since through it trauma is retroactively determined), repression serves to supply the signifier, or rather the signifying pair (S1–S2) that makes it possible to border the experience of the real by what Freud calls a boundary representation. We must now explain this initial experience of sexual passivity, in which Freud locates the origin of every defense neurosis, and see, in this connection, what role repression plays in the problematics of hysteria.

5

The Hysteric and Femininity: Disgust

What, then, is the meaning of the experience of sexual passivity that Freud identifies as the source of all neurosis, whether hysterical or obsessional? Let us begin by recalling what is at stake. We have seen that, from the beginning, the concept of bisexuality appears enigmatic and complex to Freud, while Fliess links it simply and directly to anatomical difference. In reality, Freud's approach rests on the implicit notion that, once we get beyond anatomy, we do not know what the terms "male" and "female" correspond to, or we have only approximations of this. Thus the opposition activity/passivity comes to express a relation between the two sexes that the term *bisexuality* is trying to indicate. This argument rests on a postulate that, it must be admitted, is merely a prejudice: women are naturally passive and men naturally active. This reference—most often implicit—to a male or female "nature" is obviously the problem, since it goes against the very direction of Freud's approach, an approach that seeks to show, precisely, that there is no masculine or feminine nature.

Besides, Freud quickly perceives that the pair activity/ passivity is more complex than it seemed at first. Earlier on, this pair could serve to explain the duality of the two fundamental neuroses, hysteria and obsessional neurosis, as well as the fact that more women tend to be hysterics, more men obsessionals. This is because, Freud said, hysteria is based on an original experience of sexual passivity, while in obsessional neurosis the subject's active role is evident in his original experience. But, as we have seen, this parallel collapses in 1896, when Freud discovers that even in obsessional neurosis there is ultimately a scene of sexual passivity. He makes the same point in another paper of that year, "Heredity and the aetiology of the neuroses" (1896a), noting that this experience of passivity introduces the subject to sexuality, and, more specifically, to orgasmic sexual pleasure, *jouissance*.[1]

The term *jouissance* must be emphasized. It may be just a matter of chance that Freud wrote this paper in French; in German, he uses the term *Lust*, which does not have the same connotations over and above "pleasure" as does the French term *jouissance*. A fortunate coincidence, if it is one, for it is in relocating the originary experience of sexuality in the register of *jouissance* instead of the register of pleasure/unpleasure that we come to the very heart of what Freud is trying to place into the dialectic of activity and passivity.

For on the most primary level the child's discovery of sexual *jouissance* always occurs in a passive experience, since it is always from the Other that the subject receives sexuality. Sexual *jouissance* is always an encroachment, in that it grabs hold of the child in his first relation to the Other: the

---

1. Freud would make a similar point some years later in the case of the Wolf Man (1918b).

child is at first the object, rather than the subject, of *jouissance*, for he at first gives the Other who takes care of him a *jouissance* that it would not be wrong to call sexual. This is the structural justification for the fact that Freud always connects the discovery of *jouissance* to an experience of seduction. What is important here is not whether there is or isn't a historical event in which the subject was the victim of more or less perverted manipulation, but that every subject begins by being, as an infant, given over to the caresses, the wishes, the agitations of his or her caretaker. Freud will later explain that for both the girl and the boy the primary seduction comes from the mother, who, in tending to the baby, awakens *jouissance* in it. Isn't this primary experience of passivity, in which the subject is enjoyed sexually by the Other, what Lacan has taught us to identify as the position in which the subject is reduced to being the object/cause of the Other's desire—in fantasy, but also in the real experience of dependence on that first Other who is the mother? From that time on, the experience underlying all neurosis—hysterical, obsessional, or phobic—is that of being assigned the position of object offered to the Other, a position in which the subject disappears as such and exists merely as the waste product or the instrument of the *jouissance* of the Other. We are touching here on the establishment of the fundamental structure of the fantasy in Lacan's formula $\$ \lozenge a$.

The way in which this original experience of passivity is taken up and reworked in fantasy, and recalled in repression and the return of the repressed, determines the choice of neurosis. Obsession differs from hysteria in that the active version of the trauma is repressed: what the obsessional cannot bear, the representation that seems irreconcilable, incompatible, to him, is that he in turn treats the Other as object of his *jouissance*, which amounts to killing the Other as Other. For the hysteric, in contrast, repression runs parallel to the direction of the trauma: what is unbearable is the passive position, the position of object given over to the *jouissance* of the Other. Now we are better able to understand the parallel Freud draws at the end of the paper on "Heredity and the aetiology of the neuroses" (1896a) between obsession and the masculine on the one hand, hysteria and the feminine on the other. What is at issue here is not so much assigning a hypothetical essence to both sexes as setting forth the conditions for their trying to form a relationship: "One sometimes comes across a pair of neurotic patients who were a pair of little lovers in their earliest childhood—the man suffering from obsessions and the woman from hysteria" (1896a, p. 156). This touching image is worth thinking about, since it illustrates a truth about what we call the "couple" or the alliance that is formed in the attempt to reject the traumatic element of sexuality: the reduction of the Other, and in particular the female Other, to the object of *jouissance*.

If the primary traumatic experience is that of the passivity inherent in the position of object of the Other's *jouissance*, what role does repression play? This is the question Freud discusses in two important papers written in the same year, 1896: "Further remarks on the neuro-psychoses of defence" (1896b) and "The aetiology of hysteria" (1896c). A close reading of these two texts establishes a preliminary approach to the mechanism of hysterical neurosis. In "Further remarks," Freud endorses the idea that the action of sexual trauma is belated because of repressed memory. But, in a footnote (Note 2, pp. 166–167), he raises a fundamental issue when he observes that it is only representations with a sexual content that can be repressed, representations that evoke sexual excitation. This note, brief but complex, calls for analysis.

Freud begins by setting forth the equation between the repressed and the sexual (sexual representations). This equation constitutes the rule for human sexuality insofar as that sexuality is more than a purely organic phenomenon. For repressed representations have as their main feature the power to trigger excitation that Freud describes as somatic excitation transformed into the psychic kind. This means that the effect of repression is to substitute for an organic sexuality a sexuality governed by the representation, by the signifier. Moreover, Freud continues, the excitation triggered by these repressed representations is incomparably stronger than the somatic version produced during the real experience that repression designates as traumatic.

The case of Emma (Freud 1887–1892) shows that repression serves to transform into sexual *jouissance* (with the specific meaning this term takes on for the speaking being) what had formerly been merely an indeterminate sensation. Thus, for Freud, *the signifying process of repression is a process of sexualization of the real.* He thereby inscribes the real in a trend of thought that will eventually, in his later work, become the phallic signification. And this thesis leads to two lines of questioning. First, we shall want to know what it is, in the process set up between trauma and the repressed, that triggers excitation. What is the cause of *jouissance*? Is it the repressed signifier itself, or instead the lacuna that it delimits as a trauma and somehow elevates to the rank of *sexual* trauma? We shall then go on to ask whether the equation "repressed = sexual" could not be turned around into "sexual = repressed." For the human being, only that which has undergone repression comes to take on a sexual connotation. We shall then see what clinical work with hysterics can teach us on these points.

In "The aetiology of hysteria" Freud takes a few additional steps. He describes in more detail the trauma indicated by the hysteric's repressed memories. It involves an experience of disgust, he says, twice giving the example of coming upon a corpse. This reference to a corpse seems to me to be not merely accidental, one image among others. For once again, as in the dream of Irma's injection, we find death and rotting flesh, that is, a collapse or demotion that renders the body unfit for recognition as a human body. The corpse takes on a traumatic value not so much because it is lifeless as because it lays bare what is always veiled over in human relations—brute flesh, the real part that turns the body into something that borders on filth. And though in this paper Freud claims that he invented these examples, the encounter with a corpse is a major element in the case of Emmy von N. (Breuer and Freud 1893–1895).

Then, returning to the question of trauma and repression in connection with the associative chain, Freud states that the memories of hysterics are organized like genealogical trees. But, he goes on to ask, where does this chain lead? In other words, how do we get back, through the return of the repressed and the analysand's associations, to the trauma that lies beyond the associations and the memory? Going through the chain link by link, we get to a node, as Freud says in the "Project" (in 1887–1892), that is, to a point where two series of associations intersect. This umbilical point is invariably located in the domain of sexual experience in early childhood. But the childhood scenes at which we arrive in this way must be added to the material supplied by the subject, since they form the missing piece in the puzzle constructed by the memories and associations, the piece that can exactly fill the hole represented by the nodal point and clarify the origin of the patient's neurosis.

Although at this time Freud still considers such scenes to be historical facts, we have here the beginnings of the concern with the construction of the fundamental fantasy. For the element that Freud is trying to grasp is not present as such in the associative chain but is correlative with it. And the method he invents to identify it involves extending the chain still further—in Lacanian terms, having the subject produce his master signifiers—so as to obtain something like the outline of the missing piece, the drawing of a border that makes present a hole Freud will fill in with a scene that, as he will realize later in the case of the Wolf Man, constitutes the subject's primordial fantasy. He adds that this scene, which marks the child's first experience with sexuality, cannot ultimately be other than a scene of seduction. This brings us back to the connection between passivity and trauma. For the child does not discover sexuality by himself or herself but receives it from an adult. Thus the convergence of the associative chains at a nodal point enables the analyst to see that they lead to the relation to the Other who infects the subject with his *jouissance*. This is the meaning of the seduction theory.

At another level, this attempt to fill the lacuna left (or constituted) by repression serves as a metaphor for the confrontation with the female genital. For it is surely here—and we shall be seeing this more clearly in what follows—that we find the missing piece par excellence, the hole around which Freud's entire elaboration turns. Thus, as his thinking progresses, the duality repression/trauma tends to overlap with the opposition activity/passivity and to take its place as the metaphoric approximation of the opposition masculine/feminine.

These questions raised by Freud's early papers were already implicit in the clinical material of *Studies on Hysteria* (Breuer and Freud 1893–1895). If we have postponed a consideration of the *Studies* until now, though they were written earlier, it is because they can be better understood retroactively in the light of Freud's preliminary theories of repression and trauma. For each of the cases presented there, we could supply a heading that explains the particular approach to hysteria. Thus "Emmy, or disgust" would be a way of introducing some reflections on the problematics of repression/trauma.

It is striking that, right from her first interview with Freud, Emmy presents a distinctive symptom: a hole in speech. For indeed, the first thing she says—or rather, gives Freud to understand—is an interruption that, in the chain of her discourse, literally materializes the lacuna in which Freud locates trauma. Emmy's speech is regularly interrupted by a stammer; moreover, she often stops to emit a strange tongue-click as her face expresses terror and disgust.

In its structure, this is not an unusual symptom. Breuer had already observed that words sometimes failed Anna O., to the point where she could express herself only in a language that was not her native one (she knew four or five languages), or where she would be stricken mute for days at a time. Now, this mutism had been triggered when she was confronted with a certain bodily state, specifically with an inanimate part of her body, an arm that had "fallen asleep" or was "dead" and that then seemed to change into a snake. The mutism of Anna O., like that of Emmy, seems to be related to the hole, the lacuna through which the real reveals its presence in speech. This is not merely a void but the presence of something unnamable that causes an interruption, a cut, in the chain of discourse. Emmy gives it an imaginary representation in a fantasy based on a newspaper item about a young boy who had died of fear when a white mouse was stuffed into his mouth. What does this animal, that can fill a mouth to the point where it imposes silence, correspond to? That is what we need to know.

In both cases, it is clear that the symptom conforms to the trauma through a veritable proliferation of phallic signification. Hardly had Anna O. come upon the "dead" arm when it changed into a snake. For Emmy, the story of the white mouse, together with the fact that she had heard Dr. K. say that he had sent a box full of white mice, causes her to forego her mutism and cry out in horror at the thought of finding a dead rat in her bed. Her outburst is a perfect example of the oscillation between the repressed and the traumatic that underlies hysteria. What is repressed is the rat as a penis symbol, but what is traumatic is that this symbol crumbles away and reveals the foul refuse that it was supposed to cover up: the dead rat.

The dead rat recalls the more general situation of the encounter with the dead thing that cuts off the speech for Anna as for Emmy. This is a primal encounter that the subject tries to explain in the register of the signifier by means of a series of memories, fantasies, and hallucinations[2] that constantly re-stage the abrupt transformation of the animate into the inanimate, or vice versa. Anna O.'s inanimate arm is immediately reanimated as a snake. And Emmy speaks of dead things that come to life, or of living ones that are suddenly dead. She first recalls that, when she was 5 years old, her brothers and

---

2. These are hysterical hallucinations, absolutely distinct from those of psychosis; see below for further discussion.

sisters had thrown dead animals at her head, which led to her first hysterical attack. Then, when she was 7, she had found herself, unawares, in front of her sister's coffin. In her eighth year, her brother had frightened her by playing ghost. At 9, looking at the corpse of her aunt in her coffin, she suddenly saw the jaw drop. The trauma indicated by these memories necessarily emerges as they are related: after describing the events, Emmy opens her mouth wide and speaks with difficulty. Another time, she reports that she had been violently frightened when she saw in a book a picture of Indians disguised as animals: she was afraid they might come to life. In yet another session, she relates three memories from her adolescence: at 15, she discovered her mother lying on the floor after an attack; four years later, she came home to find her dead and disfigured; at the same age, lifting up a stone, she found a toad and was unable to speak for several hours. Another time, when she entered a room she saw a doll that had been on the bed rise up, and she remained transfixed on the spot. Yet another time, she went to catch a ball of wool and found that it was a mouse trying to escape.

There were several other episodes of the same sort, and what was common to all of them was the abrupt passage from one state to another: from inanimate to animate or the opposite, corresponding to a change from the real thing to the signifying thing or the opposite. In short, the covering over of the real by the signifier is put in question each time. What is this real that left Emmy mute when it was laid bare? She indicates its emergence through the signifiers of the corpse, the dead animal, the toad, and the mouse, which function as nodal points in the chain of memories. This real is without a doubt closely connected with the body (though this seems less clear than in the case of Anna O.), since Emmy adds that at certain periods in her life she could not hold out her hand to anyone lest it change into a horrible animal. We may therefore assume that it is on the level of her own body that Emmy feels fantasmatically transfixed like a dead rat, that is, fallen away from her image and, more radically still, from her ability to maintain this image through speech.

This hole in speech that is related to the dead thing is accompanied by a lacuna in memory, an amnesia that Freud in fact consolidates by his use of hypnosis in this treatment. For Freud is compelled to admit that in Emmy he came up against something stronger than his power as a hypnotist, and this something was precisely the source of his patient's disgust. He notes that the disgust caused her to keep her mouth closed during the hypnosis, and that, despite all his suggestions, he could not really dispel Emmy's fear of animals. All he managed to accomplish through hypnosis was that she recognized his authority and was willing to be compliant with it, which of course was not what was needed. Nor did Freud get to the sexual element that would enable him to localize the trauma specifically, since Emmy gave him an expurgated version of her history.

Freud thus begins to realize that he has come up against a limit: hypnosis could certainly lead the subject to say all sorts of things he would not say when not under hypnosis, but, as Lacan astutely observed, it cannot get the subject to say what he doesn't know, and, of course, cannot get him to say what exists only as a lacuna. And hypnosis turns out to be a double-edged sword, reinforcing the lacuna that Freud wanted to fill in. Thus, when he sees Emmy again a year after the end of treatment, Freud finds that she is complaining of gaps in her memory precisely about the most important events. And when, on a walk with his former patient, he ventures to ask her whether there are a lot of toads on the path, she looks at him reproachfully and he protests that he means real toads!

What of the hallucinations that Emmy reports? Although there is a hole in her speech and a lacuna in her memory, Emmy's discourse wraps them in a flood of signifying formations of the sort that would be considered hallucinations from the psychiatric point of view but must nonetheless be distinguished from psychotic hallucinations. If Freud speaks of hysterical delusion in connection with Emmy, he nevertheless maintains that these formations have to do with compulsive associations like those of the hallucinatory visions in dreams. These productions of Emmy's are not like the verbal hallucinations of paranoia but are to be considered oneiric phenomena. They are not signifiers that arise in the real, as is the case in the psychoses; they are dreams, that is, signifiers walking around in the imaginary but accompanied by a strong sense of reality. As we shall see later on, with the dismantling of the hysterical conversion symptom the structure of hysteria is revealed by exactly this *insertion of the signifier into the imaginary of the body*. The homogeneity of the hysterical symptom with the dream process, that is, with the rebus figure, will be further emphasized in the case of Dora, which Freud originally entitled "Dream and hysteria."

Thus the case of Emmy von N., though incompletely reported, enables us to clarify the function of disgust as the primary phenomenon of hysteria. Disgust has to do with making present a certain bodily state, that of the corpse or of rotting flesh, or with the sudden passage from the state of thing to the state of body. The traumatic import of such encounters seems to stem from their causing to arise, in the subject, a *desexualized real* about which the subject can say literally nothing, as we see in Emmy's blocked speech or Anna's total mutism. What is the meaning of this dead thing or inanimate body? It seems to be the irruption of the real, organic function of the body, in other words, the fall from the erotic into the functional, that disgusts the hysteric. Anna O., for example, relates with all the signs of disgust how she went into the room of her live-in companion one day and saw the woman letting her dog drink out of a glass. Anna said nothing—out of politeness, as Breuer thinks, or because words failed her? In any case, the origin of Anna's disgust, seemingly so innocuous here, must surely be sought in the difference between a dog's drinking and a person's drinking. A human being does not drink, eat, or copulate like an animal: because of his dependence on language, his organic function is taken up into an erotic function that transcends it in such a way that everything that is of the order of need is subverted and reworked in the register of desire. From that time on, the organic function of the speaking being is pushed back to a furthest point just short of desire, as it were out of reach. Eating, drinking, even breathing—as we see in the case of smoking—become erotic activities that the body performs by relying more on the fantasy sustaining desire than on the requirements of the body.

To understand this bodily need in pure form, we have to consider extreme cases in which the person is reduced to the animal will to survive. For even the thirsty man lost in the desert, or the prisoner in the death camps, seems to want to preserve his human dignity by taking a bit of distance from the sheer claims of need. This reluctance is an essentially human quality. Thus a survivor of the camps in World War II told me that the more starvation forced him to eat roots and earthworms, the more he surrounded the act of eating with a set of small rituals, the simplest and most meaningful of which was holding back from immediately devouring what he had found and thereby preserving the idea of a meal. Placed in subhuman circumstances, he made it a point of honor to give himself an appetite, to make himself desire.

This anecdote bears on the problematics of hysterical disgust. For it is when the erotic function of hunger, or thirst—in short, of desire—is reduced to the level of organic need that we find the reaction of disgust. When Anna O. sees the dog drinking from a glass, the human function of the glass is destroyed before her eyes. Likewise, when the lips and the mouth are reduced to the upper mucous membranes of the digestive canal, a kiss becomes something absolutely obscene and intolerable. Thus, when Herr K. takes Dora unawares and kisses her on the mouth (Freud 1905b), she feels an intense disgust that leads to an aversion to food. Freud gives us the key to this symptom: the feeling is displaced from the genital area to the digestive canal. In other words, instead of feeling sexual arousal connected with an erogenous zone, instead of genitalizing this kiss, Dora experiences it as having to do with the organic function of digestion: the erogenous zone of the lips is abruptly desexualized. Freud makes this reaction of disgust the very criterion of hysteria even in the absence of somatic symptoms.

Hysteria thus raises the question of how sexualization comes to the body, how, in the human being, there occurs a change that gives the fact of *having a body* priority over *being an organism*. How does it come about that there is a boundary between the sexual and the non-sexual, and what relations can there be between these two aspects of the body? The solution to these problems requires a theory of repression. And the clinical study of hysteria proves necessary insofar as it illustrates the failures of repression.

The earliest of Freud's writings, as we have seen, present the sexualization of the body and its separation from the organism as occurring by way of repression. In determining retroactively the place of trauma, that is, of the hole through which a desexualized real makes itself known, the process of repression sets a boundary between the erotic and the organic. More precisely, it is *the failure of repression* that opens up a gap through which the trauma can be seen. To the extent that not everything becomes a memory or a representation, to the extent, therefore, that not everything is absorbed by the signifier, not everything can be said in the return of the repressed, and it remains an unsymbolized real around which the symptom forms. The hysteric's discourse ends in an umbilicus, an utmost representation that points to a beyond outside of signification: there is where we find the failure of repression. For if repression were completely successful, everything would be a memory symbolized in the unconscious. To put it another way, all the real would be brought to the state of sexual reality. There would be no more trauma, no more hole denying speech as such; there would be only the repressed, the disavowal internal to speech and bearing on speech.

It is in this sense that we have suggested a reversal of the equation set up by Freud in "Further remarks on the neuropsychoses of defense" (1896b), namely changing "repressed = sexual" into "sexual = repressed." The fact that only representations with a sexual content are repressed means that repression sexualizes the representation, or, more generally, that what undergoes repression is sexual. This argument will become clearer in the texts written from 1923 on, in which Freud affirms the primacy of the phallus. This primacy is the effect of the signifier on everything having to do with the organic, and it becomes operative through repression.

We have also seen how Freud, in these early writings, bases the process of repression on the reaction between two currents that he tries to describe in a series of oppositions ending in the rather unclear dualism activity/passivity. It was suggested that this opposition could be explained by reference to two kinds of *jouissance*. Thus the original scene of seduction, the primordial passivity of the subject that Freud places at the root of both obsessional neurosis and hysteria, expresses the condition of being given over to the Other as the object of the Other's *jouissance*. But we have to go on to view this original "being experienced sexually, being the object of *jouissance*" as the expression of a non-sexual *jouissance*, one that has not yet been grasped by the subject in its sexual signification. It becomes sexual only through the intervention of the signifier of the phallus, that is, through repression. This is what Freud seems to mean in the "Project," when he establishes the theory of the retroactivity of trauma. Once again, then, we find ourselves in the presence of the boundary established by the process of sexualization that is implied by repression. This sexualization affects *jouissance* and reorganizes it, giving it a meaning—the sexual meaning. And, as a result, sexualization entails the interdiction (or, as Lacan wrote it, inter-diction) of a non-sexual *jouissance* that Lacan first calls *jouissance* of being (1960), later *jouissance* of the Other (1972–1973).

What relation can there be, then, between these two aspects of repression, its success and its failure, that is, between what is sexualized by virtue of the signifier and what is cast out into desexualization by virtue of the real part of the body? An answer calls for a further clarification of the way in which the sexualization—that is, the derealization—of the body comes about. As it happens, hysteria is uniquely able to instruct us on this point, since, as we shall see as we continue to trace the development of Freud's thought, the typical symptom of hysteria, namely conversion, indicates a difficulty, indeed an impossibility, encountered in the sexualization of the body.

6

The Hysteric and Femininity: Conversion

We have demonstrated the function of repression in connection with trauma, identifying it with the process of sexualization and thus also with the reorganization of *jouissance*. It remains to be seen how this approach explains the symptom of conversion and the structure of hysteria in general.

Hysterical conversion reveals a certain type of bodily functioning that is the opposite of what happens in the phenomenon of disgust. While disgust causes a sort of collapse of the body from the erotic into the organic, the conversion symptom involves a hypererotization of the body. Disgust entails a desexualization of the real; conversion is a sexualization and a symbolization. But in order to understand what is at stake in this process characteristic of hysteria, we must first look at how the body of the human being is shaped and divided by the tripartition of the registers of the real, the symbolic, and the imaginary.

In very general terms, in order for a body to be sexualized, something must intervene on the level of the symbolic to ensure that the real, organic body is covered over by an erotized bodily image. But this way of putting it is not entirely accurate from a logical point of view. Observation of child development, to be sure, verifies the chronology of such a process, of which the mirror stage (Lacan 1949) is a key moment. But if we follow Freud and the lessons Lacan learned from rereading him, we must admit that the real is "already there" only in its retroactive symbolic determination. Although the real precedes symbolic organization chronologically, it can be marked out and conceived as such only from the time of this organization. Here we have a logical process exactly like the one that operates between trauma and repression: the real is actually *produced* in its function as cause by the effect of the symbolic. As a result, the symbolic system does not only camouflage or sublimate the real, but, more fundamentally, it makes it ex-sist as such, that is, as distinct. The unnamable exists only as a function of the name; there is no real of the body except with regard to the limit of symbolization. As Lacan notes in his Seminar on *The Four Fundamental Concepts of Psychoanalysis* (1964), arguing that the concept of the unconscious must be linked to the concept of lack, "The *Unbewusst* is bound to the *Unbegriff* that marks its limit . . . just as the cry does not stand out against a background of silence, but on the contrary makes the silence emerge as silence" (p. 26, translation modified).[1]

It is surely not by chance that right on the next page of the Seminar Lacan introduces the distinction between repression and censorship. Censorship is a more primitive mechanism than repression. The signifier persists when it under-

---

1. Translator's note: *Unbewusst* means "unconscious"; *Unbegriff* means "non-concept" or "unconcept."

goes repression, but it totally disappears when censored. The parallel consists in the fact that censorship is linked to repression as the concept of lack is linked to the unconscious. Because censorship points to a sort of structural failure of repression, the idea, mentioned in Chapter 5, of a complete repression, leaving no room for the rift of trauma, is inconceivable. The hysteric basically keeps on demonstrating this dialectic. If she can be said to suffer from repression, she does so insofar as this repression is never complete: the return of the repressed gives rise to censorship through which there emerges something unnamable, unrepressible, that bears witness to a failure, a limit, of sexualization.

The relation of the concepts of unconscious and repression to those of *Unbegriff* and censorship shows that the role of sexualization must be tied to a border structure, a boundary line, which is an essential element in the definition of the sexual drive. And it is precisely the theory of the sexual drive that must find a place in the background of the signifying process of sexualization and its impact on the body. This impact is expressed in the notion of the erogenous zone marking the body and, on the level of discourse, setting a boundary between the symbolic and the real.

We may recall that in the *Three Essays* (1905a), Freud understands the drive to be a boundary-concept between the body and the psyche. This boundary between the organic and the sexual is like the dualism between hunger and love. Thus the sexual drive is supported by the somatic function but is not to be confused with it. This is why Freud, in his first drive theory, makes a distinction between the sexual drives proper and what he calls the ego drives that, aiming at self-preservation, simply express the needs of the organism. Now, this distinction provides the theoretical underpinnings for a paper, "The psychoanalytic view of psychogenic disturbance of vision" (1910b), in which he attempts to analyze the structure of the hysterical conversion symptom. Though little known, this paper is important from several angles. For, in addition to a theory of hysterical conversion, it includes a discussion of drive theory and foreshadows the notion of the splitting of the ego.

Its aim is to account for the formation of the odd symptom of hysterical blindness. This symptom reveals a dramatic split between conscious and unconscious, since those who are afflicted with it both see and yet somehow do not see at the same time; visual stimuli reaching the eye register unconsciously but not consciously. The terms of this "seeing and yet not seeing" are the very ones in which, from the paper on infantile sexual theories (1908a) to the study of the splitting of the ego (1938a), Freud continued to explore the question of what the little boy does and does not know about the female genital. And, as we shall see, Freud's solution to this problem is perfectly parallel to the one that the hysteric tries to put into effect with regard to the feminine enigma.

For, according to Freud, if this split between conscious and unconscious occurs in hysterical blindness, this is the effect not of autosuggestion (as had been maintained by the French school of Charcot, Janet, and Binet) but of repression. More exactly, this symptom serves to repair a failure of repression. A representation ought to have been repressed but was not, so the symptom intervenes to compensate somehow for that failure: the representation may not have been repressed, but at least it isn't seen by the subject. Nevertheless, as Freud notes, the kind of "not seeing" brought about by repression is not the same as the "not seeing" of hysterical blindness. In the former, the intention concerns a sexual representation and hence a symbol; in the latter, there is scotomization of certain things that strike the retina. In other words, on the one hand we are in the domain of scopophilia, on the other in that of the organic visual function.

This difference between registers, oddly confused in the symptom, leads Freud to extend his reflections to a general theory of drives and a distinction between the sexual drives and those of self-preservation. He thus encounters, at this point in the analysis of the conversion symptom, the opposition between desire and need, between the drive in the service of a sexual function and the drive in the service of a purely organic one. How is this opposition expressed in hysterical blindness? Freud explains that one of these functions annexes the other, since the same organs and organ systems are involved in the sexual drives and the ego drives. Sexual pleasure is not associated simply with the genital organs; the mouth can kiss as well as eat and speak, the eyes see not only changes in the external environment that are important for the preservation of life but also the properties of objects that make them objects of romantic attraction. No one can serve two masters at one time. The more intimately an organ is involved with one of the great drives, the less available it is for the other.

Thus, in hysterical conversion, the conflict between the organic and the sexual, need and desire, is resolved by the total invasion of the organic function by the sexual one. Hysterical blindness, in short, comes from the withdrawal of the eye from external vision in order to devote itself to fantasy. Failure of repression results in the obliteration of the boundary between the sexual and the non-sexual. We may therefore conclude, *a contrario*, that the role of repression is to set up this boundary and so to prevent the loss of reality, or rather the exclusion of the real, manifested by hysterical blindness on the level of vision. In this way we can better understand the relation between the hysterical conversion symptom and the primal phenomenon of disgust or terror. For conversion is a response to disgust and terror. Disgust appears as a defense, a drawing back of the subject when confronted with the organic function of the body, a failure of the sexual in the face of the organic; conversion, on the contrary, is the response that affirms the sexual at the expense of the organic.

Thus the symptom reveals its goal of phallic imperialism. Need is completely erased by the pressure of the desire that assumes mastery over the organ, and the organ becomes purely genital, ultimately deprived of its sensory function. In other words, the sexual drive, which had been mixed, now becomes pure: instead of being propped up on the somatic, it gets hold of it and totally cancels it out. A further example of this conflict in which need and desire compete for the organ is the alternation of bulimia and anorexia that we find so often in treating hysterics. First it is the organic function of taking in food that seems to gain control over the mouth, leading the subject to stuff herself until she reaches the limit of disgust and vomiting; then, in response to disgust, it is the erotic function that gains the upper hand, and the subject goes on a hunger strike and sustains herself just on the nothingness of desire.

But the connection of the sexual drive to the body is even more subtle than what we see in this competition over the organ. For another effect of repression is to locate on the body the exact places where the sexual drive can anchor itself. These are the erogenous zones, to which the hysteric adds the hysterogenic zones. And, between the real function of the body and the symbolic function it acquires through repression, there is also the insertion of an imaginary function that Freud found to be prevalent in hysteria.

The concept of the erogenous zone appears quite early on in Freud's work. It is foreshadowed in the correspondence with Fliess (Freud 1887–1902, Letters 52 and 75), where Freud specifically links the localization of sexuality in certain bodily zones with the process of repression. The sexual drive is connected to a determinate area, localized, and partialized, at the same time as its satisfaction is bound to a representation (or to what Freud calls a mnemic trace). The ascendancy of the signifier over the drive is part and parcel of its bodily delimitation. Moreover, although this localization implies a selection—some zones being chosen, others abandoned—it is nevertheless the case that, as Freud will go on to say in the *Three Essays* (1905a), any part of the skin or mucous membranes can serve as an erogenous zone. It is not the properties of a given part of the body, but instead the mode of excitation, that determines the choice. This is why the hysterogenic zones—that is, the parts of the body in which the conversion symptom occurs—must be viewed as having the same attributes as the erogenous zones strictly speaking. In both cases, the choice of zone is based on this passage from the register of need to that of desire, this capacity of a place on the body to play more of an erotic role than a need-satisfying one.

And we may go on to observe that these erogenous or hysterogenic zones are systematically inscribed on the surface of the body. As Freud noted from around the time of the *Studies on Hysteria*, even when the hysteric complains about a particular organ or internal body part, it is always to an imaginary geography of the body that she is referring her pain, her spasm, or her paralysis (cf. Freud 1893). This primacy of the imaginary bodily topography in the hysteric's discourse obviously had to be resituated once Freud introduced his theory of narcissism in 1914 with the accompanying major reworking of the dialectic of drives.

The concept of narcissism made it necessary to revise the simple, straightforward dualistic classification of the drives into sexual and self-preservative, the latter connected to needs, that is, to organic bodily functions. For narcissism implies a division of the sexual drive itself between two kinds of object choice and two modes of libidinal satisfaction. Freud now distinguishes between object libido and ego libido, since the sexual drive is divided between two objects, one the result of the change from the organic function of need into the sexual function of desire, and the other the narcissistic object resulting from the drive's turn toward the ego, toward the subject's own image. But the most important point of this theory of narcissism is not so much the division it involves as the indissoluble link it establishes between ego libido and object libido. Freud concludes that, ultimately, ego libido envelops object libido in such a way that the subject can never aim at his or her sexual object except through his or her own image, and the narcissistic image gains substance only through the object it shelters: i(a), as Lacan writes in his notational system.

This insertion of an imaginary function of the body image between the signifying process of repression and the real of the organism takes on its full importance in the clinical treatment of hysteria and also in the examination of the question posed by femininity in general. For the hysteric never feels that she is sufficiently covered by this body image, as though this imaginary garment were always threatening to gape open and show the disgusting reality of a body that she cannot recognize as such. When the flesh breaks forth under the

B BE

dress, the makeup, or the seductive mask, the hysteric finds herself dirty, ugly, repulsive, reduced to a piece of meat. Thus the logic of the hysterical construct involves three stages:

1. A defect at the level of the body image i(a) . . .
2. reveals the real of the desexualized body (a), . . .
3. which the hysterical symbolization of the symptom (conversion or dream) attempts to repair by invading the imaginary.

Where does this defect experienced at the level of the body image come from? I have emphasized that, for Freud, the hysterical symptom originates in a failure of repression, that is, a defect in representation, in that the representation is supposed to delimit a boundary between the non-sexualized real and the sexualized symbolic. The link between this failure and narcissistic deficiencies is clarified by Lacan's account of the way the mechanisms of narcissistic identification are related to the symbolic system.

As early as 1936, Lacan had already produced the theoretical model of imaginary identification, the matrix of the ego, in the unified body image that the child discovers in the mirror stage (cf. Lacan 1949). Thereafter he placed more and more emphasis on the crucial role of the Other who holds the child up to the mirror: the constitution of the body image depends on the message of the Other, since this message can validate or nullify it for the child who is seeking the adult's approval. In his first Seminar (1953–1954), Lacan returned to this issue, analyzing it as an effect of the dependence of the human child on language. He presents an optical schema, involving two mirrors, that shows how the child now passes from the mirror stage to what might be called the two-mirror stage:

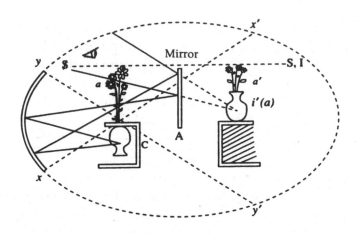

This schema distinguishes two types of narcissism: one, imaginary, fixed on the body image, corresponds to the Freudian notion of the ideal ego; the second, symbolic, fastened to a signifying trait of the Other, corresponds to Freud's ego ideal. In particular, the schema stresses the dependence of imaginary identification—the body image, i(a)—on symbolic identification—I(A). The latter is the reference point, as it were, on the basis of which the subject can see, or not see, his self-image constituted in the first mirror. What is the function of this image? In his paper on the mirror stage, Lacan (1949) shows how very different the body image, in its unification, is from the discord and fragmentation experienced by the *infans* in the grip of its drives. The image, in short, clothes the real body, whose disorder is part and parcel of the prematuration of the human being, as the vase in the schema surrounds the flowers. What is at stake, therefore, is the idea of the subject's unity or unified identity. And this identity turns out to be dependent on the ego ideal, that is, on the founding emblem that the subject discovers in the Other and that Lacan traces back to paternal identification.

Let us follow the logic of the schema and connect it with the Freudian idea of a failure of repression. If there is a defect in the constitution of the body image, there must be a corresponding defect in the symbolic identification provided by the paternal agency. It is on the level of the Other, therefore, that we have to look for the origin of the whole series of features of the hysterical problematic. What, then, is this deficiency of the Other? The hysteric herself will teach us: Anna O., Lucy R., Elisabeth von R., and Dora all tell us—each in her own manner—that their fathers failed them in a fundamental way, whether through illness, impotence, or bad character. As Miss Lucy puts it, in a formula that is the very paradigm of hysteria, they did not find in that gentleman the support they counted on. This is the central point of the clinical treatment of hysteria: the phallus that the hysteric found in her father (indeed, in the Father in general) is always inadequate. The hysteric's father is structurally impotent.

But impotent to do what? Here is where we find the hysteric's demand expressed as a questioning of femininity. If the father is structurally impotent, it is because he cannot offer her the support she needs to establish her femininity. The paternal emblem indicates only the phallus, offers no identification other than a phallic one. What is involved in the hysteric's demand to her father is an altogether radical lack: more than a failure of repression, it is the impossibility of repression. For the representation that is supposed to be repressed is utterly lacking. In Lacan's magisterial account, there is in the Other no signifier of the female sex as such.

This absence of a fulcrum for a specifically feminine identification—that is, an identification that is other than phallic—has the result that, for a woman, the body image cannot completely clothe and erotize the real of the body, or not unless she becomes "all phallic," if she "acts like a man," which does not mean that she takes on a masculine appearance, but that she approaches sexuality as a man does, in the phallic parade. But what is this real in which the properly feminine part of femininity remains? There can be no positive answer to this question, since this would involve naming what is non-representable.[2] But the hysteric is convinced that she does have the answer. What she says, in effect, is that, lacking a properly feminine identification, she can only see herself as reduced to the abject status of a commodity given over to the male's perversion.

In other words, she feels imprisoned in the male fantasy and identifies all sexual behavior with it. This conviction, after all, expresses her fantasy as a hysteric. As we shall see in the cases of Elisabeth von R. and Dora, this is the basis of her "reaction," in the strong sense of the word: made ill by the Other's deficiency, the hysteric devotes herself to repairing him, sometimes going as far as to sacrifice her entire personal life, especially her whole love life. As her father's support, madonna of invalids, she dedicates herself to a hope: not so much that she will finally get the phallus from her father—as Freud believed and expressed in his theory of penis envy—as that she will get something quite different from the phallus from him: a sign that will establish her in a femininity that is finally recognized.

This service rendered to the Other, this care taken to restore his potency at the very moment that his potency reaches its limit, goes along with an attempt to plug the defect that she experiences in imaginary identification. For the

---

2. We can thus see how an affinity for the most sublime, least namable God is part of the problematic of femininity.

hysteric, while devoting herself to her father, tries desperately to identify with a feminine image, that is, to produce an indubitable sign for woman. In so doing she cannot help coming up against her own impotence (a feeling that oppresses Elisabeth) or falling in love with another woman who embodies for her this inaccessible feminine image. But by very fact that the Other sees herself invested with this image, she deprives the hysteric of it, and this gives rise to envy (as in the relation of Elisabeth to her sister or Dora to Frau K.). So that, when the hysteric manages to grasp—at least on the imaginary level—what appears to her to be a sign of femininity, she loses the ability to use it with men and is tied up in an irremediable homosexuation of her love life.[3]

Let us return now to our original attempt to analyze the structure of hysteria, completing it in the light of these subsequent reflections. The hysterical construction has its point of departure in the Other, in the paternal identification of the ego ideal, which, on the level of the body image, takes the form of a deficit that leaves the flesh desexualized, and so forth:

The Other	Identifications	Fantasy	Symptom	Desire
Father →I(A) → i(a) →		(a) →	dream, conversion →	the other woman
(symbolic identification)	(imaginary identification)	(real body, disgust)	(symbolization)	(homosexualization)
	(phallus)			
	absence of feminine identity			

---

3. I use the term "homosexuation" because of both its proximity to and its distance from the term "homosexuality."

I(A) is the symbolic identification based on the signifying trait provided by the Other, in this case the phallus; i(a) is the specular identification or body image whose constitution and maintenance depend on the symbolic support offered by the other; a is the real of the flesh that the body image and the symbolic topography of the body are supposed to veil, and the encounter with which arouses disgust or terror.

In this construction, hysteria is not just a neurosis but also, quite simply, a way of posing the problem of femininity. For the absence of a properly feminine identity is something that all women face. It must be agreed that, unless she plays the phallic woman, a woman is always a bit off balance when it comes to her imaginary identification: her body image always seems to her to be essentially vacillating and fragile. Hence the extreme attention woman generally pay to this image, and the need to be reassured constantly about their femininity. Thus fashion is a constant concern, one that can never be more than an ephemeral realization. This is undoubtedly what led Freud (1914) to state that woman is an essentially narcissistic being:

> A different course is followed in the type of female most frequently met with, which is probably the purest and truest one. With the onset of puberty the maturing of the female sexual organs, which up till then have been in a condition of latency, seems to bring about an intensification of the original narcissism, and this is unfavourable to the development of a true object choice with its accompanying sexual overvaluation. Women, especially if they grow up with good looks, develop a certain self-containment which compensates them for the social restrictions that are imposed upon them in their choice of object. Strictly speaking, it is only themselves that such

women love with an intensity comparable to that of the
man's love for them. [pp. 88–89]

Thus it is surely in reaction to what her genital organ
represents—or does not represent—for her that a woman
turns to narcissism; she makes up for its fundamental defect
by awaiting a compensation for the beauty of her body image.
Freud's mention, here, of social pressures will be replaced
later, in his paper on "Femininity" (1933), by reference to
castration and penis envy: "The effect of penis envy has a share
. . . in the physical vanity of women, since they are bound to
value their charms more highly as a late compensation for their
original sexual inferiority" (p. 132). Thus, lacking the phallus, a woman takes special care of her body image in such a
way that it takes on the value of a phallus; for lack of the
identificatory sign of the penis, she has a *female body*. As a
result, the female body, though based on the real of the flesh,
acquires a predominantly symbolic status. Ultimately, as a
phallic symbol, it is even more valuable than a penis.

This is Lacan's reasoning, especially in the paper on "The
signification of the phallus" (1958a). If, on the symbolic level,
men tend to have the phallus and women to be it, this dis-
tribution is absorbed on the imaginary level in what Lacan
calls "the intervention of a 'to seem'" (p. 289): each man and
woman plays at seeming to possess the phallus—to protect it
when he has it, or to conceal its lack when she doesn't. Thus,
Lacan writes, "it is in order to be the phallus, that is to say,
the signifier of the desire of the Other, that a woman will reject an essential part of femininity, namely all its attributes,
in the masquerade" (pp. 289–290; translation modified). But
a bit more than penis envy is involved in this appearing feminine. According to Lacan, if a woman acts the comedy of the

phallus, this is not because she desires to possess the phallus on the same basis as the man, but rather because she uses it as a lure. As Lacan goes on to say, "It is for that which she is not that she intends to be desired at the same time as she is loved" (p. 290). In this text we find the premises that Lacan will develop in his Seminar *Encore* (1972–1973), namely that, on the feminine side, the subject is "not all" represented by the phallic function. The feminine masquerade is in fact a masque, destined to create ex-sistence as mystery—or, better still, as mystery evading the logic of the sign, as unsignifiable, a hypothetical feminine being.

Thus, for a woman, the body image has an ambiguous and essentially problematical function, different from its function in male narcissism. For this image must mask and suggest at the same time. On the one hand, it must cover over the real by which the body is attached to the organ and the object of male fantasy, and, on the other hand, it must suggest the presence, behind the veil, of a mysterious femininity. The entire art of feminine narcissism thus consists in lifting a corner of the mask in such a way that it is the mystery, and not the organ, that seems to appear. This identification with a semblance, of course, is not without its dangers. The woman-subject who takes this path can sustain an image of this sort only by staying aloof, as if separate from the mask that is brought out on the stage of the world, and doing so with nothing on the level of the Other, of the symbolic identification I(A), offering the reference point that such a distance should guarantee.

We can therefore understand that the imaginary identification of the female body is, for a woman, an essentially fragile and precarious formation, always under the threat of cracking open over a gap and always experienced as having to do with artifice, since it yields only a false identity, a stand-in. This is why women's relations with their image usually come with a question mark, indeed an uneasiness, but are also imbued with a lightness, a mobility, that is less often found on the male side. And perhaps this is why Freud attributes to women a more pronounced narcissism: if they are so concerned with their narcissistic image, it is because that image is more alien to them than it is to men.

This underlying fragility of the feminine position is the terrain for the hysteric's development. For she dedicates herself to denouncing the lack of a feminine identity, the absence in the Other of a signifier of the female genital and the resulting defect on the level of mirror identification. And she names the guilty party: the father, inadequate by definition. She is not wrong to point to this impotence, but she is nonetheless a participant in the disorder she laments, since she persists in her exorbitant demand, either devoting herself to repairing this inadequate father and placing herself at the service of his phallus that just cannot measure up, or digging in and passing from her plaintive demand to the most rageful claim. Thus, from devotion to defiance, the hysteric inevitably tends to become the standard-bearer of the phallus. But she is a standard-bearer full of treachery, requiring the phallus to give her what it cannot give, a sign of feminine identity. Thus she denounces phallic impotence only in the name of a more powerful phallus; she wants more and more and keeps on showing that she never has enough.

On this point, we have to supplement Freud's observation that this claim simply means that the hysteric wants to have the phallus she lacks. For it seems that the hysteric's logic is aimed at more than compensation: she wants tribute finally to be paid to femininity. Her demand is not reducible to a demand for the phallus; it is fundamentally a demand for "more than the phallus."

Lodged in the heart of the hysteric's reply to the precariousness of feminine identification is a fantasy whose lines of force Freud remarkably pointed out in "Hysterical phantasies and their relation to bisexuality" (1908b). This fantasy forms around the reaction of disgust or terror of which Emmy von N. has given us many examples, a reaction that has the value of "off with the masks!" The hysteric is afraid that beneath the mask of the phallicization of the body image there is only "that," the organic real to which the desexualized body is reduced. In response, she produces an excessive sexualization of the imaginary body. This, then, is the internal contradiction in the hysteric's logic: wishing to obtain a positivation of femininity and, with this in mind, denouncing the pretense of the phallic mask, she gets something, to be sure, but precisely what she did not want. For, removing the mask, she simultaneously loses its function of suggesting an enigmatic feminine presence. She finds herself confronted with the a-sexuated real of the body that Lacan calls *objet a*, which can only remind her once again of the necessity of the mask, and so on.

But if the unfolding of this process is marked by a certain failure, in that the hysteric does not get what she wants, we must nevertheless note that there is also a success. For though the discovery of *a*, of the desexualized real of the body, is accompanied by violent affects, it entails a certitude, a solidity, a fixity, that provide a true consolation for the subject. This is what makes the psychoanalysis of the hysterical subject so difficult. Whatever the effects of turmoil, emotion, or anxiety attending the hysteric's disgust, if the analysis is to bear fruit it is absolutely necessary to make the subject realize that, paradoxically, feeling like filth, or like a rotting corpse, or a pile of blubber, is much more certain, and therefore much more comfortable and practicable, than seeing an ungraspable feminine identity constantly vanishing out from under her. The depressive mode in which the hysteric often presents for analysis must not lead to an error: saying that one is a wreck or a jellyfish is much more reassuring than having to confront the enigmatic hole into which the subject falls when she asks what it means "to be a woman," that is, when she asks the question that leads to the lack of a signifier.

The hysteric manifests what Jacques-Alain Miller (1982) calls the consoling virtue of the fantasy, a virtue that brings a secondary gain in the construction of the symptom based on this fantasy. For the emergence of the body in hysterical disgust is also the starting point for a *new dream*, a dream of repairing the Other, a dream of an all-powerful phallus (with the outstanding quality of being a dream without end), a dream of sealing over the breakdown of the body image. This new dream is expressed symptomatically through symbolizations and conversions, as well as in the overvaluation of the other woman in whom the hysteric finds a convenient repository for a femininity she herself is afraid to confront too directly. But although the symptom brings a secondary gain, it is still, of course, the locus of suffering, of discomfort, or, at a minimum, of a fundamental dissatisfaction. But is satisfaction necessary? The hysteric goes as far as to raise this question, for, if the truth be told, she has to choose between two paths.

On the one hand, she can remain stubbornly on the path of her demand and her symptom, keep on positing a sexual relation between male and female, and persist in her attempt to repair both the Other and her own body image. And this draws her into an ever greater dedication to the Other, to the point where she sacrifices her entire existence; she also becomes increasingly envious of the other woman, in whom she sees the perfect femininity of which she herself feels deprived. In both aspects, symbolic and imaginary, this path leads her to reduce her life to a formula that can be expressed as "everything for the Other, nothing more for me." And it must be said that along those lines she is capable of showing an admirable degree of self-abnegation and courage. But, most often, she comes up against the limit of the "nothing" to which she is condemned. This is the moment when she suddenly gives up her heroism, falls sick, becomes depressed, and may even commit suicide, thereby bearing witness to the fact that she can repair neither the Other nor her own image except at the cost of her own existence, and to the fact that, if the only sign she gets at the very end of this sacrifice is the inappropriate mark of the phallus, then she may as well go on strike as far as human relations are concerned.

Alternatively, she may choose a second path, that of a kind of "normalization" of her hysteria. Instead of persisting in her demand, she can make the non-response to her demand the very object of her desire, a desire that cannot and must not be satisfied. If she can get no sign assuring her of her feminine identity, she will at least refuse to identify with the object of the *jouissance* of the Other. She is willing to arouse her desire but will avoid its satisfaction. In this way, she places herself in a position that enables her to define herself: she is what is lacking in the sexual relation. This promotion of desire insofar as it is unsatisfied is consistent with the hysterical fantasy and symptom. The "that's not it!" expressed in the confrontation with the desexualized, dephallicized body shows that she realizes the abjection of the object/cause of desire—and of her woman's body that can be the cause of a man's desire. Hence her wish to have her desire *recognized* instead of *satisfied*. A corollary of this is that she orients her desire more toward the pole of desire than toward that of *jouissance*, thereby sustaining her partner (and herself) in an idealization that contrasts with the initial abjection and remains continuous with her wish to deal with the Other-with-a-capital-O. Love, with its retinue of dreams and imaginary projections, is still the surest way to repair the Other, because it takes the place of what does not exist for a human being, namely the genital drive that could unite the subject and the Other. In choosing it, the hysteric is drawn toward a mode of desire similar to that of courtly love on the male side, the price to be paid being that the sex of her love object may well be indeterminate.

Our schema of hysterical neurosis thus finds its endpoint in the maintenance of unsatisfied desire. We can try to sketch out its full development, with some further points to be explained later on.

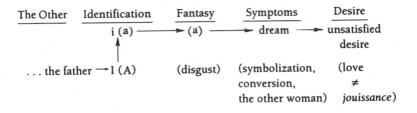

The Other	Identification	Fantasy	Symptoms	Desire
	i (a) ⟶	(a) ⟶	dream ⟶	unsatisfied desire
… the father ⟶	I (A)	(disgust)	(symbolization, conversion, the other woman)	(love ≠ *jouissance*)

The diagram needs to be completed by the introduction, at the stage of the Other, of Freud's discovery of the primary importance of the girl's relation to her mother. He calls it the prehistory the female Oedipus (cf. Freud 1925), and it will tend to appear even more often in the girl's history if she resents her father as impotent to transmit to her a true foundation for her feminine identity. The three dots preceding "father" in the diagram indicate the zone of this prehistory in which, later, we shall place the preeminent figure of the mother.

As far as identification is concerned, we still have to look into the relations among narcissism, femininity, and psychosis, an issue that is at the heart of Freud's study of the case of President Schreber (1911) and of "On narcissism: an introduction" (1914). With regard to fantasy, the crucial point is the bisexuality of the hysterical fantasy, its staging of the conflict between two *jouissances*. As for the construction of the symptom, we shall have to set out the distinctions among hysterical conversion, hypochondria, and psychosomatic manifestations. Finally, the culmination of this construction in a style of desire leads us to ask how hysteria forms structure and whether we can speak, with Lacan, of a generalized hysteria. If man's desire is the desire of the Other, this is because desire is not "desire for pleasure" but "desire for desiring." As a result, it can be argued that the very nature of desire entails something hysterical.

7

The Case of Elisabeth

The hysterical mode of putting femininity in question is beautifully illustrated by the case of Elisabeth in *Studies on Hysteria* (Breuer and Freud 1893–1895). As in the case of Emmy von N., the reflections prompted by this material can be grouped according to several major themes. The first concerns the connections and distinctions between hysterical conversion and hypochondria, and I shall consider this later on after further discussion of what I have called the process of sexualization. The second concerns the hysteric's relationship with her father; the third, the question of femininity and the indirect way in which Elisabeth poses it; the fourth the problematics of hysterical identification and the role of the other woman.

Let us first consider Elisabeth's relation with her father and, beyond that, with the Father as such. It is remarkable that, in this relation, her position evolved between two poles, that of the friend and confidant,[1] and that of the devoted

---

1. Compare the case of Dora (Freud 1905b).

nurse, a role she took on as soon as her father fell ill. Elisabeth's first function was that of confidant—in the masculine, since it was as a son, not a daughter, that her father first considered her, someone with whom he could exchange ideas. This was therefore a special position but an ambiguous one; we soon learn that her father often said that she would have a hard time finding a husband. Here was a father who willingly and generously passed on to his daughter the heritage of the phallus, to the point where he made a little man of her. For Elisabeth did not welcome suitors and was reluctant to make any sacrifices in order to marry, especially the sacrifice of her much-cherished relation to her father.

The mother was set aside with regard to this duo, her physical illnesses making this all the easier, nor did Elisabeth's two older sisters count for much in their father's eyes. Elisabeth made an effort not to antagonize her mother and sisters, which suggests that she was sure enough of her position to grant them this favor. But her share in the paternal phallus was not to last. Her father collapsed one day, a heart condition having led to pulmonary edema, and became a bedridden invalid. For a year and a half Elisabeth devoted herself to him, sleeping in his room at night so that she could be of service when needed and trying to keep up his spirits. In other words, the complicity between Elisabeth and her father was based on a pretense, on maintaining a facade of hope while knowing full well that the situation was grave.

Elisabeth discovered her calling as her father's nurse in nostalgia for a lost cause. It is a calling that she shared with Anna O. and Dora, and Freud notes the affinity between the position of the hysteric and the role of the nurse. He does so a bit awkwardly, reversing cause and effect, but he sees the relation of causality:

Anyone whose mind is taken up by the hundred and one tasks of sick-nursing which follow one another in endless succession over a period of weeks and months will, on the one hand, adopt a habit of suppressing every sign of his own emotion, and on the other, will soon divert his attention away from his own impressions, since he has neither time nor strength to do justice to them. Thus he will accumulate a mass of impressions which are capable of affect, which are hardly sufficiently perceived and which, in any case, have not been weakened by abreaction. He is creating material for a "retention hysteria." [pp. 161–162]

This concept of retention hysteria reflects the still largely unformulated state of the theory of repression at the time Freud wrote up this case (in 1892). For in fact it is not because the subject practices the profession of nursing and undergoes its constraints that hysteria occurs. On the contrary, as we see with Dora as well as Elisabeth, it is because she is a hysteric that she is particularly well suited to nursing, for nursing, as Freud describes it here, is an extension of the problematics of hysteria in two directions. First, the Other must be made well or a facade must be kept up of repairing him, and second, the devoted nurse must entirely devote herself to the demand of this Other. The retention of which Freud speaks, the muffling of the subject's expression of her own desires, finds its meaning in the abnegation before the demand of the Other, an abnegation in which the subject assumes the image of the person, male or female, whom the Other cannot but love and prefer to everyone else.

By devoting herself to her father in this way, Elisabeth ultimately did for him what he had formerly done for her. It was as though, by offering herself without limit to his demand, she were telling him: "Keep on demanding; there's more where

that came from." The father had loved his daughter in her
capacity as possessor of the phallus, and the daughter, in turn,
proved to him that one can love someone who no longer has
it. This response was a new way of maintaining the phallic
alliance that they had formed between them. The father's
death, when it occurred, did not compromise this structure,
since Elisabeth immediately replaced him with her mother as
the object of her dedication. In turning toward her mother,
whom up to now she had completely ignored, Elisabeth
showed that the torch had been handed on to her by her father: she occupied his place, as if she had inherited the dead
man's power.

In this process, Elisabeth systematically denied her feminine position, starting with the fact that a woman does not
have the phallus. Already in the days when she was her father's
friend and confidante, she had been uncomfortable with her
femininity, and now she preferred to carry the banner of the
phallus, even if this involved the arduous task of being a nurse
first for her father, then for her mother. The outcome of this
frantic self-abnegation is unsurprising, for the wish always to
be ready and able to meet the Other's demand leads to exhaus-
tion and depression. And this is just what happened to
Elisabeth when she became not only her mother's nurse but
her faithful knight as well, fighting with a brother-in-law who
had been discourteous to the old lady. But the brother-in-law
escaped, moving far away with his family and thereby depriv-
ing Elisabeth of the opportunity to display the power of her
weapons.

The marriage of her second sister, however, made a chink
in the armor of this phallic knight, one that Elisabeth experienced not as a weakness or a wound but as an opening toward femininity. This second brother-in-law was refined and

attentive to women, someone who seemed not to want to infringe on their power. Elisabeth was suddenly reconciled to the thought of marriage, and, naturally, the first child of this union became her favorite. After having loved the man or woman who lacked the phallus, she now seemed to identify with it overtly.

However, during the year of the child's birth, Elisabeth's mother became ill, and the family accompanied her to a vacation spot where she could convalesce. It was here that Elisabeth found the ground no longer firm under her feet. Her phallic identification broke down, and she began to relinquish her role as heir. Things "weren't going well," as it were, and this was expressed in Elisabeth's problems with locomotion. Soon she had switched roles completely and become the sick one in the family. And, worse still, shortly after the vacation the sister died of the same illness as the father, and the brother-in-law, inconsolable, withdrew from the family. Thereafter Elisabeth lived as a recluse, solely concerned with caring for her mother and for her own distress.

Freud is able to explain the abrupt shift in Elisabeth's attitude during this family sojourn. As she told him about her state of mind at this time, she confided how she had felt in the presence of the happiness of her sister and brother-in-law: she, who had not needed a man up till then, now felt herself dissolving in feminine weakness and longing. On a walk she managed to take alone with her brother-in-law, she found herself speaking of personal things in a way that could not fail to recall her close relationship with her father. She was now overcome with the desire for a husband like this. On the day after the walk, Elisabeth retraced the path the two of them had taken and began to feel a pain that Freud recognizes as the beginning of a conversion symptom, a repetition of a pain she had experienced when she was caring for her sick father as he placed his foot on her thigh so that she could bandage his leg. This had been a muscle pain that was not at all hysterical in itself, but it became the nucleus of trauma via signifying repetition.

Asked about the circumstances surrounding the first occurrence of the pain, Elisabeth told Freud about a romance that she had felt to be in competition with the attentiveness she showed to her sick father. For, at the time she was caring for the invalid, she had fallen in love with a young man who happened to be likewise devoted to Elisabeth's father. What had commended him to her, therefore, was his choice of her father as a mentor and the celebration of the paternal phallus that he shared with her. This is no doubt why, when she came to believe that this young man was in love with her, Elisabeth had felt that marriage to him would not entail the sacrifice she had dreaded, the sacrifice of the paternal phallus, since the young man was clearly intent on keeping it in its place with the lord and master.

When this structure was endangered, the equilibrium of the situation was broken and Elisabeth dropped her lover. This occurred at the very moment when, for once, the young man stepped ahead of the father. He had persuaded Elisabeth—with the father's assent, as it happens—to leave the bedside and go out with him. She did so with joy, but the next day, returning home, found her father sicker than before. Full of self-reproach, she all but stopped seeing her boyfriend. It is clear that she was unwilling to have him compete with her father. This encounter with the father—wretched, weakened, the phallus in defeat— was the trauma that would be defined retroactively when Elisabeth dreamed of the happiness of her sister and brother-in-law, that is, at the moment when she saw opening up before her the path of femininity instead of the path of fighting for the phallus.

Let us look at the mechanism of hysterical identification, with emphasis on the role of Elisabeth's sister. Elisabeth told Freud that she wanted to find happiness like her sister's; are we to interpret this as an identification with her? This is the way Freud understood it, which led him to conclude that Elisabeth was unconsciously in love with her brother-in-law. But, when he interpreted this to her, his patient cried out and said that she was in great pain. In other words: everything but that! This refusal does not seem to be merely a resistance. Elisabeth was not wrong to reject Freud's reasoning, reasoning that involved a misjudgment he was to repeat several years later in the treatment of Dora (1905b), when he tried at all costs to persuade the patient that she was in love with Herr K. But the process of hysterical identification, and the role played in it by the choice of love object, are more complex. Elisabeth's subjective position, like Dora's, their identifications, and the role of the other woman cannot be correctly situated unless we write them in a four-way schema like Lacan's Schema L (1966, p. 53):

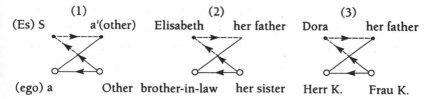

The sister who fascinated Elisabeth in the way in which Frau K. fascinated Dora, was not just an identification but the very incarnation of the femininity that up to now she had experienced as weakness or impotence. The sister took on this enigmatic value as the object of desire of her husband, this man who was so pleasing to women, this faithful knight, a role that Elisabeth had played for her father. The sight of the happy couple thus reminded Elisabeth of the relationship with her father, but with the additional aspect that the sister was treated as a woman, not as a male friend. Thus Elisabeth's desire cannot be reduced to desire for her brother-in-law; it was more the desire to be loved by her father as the sister was loved by the brother-in-law. As Lacan observes, "The hysteric experiences herself in the tribute paid to another woman and offers the woman in whom she worships her own mystery to the man whose role she takes without being able to feel pleasure in it" (1966, p. 452). With regard to Elisabeth, this dictum enables us to understand that she was motivated by an identification with the brother-in-law's desire, not by a direct desire or romantic wish. It was the relation between the brother-in-law and the sister that was so precious to her, because it presented the mystery of a femininity maintained by male desire. So it is not surprising that Elisabeth protected this relation: what she loved was not her brother-in-law but his desire for her sister.

This dimension of the four-way schema, in which there is one position that is beyond the identifications, is precisely what was missing in Elisabeth's first romance. The structure did not develop beyond the triangle formed by Elisabeth, her father, and the young man:

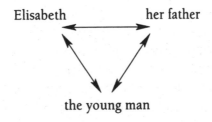

Elisabeth   her father

the young man

In this triangle, nothing opened out into the mystery of femininity. On the contrary, the three partners remained completely bound together in the same identification with the paternal phallus. The comparison shows both the strength and the weakness of the four-way schema. Its structure is valid only if Elisabeth's own desire—which Freud is overly hasty in emphasizing—remained unsatisfied, in other words, if she had no relationship with her brother-in-law outside of the couple he formed with her sister. This problem is, much more than the death of the sister, at the root of the second catastrophe in Elisabeth's life. For at the very moment she entered the room in which the dead woman was lying, the thought that crossed her mind had less to do with the loss of her sister than with the loss of the couple that the sister had formed with the brother-in-law: it occurred to her that her brother-in-law was now free and could marry her. This "could" entailed not a wish, as Freud is too quick to conclude, but rather a threat. The death of the sister left Elisabeth without her feminine guideline with regard to the brother-in-law, and this absence of mediation was, for her, the unbearable representation par excellence, since it imperiled the necessary unsatisfaction of her hysterical desire.

The necessary unsatisfaction of desire as a precondition to love is also perfectly illustrated in the case of Miss Lucy R. (in Breuer and Freud 1893–1895). A young English governess, Miss Lucy was in charge of the children of a widower, a businessman in a suburb of Vienna. She had, oddly, promised the children's mother that she would be a mother to them when the real mother died, which in effect made the governess the wife of the children's father. Freud, who saw this connection, was quick to interpret her symptoms: you are in love with your boss without knowing it. Miss Lucy agreed. And

when Freud asked why she was unwilling to admit this inclination, her reply clearly showed the little difference that marks
hysterical desire. What distressed Lucy, she said, was that she
was a poor woman in service in the house, not an independent woman who could aspire to such a match. Thus her desire
was to love the master, but without going further, that is,
without satisfying the desire that she felt. And this was in fact
the balance she achieved at the end of treatment, when she
confessed to Freud that she was happy to be able to continue
to love her boss in secret, remaining in his service and caring
for his daughters. We must no doubt add that this situation
allowed her to get children from a father without having to
have sexual relations with him.

   We can now return to the theme of the sexualization and
the manifestation of the body in the different registers of the
symbolic, the imaginary, and the real. The case of Elisabeth
von R. raises a number of points that Freud develops into a
clear distinction between the hysterical conversion symptom
and the symptom of hypochondria. In this case, he states, the
diagnosis is not easy to establish. Here is his description of
Elisabeth's somatic symptoms:

> Her gait was not of any recognized pathological type, and
> moreover was by no means strikingly bad. All that was
> apparent was that she complained of great pain in walk-
> ing and in standing, and that after a short time she had to
> rest, which lessened the pains but did not do away with
> them altogether. The pain was of an indefinite character;
> I gathered that it was something in the nature of a pain-
> ful fatigue. A fairly large, ill-defined area of the anterior
> surface of the right thigh was indicated as the focus of the
> pains, from which they most often radiated and where
> they reached their greatest intensity. In this area the skin

and muscles were also particularly sensitive to pressure
and pinching (though the prick of a needle was, if anything, met with a certain amount of unconcern). This
hyperalgesia of the skin and muscles was not restricted
to this area but could be observed more or less over the
whole of both legs. The muscles were perhaps even more
sensitive to pain than the skin, but there could be no
question that the thighs were the parts most sensitive to
both these kinds of pain. The motor power of the legs
could not be described as small, and the reflexes were of
medium strength. There were no other symptoms, so that
there was no ground for suspecting the presence of any
serious organic affliction. The disorder had developed
gradually during the previous two years and varied greatly
in intensity. [pp. 135–136]

It is the systematic imprecision of Elisabeth's account of
her pains that leads Freud to make a diagnosis of hysteria. He
distinguishes among three discourses, three ways of speaking of a somatic pain. The person afflicted with an organic
problem speaks of his illness calmly and with assurance, describing his pain in detail and with precision. The hypochondriac, on the contrary, gives the impression of making a mental
effort beyond his means:

> His voice grows more shrill and he struggles to find a
> means of expression. He rejects any description of his
> pains proposed by the physician, even though it may turn
> out afterwards to have been unquestionably apt. He is
> clearly of the opinion that language is too poor to find
> words for his sensations and that those sensations are
> something unique and previously unknown, of which it
> would be quite impossible to give an exhaustive descrip-
> tion. For this reason he never tires of constantly adding

fresh details, and when he is obliged to break off he is sure
to be left with the conviction that he has not succeeded
in making himself understood by the physician. [p. 136]

As for the hysteric, she presents an account like Elisabeth's, an account of a very different kind. In contrast to the
hypochondriac, she speaks of her pain with indifference. This
so-called *belle indifférence* typical of hysteria means, Freud tells
us, that her attention is focused on something else, and that
the pain is incidental to her true interest. What is this something else? We can understand it, says Freud, in the thoughts
and the feelings that accompany the pain.

There are three types of discourse, then, and hence three
styles, that enable us to distinguish three types of symptoms.
Freud then goes on to add a further criterion on the level of
the body and *jouissance*, namely the sexuality of the body. For
if we stimulate the part of the body described as painful, the
reactions differ according to whether we are dealing with an
organic illness, hypochondria, or hysteria. The patient with
an organic illness and a hypochondriac will express discomfort or physical pain; they will flinch and try to avoid the
examination. But, instead of pain, the hysteric will show satisfaction, indeed sexual pleasure. Thus, when Freud pinched
the skin and muscles of Elisabeth's thigh, the patient cried
out as though she were being sexually titillated, blushed,
turned her head and torso aside, and closed her eyes—in short,
she behaved as though the painful area were an erogenous
zone and as though the medical examination were a caress
designed to bring her to orgasm. However, Freud notes, her
expression of pleasure could not be caused by the physical
sensation as such, since this would be a feeling of pain; it must
have been caused by the content of the thoughts in the back-

ground of the pain, thoughts that were reactivated by the stimulation of the part of the body associated with them.

The essential point about these distinctions is their structure. Hypochondria expresses a defect of symbolization (the lack of a word for what, in the body, escapes language) and a defect of sexualization (hypochondriacal suffering is tied to the real body), while hysterical conversion reveals an excess of symbolization (the signifier annexes the body and robs it of its organic function) and an excess of sexualization (the organs or body parts annexed by the symptom are induced to play the role of erogenous zone, to which they are not destined). Thus Elisabeth cannot stand up "by herself" (*allein stehen*) because she suffers from being "by herself," alone (*allein*); she cannot move from the spot in the literal sense of walking because there is a figurative impediment in her way. These examples, along with others that Freud notes in the case of Cäcilie M., show that Elisabeth's abasia is a symbolic translation in the manner of the rebuses encountered in dream formation. The body's organic function (for example, walking) becomes subject to the signifying process: when something "isn't going right" on the level of unconscious thought, the patient cannot take a step with his legs. The complaint of the hypochondriac, on the other hand, indicates that he finds in his body something impossible to symbolize and to sexualize. For lack of a signifier to name it, a body part remains in suffering,[2] for the subject cannot even "imaginize" it, that is, project it on the surface of the body image.

The hypochondriac clings tenaciously to the existence of this bodily area that cannot be symbolized, while the hys-

---

2. Translator's note: *en souffrance* means "in suffering" and "in abeyance."

teric constantly flees it by giving herself over to unbridled symbolization. The problematics of hypochondria can thus be located at the intersection of the registers of the real and the symbolic, whereas hysterical conversion is played out between the symbolic and the imaginary (the body image). The hypochondriac is fixated on what, in the real of the body, puts a stop to the power of the symbolic; the hysteric is bent on denying that there can be such a stop. She is not fixated but instead moves in a play of extreme bodily plasticity. In each case, the result is a relation to the doctor, and more specifically to medical knowledge, that is odd to say the least. The hysteric's tendency to show up the doctor's impotence is well known. The hypochondriac does this as well, but in a way that is subtly different from the hysteric's maneuver.

Molière, a notorious hypochondriac, represents his imaginary invalid, Argan, as contemptuous of medical knowledge. Nevertheless, Argan does not reject the doctors who crowd around his bedside. And when his brother tries to persuade him that the Greek and Latin terminology deployed by the doctors is of no avail in curing the illness, he replies that one must trust their professional judgment. It would be a mistake to see this statement as mere farce. The hypochondriac's entire position is summed up in the disjunction between terminology and cure; it is to the extent that the terms of medical knowledge remain without effect for his illness that he loves doctors and will do anything, including give them his daughter, to keep them at his side. Through his illness, Argan shows that his urgent concern is not to be cured but to be recognized as ill. The hypochondriac seeks not so much to show up the doctor's impotence as to be assured of it in order to guarantee his essential suffering. He is often preoccupied with medical books, but his sole aim is to confirm and reinforce their lacuna. No word will name his illness, which will always escape medical knowledge. He demonstrates the necessity of an unnamable and refutes any symbolic power on this point, since the lacuna serves as a protection for him. Freud himself (1914) noted the parallel between the role of hypochondria with regard to paranoia and that of anxiety with regard to hysteria; if the hypochondriac ever gives in—for example, if the unnamable body part in which the suffering is localized comes to be symbolized by some signifier—the subject is at great risk of becoming delusional, because the symbolic no longer encounters the stopping point that prevented it from invading the real.

These reflections are relevant to our discussion of femininity, since they raise the crucial question of the nature and function of the female body, or of what goes by that name. What is a woman's body? Everyone wonders about this, women as much as—if not more than—men, and no one has a satisfactory answer. The so-called "female" body is defined as at least partly outside of knowledge, there being no signifying articulation to vouch for the difference that anatomy indicates. Isn't it this aspect of the female body that is unsayable, incapable of symbolization, that makes men ill in their romantic relationships? It is as though the female body, the body of Woman, presented itself in the manner of a hypochondriacal object.

8

Dream and Desire in Hysteria

Men, sick because of woman, are very careful to maintain her enigmatic status. Femininity is revered as a mystery, as the incomprehensible hollow object whose center is everywhere and whose circumference is nowhere. Nothing leads to more extravagant pondering than the desire to know that is turned toward the female genital organ, especially in its relation to *jouissance*. In the face of this enigma, several attitudes are possible. There is the essentially "hysterical" solution, the form of love that raises Woman to the status of the Other. The tradition of courtly love is the most striking example of this idealizing of the Other at the expense of the satisfaction of one's desire. Or else, as when hypochondria veers toward psychosis, the relation to "The" woman can go in the direction of that madness, not always benign, that is passion. In its querulous or erotomaniacal form, passion is organized round a name that makes its appearance in the real as the name of Woman, and the subject must subject himself to it absolutely. Finally, there is the perverse solution, in which something, a fetish or an instrument of *jouissance*, is put in place of the partner's femininity; this maintains another form of passion, that of the ignorance of femininity.

Psychoanalysis exposes the impasse of these three attempts, revealing what each of them, in its own way, misrecognizes: the dialectic of desire. For desire is never desire for Woman; it is never addressed to the Other as such but rather comes from that place. What desire aims at is the signifier through which the Other itself appears as desiring and hence as desirable. The term *desire* is thus the ultimate signifier of the Phallus. Femininity can only be situated in a beyond of desire, as if still owing something in regard to what desire can attain. Hence the fundamentally unsatisfying, and moreover fundamentally hysterical, character of human desire.

Let us take a look at the connection between the hysteric and desire. Their relation is immediately apparent in dream formation: the dream fulfills a desire, but only in the register of the imaginary, leaving in abeyance the satisfaction it would find in *jouissance*. To this the hysteric adds her own twist. It is appropriate for us to try to locate what the hysteric expresses in her desire from the perspective of an identification with the masculine position of the man ill because of Woman. If the hysteric acts like a man, as Lacan claims, it is insofar as she tries to define femininity in the male way, raising it to the rank of a mystery hidden in the hollow of the body. This, of course, leads to a distinctively hysterical conception of the female body; Dora is the purest illustration of this.

The structural homology between hysterical neurosis and dreamwork was quickly emphasized by Freud. We find it as early as the *Studies on Hysteria* (Breuer and Freud 1893–1895) in connection with the case of Emmy, whose hallucinations and delusions he compared to those found in dreams. This first intuition develops into a thesis that Freud is at pains to demonstrate in the years 1899–1901. "The key to hysteria really lies in dreams," he writes to Fliess on January 3, 1899, adding, " If I wait a little longer I shall be able to describe the mental process in dreams in such a way as to include the process in hysterical symptom-formation" (1887–1902, p. 271). A few days later, he writes: "It is not only dreams that are fulfillments of wishes, but hysterical attacks as well" (p. 277). This thesis is the subject of a short paper of 1909, in which Freud analyzes the hysterical attack as a pantomime calling for the same interpretative elaboration as the dream. We shall see how this homology between the dream and the hysterical symptom operates in the case of the witty butcher's wife and the case of Dora.

The dream of the butcher's wife (Freud 1900, pp. 146–151) highlights a particular feature, the value placed on lack, on the nothing as such. Here hysterical desire appears in pure form, as the desire to have a desire without object, hence a desire that can never be fulfilled. Freud tells us right away that this is the dream of a hysteric, and, moreover, that it is to be located in the transference. It is, in effect, addressed to him as a clear challenge to his knowledge. "'You are always saying to me,' began a clever woman patient of mine, 'that a dream is a fulfilled wish. Well, I'll tell you a dream whose subject was the exact opposite—a dream in which one of my wishes was *not* fulfilled. How do you fit that in with your theory?'" (p. 146). It fits in all the better, Freud will show, because it fulfills the desire not to fulfill (or satisfy) her desire.

The text of the dream is simple: "*I wanted to give a supper-party, but I had nothing in the house but a little smoked salmon. I thought I would go out and buy something, but remembered then that it was Sunday afternoon and all the shops would be shut. Next I tried to ring up some caterers, but the telephone was out of order. So I had to abandon my wish to give a supper-party'"* (p. 147; emphasis in original). Freud very skillfully begins by agreeing wholeheartedly with the patient, subscribing to her opinion that this dream shows the non-fulfillment of a desire. But he does so only to reverse the perspective by asking her why, if she must have an unsatisfied desire, it is precisely this one? The patient's associations provide the material for this reversal. She first describes her husband. He had felt he was too fat and wanted to go on a diet, and to this end had announced that he would no longer accept dinner invitations. The rather coarse realism of a man who has no doubt about the object of his desire appears in an anecdote: the husband said that he had replied to an artist who wanted to paint his portrait that he, the artist, would surely prefer to paint a piece of a beautiful girl's behind. But the wife's desire seems more complex. She is dying to have a caviar sandwich every morning, but she had asked her husband not to give her one. In this way she teases her husband, of whom she is very fond, by asking him to prove his love by not fulfilling her desire for caviar.

Freud then elicits the day residue that accounts for the wish on the part of the butcher's wife to create an unsatisfied desire for herself. Another woman now enters the scene, a friend whom the butcher's wife had visited and who, unhappy with her thinness, had confided the desire to put on weight. And she had asked the butcher's wife, "'When are you going to ask us to another meal? You always feed one so well'" (p. 148). We see the makings of a sort of intersection between the desire of the butcher—who wants to be on a diet and accept no invitations to meals—and that of the friend, who wants to gain weight and hopes to be asked to dinner. Now, at the point where these two desires meet, in the mind of the butcher's wife, there arises an enigma concerning the truth of desire. For, as it happens, the butcher, who claims that he wants to lose weight, makes no mystery of his preference for a full figure and yet seems to have a soft spot for this friend, who, for her part, claims that she wants to gain weight yet remains thin. On first reading, the dream could thus be interpreted as expressing the jealousy of the butcher's wife. Its sense would be the refusal to help make the friend more attractive in the butcher's eyes by giving parties at which she might gain weight.

But there is an element of the dream that is not covered by this initial decoding: the smoked salmon, the only foodstuff the butcher's wife had on hand. Replying to Freud's question on this matter, the patient admits that this is her friend's favorite dish. So the friend is behaving with regard to her desire for salmon the same way as the patient with regard to her desire for caviar: she refuses to have it fulfilled.

Then the knot of the dream shifts yet another time. Its enigmatic point ultimately turns out to be not so much the intersection of the desires of the butcher and her friend as that of the two unsatisfied desires of the wife and the friend. These two desires have in common the wish to be recognized but not fulfilled. Thus the two demands that the two women articulate can be juxtaposed and interpreted as the desire to feed on a desire as such instead of on the object that could satisfy the demand for food. And the butcher's wife has to question the desire of her husband, who, though seeming quite sure that he is satisfied by a full form, nonetheless remains attentive to his wife's thin friend: what does this friend have, then, that appeals to the butcher?

A new path of interpretation now opens up. It is in her friend that the patient is seeking to grasp and decode her true desire. The hysterical identification with the desire of the Other underlies what this dream presents as the non-fulfillment of a desire. If, in the dream, the butcher's wife must give up the idea of having a dinner party, it is not to oppose her friend's desire, as we might think on first reading, but, on the contrary, to sustain it as an unsatisfied desire, insofar as the friend's desire has been substituted for her own.

It is important to define accurately the process of this hysterical identification. This is not an *imitation*, Freud emphasizes, not a sympathy that would lead to a reproduction. In other words, this is not an identification with the person of the friend. There is, to be sure, a process of contagion and a certain jealous sympathy between the two women, but these are merely the effects of the identification whose basis is "a common *sexual* element" (p. 150), that is, a common position with regard to sexual relations in the broad sense of the term: the real or virtual place to which the butcher's desire is addressed. Here there rises an issue that Lacan pinpoints in his remarkable commentary on this dream: "But how can another woman be loved . . . by a man who could not be satisfied by her (he, the man of the slice of backside)? That's precisely the question, which is usually that of hysterical identification" (1958b, p. 262). And Lacan goes on to explain what marks the hysteric's subjective status: "The subject becomes this question in this very place: in what respect the woman identifies with the man and the slice of smoked salmon substitutes for the desire of the other" (p. 262, translation modified).

Thus the motivation behind hysterical identification reveals a complexity stemming from vacillation in a sexual bipolarity. It is not so much with her friend that the witty butcher's wife identifies, as with the latter's desire. But—and this is the second phase—if she identifies with this desire, it is because it offers her a position from which to question the desire and the love of her butcher husband. And this, in a third phase, opens onto a reinterpretation of male desire: if the fat butcher who wants to get thinner can desire a thin woman who wants to put on weight, isn't this because he is less satisfied than he seems with slices of his wife's backside? As the questioning proceeds in these three phases, we can see the hysteric's characteristic bisexuality falling into place. On the one hand, the butcher's wife sides with her friend, in whom she is trying to grasp the incarnation of a mysterious femininity of which her husband seems to be aware, and, on the other hand, she adopts the masculine position of the butcher to put forth her question about her friend: who is she that he should love her? Thus she puts herself in the place of her husband to interrogate the femininity of her friend (the masculine position), because she would like her husband to love her as he loves the friend (the feminine position).

We may note that, in the development of this analysis of the dream, an element has not been touched upon: its pervasive orality. Neither Freud, in the *Interpretation of Dreams*, nor Lacan, in the brief commentary in "The direction of the treatment and the principles of its power" (1958b), looks at the aspect of the dream that concerns the object/cause of our hysteric's desire. It is true that, at the time they wrote their respective discussions of this dream, neither Freud nor Lacan had yet taken note of the crucial role of the object as cause of desire and condenser of *jouissance*. Nevertheless, a bit further on in "The direction of the treatment," Lacan identifies the problematics of anorexia nervosa in a way that we can use to define the object leading to the dream of the butcher's witty wife:

> But the child does not always fall asleep in this way in the bosom of being, especially if the Other, who has his own ideas about its needs, interferes, and in place of that which he does not have, stuffs the child with the choking pap of what he does have, that is, confuses his caretaking with the gift of his love. It is the child fed with the most love who refuses food and plays with its refusal as with a desire (anorexia nervosa). On these borders we grasp as nowhere else that hate pays the coin of love, but that it is ignorance that is unforgivable. When all is said and done, isn't the child, by refusing to satisfy the mother's demand, requiring her to have a desire outside the child, because that is the path he lacks toward desire? [1958b, p. 264; translation modified]

We scarcely have to change this passage to apply it to the case of the butcher's wife. It is the woman fed with the most love who refuses food (caviar or smoked salmon) and plays with her refusal as with a desire. By asking her husband not to give her caviar (which she would immediately get if she did ask him), the butcher's wife transforms it from an object of her demand to a signifier of her unfulfillable desire. She makes it *the nothing on which her desire feeds* instead of food to fill her mouth. The result of this process is the very image of the desire she interrogates in her husband, the desire directed to a thin woman. Like the smoked salmon, the caviar here becomes the signifier of a desire articulated around the lack, as such, of an object. The anorexic simply pushes this logic to its limit. For her, lack itself becomes an object, and specifically what Lacan calls *objet a*, cause of desire—in other words, the void, the hollow to which the anorexic's mouth and stomach are dedicated, abandoning their physiological function to be at the sole service of a purely erotic one.

Our butcher's wife thus illustrates the function of the orality so often found in the clinical treatment of hysteria. In accordance with the model we have been developing of a sexualization of the organic body, what occurs in hysterical orality is the emphasis on desire over need and appetite over nutritional satisfaction, and a demonstration that the fulfillment of the oral function by food can only leave something over—a nothing—that forever remains to be desired. It is this nothing that must be preserved, at the cost of unsatisfaction. A nothing as unswallowable as it is unvomitable, a nothing that has no materiality other than what remains of the breast or the thumb when it has left the baby's mouth. It is to this nothing that the hysteric is radically reduced in fantasy when she questions the desire beyond the demand of the Other.

This fantasmatic position of the hysteric is especially evident in the unfolding of the analytic relationship, where it enables us to understand the structural reason for a number of difficulties or impasses in which the analyst can find himself. For, of course, it is with regard to her analyst that the hysteric deploys the structure of her fantasy. We find this right at the beginning of the butcher's wife's dream: the patient presents as someone who cannot meet Freud's demand, who can only leave unsatisfied his desire to know, since she cannot bring him a dream that corresponds to his theoretical expectations. More generally, we see the relation of the subject to the nothing within the psychoanalytic session, in a series of behaviors revealing the hysteric's privileged relation to the interruption of the session or of the analysis (for example, during the analyst's vacation). In all these cases, her behavior indicates that she places her very being in these times of interruption, of vacation or vacancy.

It is in this outside-of-discourse, this extra-session remainder, that she realizes herself as such, beyond any subjective identification. Thus the patient may arrive so late that the session is reduced to the question, "Where were you?" Or she cannot leave the analyst when he has ended the session; or she remains silent throughout the hour but phones constantly between hours. In all these behaviors—which we may well call "acting out" because they are appeals for interpretation—the hysteric places herself in a certain position vis-à-vis the analyst: she shows that she is, for him, what remains when she has left him, that she is that void that makes room for desire beyond the sessions. This void can sometimes be perfumed with a singular *odor di femmina*. Thus a female analysand, who was unable to continue with her sessions once the doorbell indicated the arrival of the woman patient after her, found herself totally preoccupied with the place this other woman might occupy for me. No sooner did the bell sound than she was already in the interruption, the vacancy, the expectation of the other. She knew, by the way, how to keep me waiting, in the knowledge that a woman is never so desirable as when she occupies that intermediate place between presence and absence, that place of awaiting in which she is, literally, present insofar as she is absent.

All of the structural features of hysteria that we have noted in the case of the witty butcher's wife are to be found in the study of Dora that Freud recorded in 1899 (Freud 1905b): the homology between dream and hysteria; the constitution of an unsatisfied desire in which the subject is located by means of identifications; the bisexuation of these identifications; and the convergence of all these on a question about femininity, and more specifically about the female body.

Recall the four-way situation in which Dora found herself before she was brought, at the age of 18, to consult Freud on her father's orders. The friendship of Dora and her father for the couple Herr and Frau K. concealed a web of complex relations. Frau K. had taken care of Dora's father during a severe illness he experienced when Dora was still a small child. Later Frau K. became his mistress, although he was impotent. Dora thus found herself in some sense being offered to Frau K.'s husband, who had always been very friendly to her, taking her on walks and giving her little presents. Dora's father closed his eyes to this. The situation became even more entangled when, during vacations, Dora was a most attentive caretaker for the K. children, thereby assuming the position of their mother.

In reality, each member of this quartet was in complicity with the other couple. The father left the field open for Herr K. as far as Dora was concerned, to the point where the girl came to believe that there was a formal agreement that made her an object of exchange between the two men. For her part, Dora protected the relationship between her father and Frau K., looking after the latter's children so that the couple would be left undisturbed. The apparent harmony of these arrangements ended abruptly when, one day, Herr K. made more insistent overtures to her; furious, Dora smacked him, and, returning home, demanded that her father immediately break off relations with Frau K. and her husband. When her father refused, Dora became unbearable; when she threatened suicide, her father decided to have her see Freud.

This case has been so thoroughly discussed in the psychoanalytic literature that there is no need to repeat its details. We shall focus on only those points that reveal the hysteric's approach to the question of femininity, especially the role Dora assigns to Frau K. and the two dreams through which she shows Freud the very place of the enigma, the female body.

Freud's analysis of this case articulates three major themes: the love that Dora denies Herr K., her unconscious love for her father and her jealousy of Frau K., and the predominance of orality in the subject's sexual fantasies. In the notes that he later added to the case, Freud acknowledges that he had underestimated Dora's homosexual love for Frau K. and sees this as the reason for the premature termination of the treatment. Lacan's commentary on this case in "Intervention on transference" (1951) is devoted to explicating the motivations underlying this relationship between Dora and Frau K. that Freud failed to understand.

Dora's fascinated attachment to Frau K. and unshakable loyalty to her are what, according to Lacan, show "the real value of the object which Frau K. is for Dora. That is, not as an individual, but a mystery, the mystery of her own femininity, by which I mean her bodily femininity" (p. 67, translation modified). Thus, discussing the scene at the lake in the course of which Dora slaps Herr K., Lacan stresses not Herr K.'s advances but his statement that his wife is nothing to him. The slap Dora gives him by way of response thus shows her taking the side of the other woman: if she is nothing to you, then what are you to me? For indeed Herr K. has no value for Dora except insofar as he appears to desire Frau K. His words effect a clean rupture of Dora's hysterical identification, an identification whose double polarity is easy to discern. On the one side, there is the masculine identification through which she had taken the position of Herr K. or of her father in order to contemplate Frau K.; on the other, the feminine identification through which she had wanted to be loved by Herr K. and by her father in the same way that Frau K. was loved by the father. To see what is going on in Dora's question, we can recall what the butcher's wife wanted to know: how can another woman (in this case, Frau K.) be loved by a man who cannot be satisfied by her (the absent husband or the impotent father)?

Lacan also emphases the unconscious connection Dora makes between her question about femininity and the trace that sexuality retained from her childhood relation with her brother. The brother, a year and a half older, had been the object of her emulation. Freud records her memory of sitting in a corner as a small child, sucking her thumb and, with the other hand, pulling on her brother's ear. She had been a thumbsucker, and her father had tried everything in order to break her of this habit. According to Lacan, this childhood memory represents "the imaginary matrix in which all the situations developed by Dora during her life have since come to be cast" (p. 67). This matrix involves a dialectic among three terms, since the thumb, which Dora is busy sucking, has the value of a third term added to the brother and Dora herself to constitute them as a man/woman couple. As Lacan says succinctly, "Woman is the object which it is impossible to detach from a primitive oral desire, and yet in which she must learn to recognise her own genital nature" (p. 67). This description of the function of orality is essential to the understanding of Dora.

On the basis of what Freud reports, we can state two conclusions. First, Dora found in her brother her first masculine identification, and, second, she had what might be called a sexual relation with him based on *jouissance* of the oral type. But what is Dora's place in that childhood scene? Is she a girl, taking pleasure in her orality and stimulating the desire of the boy sitting beside her? Isn't she rather identified with the boy, sucking the girl in herself and wondering what might be the relation of a boy to a girl conceived as an oral object? In short, Dora's question might be as follows: What happens to a woman if the relation of a man to a woman can be reduced to the relation of a man to a breast? And indeed Dora's symptoms—a nervous cough, aphonia, hallucination of the smell of smoke—show the summons to the oral drive experienced when she finds herself placed in a couple situation. Lacan's speculation about whether the symptom is related to a fantasy of fellatio performed on her father or of cunnilingus he performed on Frau K. is the result of the bipolarity of the identification through which the hysteric questions femininity. Thus this question points to a beyond of the fantasy object.

It is this "beyond," this absolute Other of which a woman can serve as support for a man, that Lacan discusses twenty years later in his seminar *Encore* (1972–1973). In "Intervention on transference" he had scarcely gone further than Freud in his assertion that a woman's destiny can follow no path other than that of accepting herself as the object of male desire. He had written, in a passage to which we shall return,

> But this homage, whose beneficial value for Dora is sensed by Freud, could be received by her as a manifestation of desire only if she could accept herself as an object of desire, that is to say, only once she had worked out the meaning of what she was searching for in Frau K.
>
> As is true for all women, and for reasons which are at the very basis of the most elementary forms of social exchange (the very reasons which Dora gives as the

grounds for her revolt), the problem of her condition is fundamentally that of accepting herself as an object of desire for the man, and this is for Dora the mystery which motivates her idolatry for Frau K. Just as in her long meditation before the Madonna, and in her recourse to the role of distant worshipper, Dora is driven toward the solution which Christianity has given to this subjective impasse, by making woman the object of a divine desire, or else a transcendent object of desire, which amounts to the same thing. [1951, p. 68]

What does *Encore* add or change with regard to the arguments put forth in this passage? This seminar has given rise to one of the greatest misunderstandings concerning Lacan's doctrine. The fact that Lacan tried to conceptualize femininity as a beyond of the phallus and of the object of male fantasy has led certain authors to see femininity as truly hysterical, with the woman summarily rejecting the role of object of male desire and becoming a transcendent object. It is not surprising that the allusions to mysticism that Lacan makes in this seminar have given support to these errors and to a return to the Christian solution. But the fact is that, while nothing in the passage from "Intervention on transference" needs to be changed or corrected, something does need to be added. For, if *Encore* views femininity as not-all determined by the phallic function, and hence not-all reducible to its condition as the object of male fantasy, this does not mean that that phallic function and that condition are alien or contrary to woman's destiny. What Lacan says in the seminar is that woman's destiny is not exhausted by the phallic reference, that we must add the dimension of a "supplement," a dimension through which women have a relation to the real that men can establish only by the intermediation of fantasy.

This "supplement," however, has nothing transcendental about it. It in no way implies the consecration, in Lacan's thought, of woman as the Other of the phallus. Furthermore, in order for this supplementary dimension to be opened up, the subject must assume the phallic position and the condition of object that structure the castration complex. Thus *Encore* cannot be held to refer to a new feminine condition in which the woman receives the status of Other than what she is in male fantasy. What this seminar does is develop the concept of this condition in a new way, insofar as woman is not-all determined by sexuation. We shall be returning to this argument later.

But because he had not made this advance in 1951, Lacan could envisage Dora's attachment to Frau K. only in terms of homosexuality, thereby agreeing with the self-criticism Freud expressed in his addendum to the discussion of the Dora case. But rather than speak of homosexuality in the clinical sense of the term, it would be more appropriate to think of the *homosexuation* of Dora's desire, a homosexuation bound up with the detours of identification through which she must pass in order to interrogate her own femininity. For Dora must initially adopt the position of a man (her brother or father) in order to take the measure of the desire that this man can have for a woman and hence to appreciate the value that the woman receives in this desire, and it is because she must do so that she is finally confronted with the enigma of Frau K. This confrontation does not amount to the establishment of a sexual couple; Frau K. is not Dora's sexual partner. On the contrary, this process ends in an identificatory reversal: having viewed Frau K.'s position from a man's perspective, Dora concludes that she wishes to be loved by a man, first of all by her father, as Frau K. is loved by him.

For that to be possible, nothing must be changed in the four-way situation. Frau K. must continue to appear to Dora as that which her father loves *beyond herself*, that is, as the supplement of femininity she herself feels she is lacking. By the same reasoning, Dora can very well accept the advances of Herr K., but only on condition that he keep on loving his wife, thereby assigning Dora to the position of a beyond of Frau K., the position of supplement to femininity that is reserved for Frau K. in the first couple of the quartet. What is to be denounced in this process is not so much a homosexuality, in the strict sense, of Dora's desire as it is her overvaluation of Frau K. as the very incarnation of femininity, which results in a split between the condition of object of male desire and the condition of woman. The overvaluation and the split ultimately lead Dora to adopt a trait that Freud finds typical of the man's romantic life, namely a division between two women, the one, overidealized, supporting the figure of the respected and untouchable mother, and the other, debased to the rank of prostitute, symbolizing the sex object strictly speaking. It is because the logic of hysteria tends to be modeled on the rules of a man's love life that Dora cannot find an answer to her question: What is a woman?

The two dreams at the end of the case discussion reveal the way in which Dora frames this question, a way I would characterize as masculine in the sense that femininity is seen as a contents or an inner secret, instead of as the supplement I have described. The first dream concentrates the issue of femininity in the symbol of a jewel box. With the father, the mother, and Dora herself this precious box forms the quartet in which Dora seeks her place. In the dream, the mother wants to save her jewel box, but the father is opposed. This conflict brings to mind a real episode in which Dora's mother wanted some pearl earrings, but the father, who did not care for them, bought her a bracelet. The mother, furious, refused it, saying that since he had spent so much money on something she didn't want, he might as well give it to someone else. Freud observes to Dora that she would have liked to get the gift from her father that the mother had refused. And a more recent episode also involved a jewel box; Herr K. had offered one to Dora.

Finding the common element in the two episodes and the dream, Freud concludes that Dora was prepared to give Herr K. what his wife refused him: her "jewel box" in the figurative sense of the term. Thereafter, as if to defend against this lack of restraint, she recalls in a dream her old love for her father. Dora, however, does not accept this interpretation. It seems that Freud was a bit to quick to understand the "jewel box" as a reference to the female genital, or rather that he did not stop to find out what it meant for Dora. As it turns out, in her associations the jewel and the box represent objects of exchange between a man and a woman, things that can be given and refused and, if refused by one person, given to another.

In short, this motif represents for Dora the enigma of the gift between men and women, and especially the gift as a love token. Doesn't Dora's question have to do with knowing what a woman wants and with how she is to accept what a man may want from her? And then with knowing how what one woman rejects can satisfy another? The pearls her mother had hoped for were associated with the father's damaged sexual potency and with disgust regarding sexual secretions. Dora's question thus also has to do with Frau K.: How can she be satisfied by an impotent man? What does she get from him? The fact that she herself accepted a gift from Herr K. puts her in the position of the one who receives the token of exchange between men and women. But this position is ambiguous: Is it that of her mother, or that of Frau K.? And, if the latter, is it the Frau K. who receives homage from the father or the one who refuses herself to Herr K.?

The true enigma before which Dora finds herself is what she would have to give in exchange for the sign of love represented by the man's gift. If the initial interpretation of her dream led Freud to conclude that she would have liked to receive the gift from her father that her mother had turned down, the scene with Herr K. introduces a new quartet and thus calls for a new interpretation. The four terms in play are no longer Dora, the father, the jewel box, and the mother. They are now Dora, Herr K., the jewel box, and Frau K. And the meaning of the exchange has shifted; here it is Herr K. who would like to receive from Dora what Frau K. refuses him. Because she accepted the gift of the jewel case from him, Dora finds herself in the position of being able to give—that is, in the position occupied by her mother in the first scene. But what does she have to give? Exactly what Frau K. can refuse. It is this ability to refuse that, for Dora, puts Frau K. in the position of mistress of desire and possessor of femininity.

The second dream offers an even more direct illustration of the mystery that Frau K., and especially her woman's body, represents for Dora. This dream constitutes a veritable topography of the female body, a symbolic sexual geography, as Freud calls it. And indeed Dora's associations reveal that all of the designations of place in the dream relate to the female body and culminate in a question about the genital organ. Woman appears in the idealized form of the Madonna, a figure who, as virgin and mother, combines the incompatible. How to "deflower," how to penetrate the secret of this virgin? How to open the box of this woman's body represented by Frau K.?

This is what Dora tries to resolve in the dream. The moment she gets to the heart of the matter, she cannot go further; it is as though she were paralyzed before the risk of discovering the female genital. Here there is a gap in the dream report, a blank or a censoring that is the thing itself. She then attempts to fill this lacuna by consulting a reference book that treats forbidden topics. This construction clearly shows the two-phase mechanism by which the subject attempts to fill, by sexualizing it, the lacuna of the representation of the feminine. In place of the lacuna there appears a sexual explanation that is not censored but forgotten, that is, repressed. (It does not emerge into awareness until after an interpretation by Freud.)

What is this explanation? It develops in three successive stages. First, Dora recalls how, when one of her cousins had appendicitis, she ran to the reference book to find out about the symptoms of this illness. Then an unconscious fantasy comes into awareness. After she herself had undergone an appendectomy, Dora was left with an odd symptom: she dragged her right foot. Freud interprets this as the displacement of a fault for which she punished herself, since by consulting the book Dora had made a faux pas, a false step. She had taken an interest in other passages in the book besides those that concerned appendicitis. And the appendicitis had appeared nine months after the scene at the lake with Herr K. Freud therefore concludes that this was an unconscious fantasy of pregnancy, in which the operation Dora underwent was equivalent to childbirth. But—and this is the third phase of the explanation—Dora is not satisfied with Freud's inter-

pretations. She scornfully refuses what he gives her and ter-
minates her analysis at the next session.

How are we to understand this sequence? It must be
placed in the context of the transference surrounding Dora
and Freud in the course of the analytic relation. For it is obviously to Freud that this dream, like that of the butcher's wife,
is addressed, and it is therefore in the framework of an expectation regarding Freud that Dora's question must be asked
anew. It is he who can give Dora what she is trying to grasp,
or refuse it to her. This puts him in the same position, and
with the same function, as the reference book to which Dora
had had recourse without finding there the answer she sought.
Dora's demand is a desire to know—knowledge of the body
or a body of knowledge, the book symbolizing this corpus—
but at the same time a refusal to know, since no knowledge,
no symbolization, will ever be enough to name the empty heart
of her fascination, that is, the female genital organ censored
in the dream. Freud's reply, inviting her to recognize in her
demand the expression of a wish to receive a child, can only
disappoint her. For the wish for a child is always a substitute meant to plug the unspeakable gap of femininity. Dora,
in short, was waiting for Freud to tell her what a woman is.
He answers: a mother. There is no way out for her now except to abort her analysis. The only correct response to Dora
would have been not knowledge but non-knowledge, not interpretation providing meaning, but invention conveying
non-meaning.

9

A Change of Sex?

Between 1919 and 1925, Freud's thinking on the question of femininity changes completely, passing from a notion of the girl's parent complex—as in the case of Dora—to a diametrically opposed notion. Three fundamental texts are the landmarks of this transition: "A child is being beaten" (1919a), "The psychogenesis of a case of homosexuality in a woman" (1920a), and "Some psychical consequences of the anatomical distinctions between the sexes" (1925). After this last paper, the way will lie open for the final elaboration of the two great texts of 1931 ("Female sexuality") and 1933 ("Femininity").

To understand what is at stake, let us note only the most flagrant contradictions. In 1919, the origin of the feminine problematic is said to be the romantic fixation on the father and its endpoint a masculine identification; in 1925 the origin becomes a fixation on the mother and the endpoint a detour through the father with regard to whom the feminine position is secured. On the one hand, the Oedipus complex seems to establish perversion, on the other, it is what guarantees the girl's normal position. We shall try to follow step by step the logical progression that obliged Freud to make these crucial revisions.

"A child is being beaten" presents an initial outline of the fundamental upheaval that, for Freud, accounts for a woman's fate: what he calls, quite simply, a change of sex. In order to arrive at the final position that will insert her in her sexual role, the girl must change sex, that is, abandon the sexuated position that was hers in the Oedipus. Freud will maintain this idea throughout his work, but, as we shall see, he will give it a totally new meaning between 1919 and 1925. In "A child is being beaten," this change involves a masculinization, inscribing feminine destiny in the development of a masculinity complex. This is clearly a paradox, one that the case of the young lesbian will enable us to resolve.

Let us recall the major points of the 1919 text. Having observed how often the fantasy of a child being beaten appeared in the conscious discourse of his women patients, Freud came to recognize that this fantasy does not appear before the age of four or five. He conjectured that it had a prehistory and represented the end of a lengthy development and elaboration. This hypothesis was confirmed by the emergence of three strata, or sequential phases, in which the fantasy constructs its utterance: father is beating a child (hated by me); I am being beaten by father; a child is being beaten.

The first phase is not necessarily a fantasy; it might be the content of a memory. The second, which is the most important, did not reach consciousness and never had a real existence. We are not dealing with a recollection here, Freud explains, but with an analytic reconstruction. The person doing the beating is still the father, but now the child is no longer the rival but the subject himself, taking the place of the sibling believed to be the father's favorite. In the third phase, both the father and the subject have disappeared from the scene; the person doing the beating is indeterminate (or is sometimes specified as a father substitute—a teacher, for example), and the child is interchangeable. In the case of girls, however, the fantasy has a particular feature in this phase, namely that the child being beaten is always male. How does it come about that the beating of a little boy becomes the fantasmatic fulcrum for the sexual desires of a little girl?

To discover the solution to this enigma, as he called it, Freud studied the girl's parent complex at the time of the construction of the fantasy, that is, between the ages of two and five years. We may compare the structure he discerns here with the one described the following year in the case of the young homosexual woman and with the prehistory of the female Oedipus whose lines of force he would articulate in 1925. Here, in 1919, he starts out, as he had done in the analysis of Dora, with the little girl's tender attachment to her father and the resulting hateful competition with her mother. The girl's situation, in this approach, thus corresponds symmetrically to that of the boy, who loves his mother and is jealous of his father. In the female Oedipus, the mother has no role other than that of rival, and she is excluded from the construction of the fantasy. At this point, there is no mention of an early attachment of the daughter to her mother; the parent complex and the fantasy that sustains desire are oriented entirely toward the relation to the father and the guilt that accompanies this incestuous love. Thus being beaten by the father means, in the first phase, having lost favor with him, while in the second phase it means being the favored recipient of his love, a love that, having been repressed, can appear only in the form of atoning for guilt. "Father loves me" becomes "father is beating me": the incestuous love is concealed, and the punishment it deserves is inflicted. The first two phases of the fantasy thus express the same oedipal attachment of the girl to her father.

Yet we find that there is a limit to this fixation to the father, since, in the third phase, the father–daughter relation disappears and is replaced by that of a father substitute to a boy. This enigma leads Freud to introduce the notion of a masculinity complex in the girl. Noting that in the fantasies of children of both sexes it is almost always boys who are being beaten, he concludes that the girl, turning away from incestuous love for her father, also turns away from her femininity and wishes to be a boy. In other words, the outcome of the Oedipus for the girl is perversion. Freud apparently feels that this conclusion is untenable, for he immediately goes on to discuss the origin of perversions and new contradictions appear. If the elaboration of the fantasy "a child is being beaten" is supposed to teach us about the root of perversions, especially of masochism, how does this square with the fact, noted at the beginning of the paper, that five of the six cases that prompted his reflections were cases of neurosis? And, moreover, how can we correctly understand the Oedipus complex, if it can be simultaneously the basis of both perversion and neurosis?

A solution is suggested in the distinction Freud draws between infantile and adult perversion. Although perversion in the adult, homosexuality in particular, stems from the Oedipus, it does so less from the complex itself than from its traces, or, as Freud calls them, the scars it leaves in the unconscious. Beating fantasies are among such scars. In other words, it is the fantasy that is perverse, but not necessarily the subject himself; the beating fantasy can—but need not—support the eventual appearance of a perversion in adulthood (when the scenario will be played out in the real and no longer on the imaginary stage of fantasy life).

The question then concerns what has to be added to the oedipal scar, here the sadomasochistic fantasy with masculine identification, in order for the subject to choose perversion, in particular homosexuality. This question arises in the following year in the case of the young lesbian (Freud 1920a). For, after "A child is being beaten," the problem becomes knowing how the girl can orient herself correctly in her sexual life if her fantasy, a scar of the Oedipus, guides her toward a masculine position, that is, leads the way toward homosexuality. And Freud goes straight to the point. In the fourth section of "A child is being beaten," he writes that the female fantasy culminates in a change of sex, a change totally contrary to the femininity that the oedipal girl was supposed to want her father to acknowledge. How then, can the girl not become homosexual?

To answer this question, we must follow the development of Freud's thought in his discussion of the case of the young homosexual woman. This case leads Freud to make a fundamental alteration in the argument presented in "A child is being beaten," one that enables him to resolve the difficulty of connecting the oedipal position with an outcome in a masculine identification. The case of the young homosexual woman shows that perversion is not a simple derivative of a father fixation in the Oedipus complex; instead its basis is a prior romantic fixation that Freud discovers here: the primal fixation to the mother. And with this, another dimension appears in the background of feminine destiny, the dimension of what Freud calls the prehistory of the Oedipus. The revelation of

this prehistory will lead him, from 1920 to 1925, to reconsider the girl's love for her father as a more or less opaque
concealment of a more fundamental love for her mother.

The case involves a girl of eighteen, beautiful and intelli-
gent, from a well-off family. This young person is ardently
pursuing a woman ten years older, a "woman of the world"
or high-class prostitute, who lives with a married woman
friend and is conducting an intimate relationship with her.
The young woman is completely indifferent to unflattering
gossip about the lady and to her father's scorn for this "loose
woman." On the contrary, the depravity of the object is an
essential condition of the love the girl feels for her. The
patient acts like the lady's loyal knight, following her everywhere, camping on her doorstep, sending her flowers and
the like, dedicating her entire life to this adoration (as Freud
calls it) and abandoning all other interests. The lady, for
her part, seems annoyed by the excesses of her young ad-
mirer and never grants her any favor other than allowing her
to kiss her hand. Moreover, she constantly reproves the
patient, urging her to turn away from her and from women
in general.

The girl's parents—especially the father—are angry and
upset at the provocativeness of her behavior. On the one hand,
she does not hesitate to parade in the street on her beloved's
arm, caring nothing for her reputation and that of her family;
but, on the other hand, at home she resorts to all kinds of lies
in order to hide these meetings from her parents. One day
there occurs an incident that leads the parents to take their
daughter to Freud. The father comes upon the girl walking
in the street with the lady and glares at them angrily; the next
moment, the girl tears away from her companion's arm, climbs

on a parapet, and jumps over, crashing onto the train tracks below. Six months later, having recovered from her injuries, she comes to Freud.

How did this young woman become a homosexual? And what could have led her to jump from a bridge after encountering her father? Freud begins by pointing out that this inclination of the patient's toward a woman was not her first; the present love affair simply illustrates in a particularly striking way a tendency that had been apparent in former years. In tracing the young woman's love life from its onset, Freud comes to articulate the bipolarity of the feminine Oedipus. He begins by considering his patient's Oedipus complex solely from the perspective of her attachment to her father, noting that she had experienced a normal feminine Oedipal passage and has subsequently replaced her father with a brother a bit older than she is.

Penis envy is conspicuous in her and has been so for a long time, since the comparison of her genitals with those of her brother, around the age of five, had left a strong impression. But, apart from this, there seems to be nothing abnormal or noteworthy about her account of her childhood. She has never been neurotic and shows no hysterical symptoms. When she was around thirteen or fourteen, penis envy resurfaced and took the form of a desire for a child; at that time the girl showed an excessive tenderness toward a little boy of three whom she met. Nevertheless, shortly thereafter, the little boy ceased to interest her and she began to turn her attention to mature women, something her father disapproved of. How to account for this change? Freud observes that it coincides with her mother's new pregnancy and the birth of a little brother. The patient was around thirteen at the time.

The girl's libido, then, was first directed toward maternity, and, from the time of her mother's pregnancy, she became homosexual. A series of dreams clearly shows that the beloved lady is a substitute for the mother. Moreover, the women who had preceded her in the patient's heart had all been mothers whom she had met together with their children. But matters are complicated by the fact that the lady also seems to be a substitute for the older brother, whom she resembles in her slim figure, her severe beauty, and her brusque manners. Thus, Freud notes, the lady corresponds to the patient's masculine as well as to her feminine ideal, combining homosexual and heterosexual object choices. Who, or what, does the patient love in the lady? The mother? The brother? And what has become of the desire for a child that was so strongly in evidence just recently and that must have been disappointed by the mother's new pregnancy?

Freud is well aware of these difficulties and is therefore surprised that, frustrated in her hope for a child, the girl nonetheless turned to a mother substitute. Why did she not, as would normally be expected, rebel against her mother and hate her as a rival? Her choice is all the more surprising because her mother in fact behaved toward her like an annoying competitor, taking pains with her own appearance and jealously making sure the girl did not get too close to her father. The patient really had no reason to feel affection for her mother. This complex and mysterious process leads Freud to set forth two lines of thought.

First, he emphasizes the existence, in the background of the relationship of the girl to her father, of a more primary relationship to the mother. Second, he distinguishes between two orders in the subject's love life: on the one hand, the subject's *sexuated identification*, that is, the masculine or feminine position that the subject adopts (does he or she love as a man or as a woman?), and, on the other hand, the *object choice* (does he or she love a masculine object or a feminine one?). Applying this distinction to the case of the girl, Freud shows that from either point of view the mother plays the central role. The mother both guides the girl's sexuated identification and embodies her romantic object choice. And, as we shall see, she is also the one who is involved in the acting out to which her daughter's behavior leads. As for the father, he seems to be relegated to a minor role, that of the witness before whose eyes the bond between two women is formed.

Thus Freud begins by observing that it is just at the time when her desire to receive a child—especially a boy—from her father is at its most intense that the girl finds that her mother, the unconsciously hated rival, is pregnant by him. Bitter and indignant, she turns from her father and from men in general. It is thus resentment in matters of love that leads the girl to reject, all at the same time, love for a man, the desire to have a child, and the feminine role. (We shall, however, see that in the suicidal acting out she reveals certain elements that she had wanted to repudiate.) But the girl does more than show her resentment and deny some of her desires. Not content just to avoid men, she goes as far as to direct her love toward a mother substitute. This is the mystery that we have to penetrate. As Freud strikingly sums up what happened, "She changed into a man, and took her mother in place of her father as a love object" (p. 215). The distinctions we previously noted explain this upheaval: the girl, at this moment, changes both her sexuated identification, becoming a man, and her love object, choosing the mother over the father. This double reversal is possible only on one condition that Freud introduces as if in passing, but that is to become crucial to his entire conception of feminine desire: "Her relation to her mother had certainly been ambivalent from the beginning, and it proved easy to revive her earlier love for her mother and with its help to bring about an over-compensation for her current hostility towards her" (p. 215).

This hypothesis completely changes the position Freud had up to then defended regarding the girl's classic oedipal love for her father and her wish to receive a child from him. It now turns out that, behind this love for the father, there lies hidden an even older one for the mother. This primordial relation is far from being extinguished by the love for the father, since all it takes is one disappointment of the love the girl had hoped for from him to cause the earlier love to regain the upper hand, despite whatever hostility she may feel for this first object. This original love for the mother is all the more solid because it sustains narcissism; the girl can identify with the object of her love and thereby blur the separation of the levels of sexuated identification and object love.

However, although the former love for the mother returns after the disappointment the girl experiences from her father, it is important to note that it does so only in a different form. This transformation presents the most difficult obstacle in the case report. In the movement by which the girl turns toward the lady, there is a kind of sleight of hand or inversion. The girl preserves her identificatory schema as the path of access to love, but the other, with whom she identifies, changes. During the phase that Freud characterizes as that of the normal Oedipus, she had identified with her mother in order to be loved by her father; after the disappointment, she identifies with the father in order to love the mother. There is a crossing over between the poles of identification and object and a simultaneous inversion of the subject's position as lover or beloved.

	identification	*object*	*libidinal aim*
Phase 1 :	the mother	the father	to be loved
Phase 2 :	the father	the mother	to love

In this crisscross, the erotic/aggressive ambivalence characteristic of any imaginary identification is transferred from the mother to the father. As Freud stresses, "The attitude of the libido thus adopted was greatly reinforced as soon as the girl perceived how much it displeased her father" (p. 217). In short, she is taking revenge on her father, remaining homosexual in order to defy him. This is why she has to parade around publicly on the lady's arm, making sure the father will learn of the relationship.

Two further elements have to be clarified before we can completely untangle this skein. The first is the double role of the lady, and the second is the specific nature of the love the girl feels for her. As we have already seen, the lady is a substitute for both the mother and the older brother; it might be said that she is a mother, but one who has certain features of the brother and can therefore gratify the heterosexual part of the girl's libido. But this explanation seems to make matters more obscure. For what we need to know, after all, is whether this young person is in love with a woman or with a man. It will not help to say that we are dealing with a combination of the two. We may be closer to a solution if we recall that, in 1920, Freud had not yet analyzed the mechanisms of fetishism. For the object, at the same time homosexual and heterosexual, represented by the lady reveals its identity once we become aware that it is a fetishized mother. Recall that the brother's penis had made a great impression on the patient when she was still a small child. The fact that the lady has certain traits of the brother inevitably reminds us of this very typical penis. The attachment to a phallic mother also indicates the girl's perverse structure.

As for the nature of the love that the girl lavishes on the lady, it is clearly a form of courtly love. In other words, the girl loves the lady in the way a man loves a woman according to the masculine type of romantic object choice that Freud brilliantly described in 1910 (see Freud 1910a). Certain details of the patient's object choices following her mother's pregnancy are consistent with this argument. The women with whom she fell in love were not necessarily known to be lesbians but were, in each case, of bad reputation. Thus the girl shared the typically masculine wish to "save" the beloved woman from her depravity. This attitude no doubt concealed an unconscious condemnation of the mother for having received a child from the father: "my mother is a whore." Thus it is not only the other of sexuated identification and the romantic object choice that change after this pregnancy, but also the kind of love that the girl feels for this object. When she takes the mother as object and identifies with the father, the subjective position she adopts in her love life undergoes a change: she passes from a feminine way of loving (that is, from the role of the beloved) to a male way (the role of lover). We may note, moreover, that this inversion serves only to sustain the proposition that her mother is loved by her father.

Now that we have traced the subjective journey of the patient between the ages of fourteen and eighteen, two questions remain: What is the cause of this journey, and what is its aim? Let us begin with the second. It is clear that the unconscious goal of the young homosexual woman is a sort of demonstration with regard to her father. She shows him how he should have behaved toward her, what kind of love he should have offered her. She challenges him to pick up the gauntlet, to love her as perfectly as she herself loves the lady. But over and above this, she also has a goal as far as her mother is concerned. Consider her suicidal acting out and exactly how it occurred. The girl is out walking with the lady in a neighborhood that she knows her father is likely to be found in at that hour. They do indeed cross paths, and he glares at them. The girl tells the lady that the man who had just looked them up and down was her father; the lady becomes angry, demanding that the girl leave her at once and never speak to her again. The girl immediately flings herself over the parapet.

Two facts stand out in this sequence. First there is the father's gaze that makes the girl feel as though she has been reduced to nothing, or, at any rate, distanced from the all-powerful phallus that she would like to be. She returns to a position in which the subject feels fundamentally excluded; she is merely *objet a* for the father who repudiates her. To add insult to injury, the lady, too, is angry at her. This change upsets the poles of identification and love object. The lady, who had been in the position of the love object as a substitute for the phallic mother, suddenly assumes the paternal role, and this at the very moment when, confronted with her father's scornful gaze, the girl can no longer sustain her identification with him. The rejection is complete, and the girl has no recourse but to actualize the repudiation she had encountered on the symbolic level.

However, as Freud subtly observes, this desperate acting out also enables her to retrieve something of her desire. Suicide represents not simply a loss, but also what Lacan calls a *plus-de-jouir*, an excess of *jouissance*. According to Freud, her act fulfills both desire and a need for punishment. The desire in question is her deepest one, the one whose dis-

182 WHAT DOES A WOMAN WANT?

appointment marked her entry into homosexuality, namely her desire to have a child by her father; in "falling" from the bridge because of her father, she also gave birth because of him, the German verb *niederkommen*, which she had used to describe her action, means both "to fall" and "to be delivered of a child." This signifying equivoque is thus the key to the act. And this analysis proves that the desire of the child was in no way abandoned by the girl at the time of her mother's pregnancy.

As for the bringing about of punishment, this is both a self-punishment (ordered by the paternal gaze and the lady's reproaches) and a punishment of the woman in childbirth, that is, of the mother. As Freud says, "[P]robably no one finds the mental energy to kill himself unless, in the first place, he is in doing this at the same time killing an object with whom he had identified himself, and, in the second place, is turning against himself a death-wish which had been directed against someone else" (1920a, p. 220). Thus, in attempting suicide, the girl is also punishing her mother, with whom she was identified and who should have died in giving birth to the little boy whom her daughter envied her. Thus the fulfillment of the wish for punishment is itself a fulfillment of desire.

But the same question keeps coming up whenever we try to explain this case: Why does she have to become a homosexual in order to attain this goal? She had identified with her mother and subsequently wanted to kill her when she felt humiliated by the mother's pregnancy. So far, so good. But why does this identificatory hate entail the mother's becoming a love object? The paradox at the center of the case report is this: the girl kills her mother as a pole of identification but continues to love her as an object. We must therefore conclude that the mother's pregnancy, although it was the *catalyst* for the girl's overt homosexuality, was nevertheless not its *cause.*

Taking up the discussion of the cause of this structure at the end of the case report, Freud highlights the importance of a position prior to the ones illustrated in the schema above (p. 172). Although there are indications in the patient's history of a classical oedipal position (such as the interest in the little boy), these must, he says, be counterbalanced by other elements that, from early childhood, pointed to her homosexuality. For example, when still a schoolgirl, she had fallen in love with a woman teacher who was clearly a mother substitute. The girl's homosexuality did not begin in adolescence but was "probably a direct and unchanged continuation of an infantile mother-fixation" (p. 228). Here we see the meaning of the strong penis envy that the patient, as a child, had felt with regard to her brother. Ever since childhood, she had taken the path of the "masculinity complex."

This case report, then, ultimately teaches us that, before the oedipal position in which the daughter identifies with the mother, takes the father as her object, and wants to be loved by him and to receive a sign of his love (a child), there is an earlier, masculine position in which the daughter actively takes her mother as a love object. We must therefore complete the diagram by adding a "zero stage":

	identification	*object*	*libidinal aim*
Zero Stage	the father	the mother	to love
Stage 1 (Oedipus)	the mother	the father	to be loved
Stage 2 (homosexuality)	the father	the mother	to love

In the years following the paper on the case of the young homosexual woman, Freud was to focus his investigations on this infantile fixation of the girl on her mother, especially starting in 1925, when he introduced the notion of a pre-history of the feminine Oedipus complex. Let us try to follow this development and to understand its results.

10

A Daughter and Her Mother

In considering "A child is being beaten," we wondered
why it is that a masculine position in a girl can stem from an
erotic fixation on the father. The case of the young homosexual woman enables Freud to respond to this question but
also to make it more complex by revealing a dimension that
he had not noted before, the more archaic fixation on the
mother. This paper, then, presents its own enigmas. The girl's
homosexuality now becomes a possibility inscribed in the
structure of the feminine Oedipus complex, and indeed a basic
element in that complex (the masculine position vis-à-vis the
mother). What will determine whether or not a girl goes on
to become homosexual? What will determine whether or not
the archaic relation to the mother will resurface through the
relation of the daughter to the father? In other words, the
question is whether the relation to the father that is established
in the girl's Oedipus complex functions as a metaphor or just
as a metonymy with regard to the relation to the mother.
Freud's young homosexual patient moves in the direction

opposite to the one he now specifies as the trajectory of feminine development. Under what conditions is this regression toward the mother possible? Freud did not really answer this question in the case report. But we may note that the question takes on a more general scope if we rephrase it as: under what conditions is this regression *impossible*?

This is the problem that Freud addresses from 1925 on, in an odd echo of his preoccupation twenty-five or thirty years earlier, when he had undertaken to curb the dark power of the female sex. From that time on, as he wrote to Fliess, at each phase of the development of his thought, he came up against the same obstacle, namely that the daughter's relation to the father does not really cause the disappearance of her primary relation to her mother. The question of female homosexuality is thus one of structure; there is something close to a natural homosexuality in women. That is why it is difficult to consider female homosexuality to be a perversion pure and simple.

And so we need to look, with Freud, at the relation between mother and daughter in that "prehistory" of the feminine Oedipus complex, beginning with the 1925 paper "Some psychical consequences of the anatomical distinction between the sexes." Here Freud explicitly formulates the girl's relation to her father, which up to now he had defined as her Oedipus complex, as the *transference* of an earlier relation to the mother, a transference in which the father functions as a metaphor. Hence Freud must fundamentally revise his theory of the Oedipus complex, introducing an essential asymmetry between the boy and the girl, one that will be expressed primarily in the role of the castration complex.

The terminology of the paper's title indicates right from the start a split between the psychic and the anatomical; the difference that is observable on the anatomical level is not inscribed as such in the psyche. All that is inscribed there is *what follows from* this difference, namely the castration complex. What matters, though, is not this split but the use made of it by the boy and the girl to determine their attitude. One of the psychic consequences of the absence of unconscious inscription of the anatomical difference between the sexes is thus the tendency to establish a male way of thinking and a female one. This is just a tendency, but it is a striking one. Placed in front of anatomy, the boy does not know what to say; he is as it were condemned to inquiry and doubt, whereas the girl, according to Freud, knows from the outset what she ought to think, because, when it comes to the opposite sex, she can line up behind evidence that exempts her from masculine ruminations.

The paper begins with a review of the arguments set forth in the paper "On the sexual theories of children" (1908a) and initially revised in "The infantile genital organization" (1923). For up to that time, Freud had never envisaged the discovery of anatomical difference except from the little boy's perspective. In 1908, he had proposed that, confronted with the female genital area, the boy did not act in accordance with his perception of the lack of a member but consoled himself with the thought that the girl's penis would grow when she got older. In other words, the boy who discovers feminine anatomy *does not see* that the penis is missing, but *he says* that it is there, hidden. Freud added that the little girl shares her brother's opinion and takes great interest in the boy's member, feeling herself to be at a disadvantage and envious. In short, at this stage of the development of Freud's thought, both boy and girl celebrate *the universality of the penis*, at the price of castration fear on the boy's side and penis envy on the girl's.

By 1923, in "The infantile genital organization," Freud has already modified this argument. It is no longer the universality of the penis that is to be found in the attitude of children but, more subtly, *the primacy of the phallus*. This term introduces a nuance: if the phallus is in direct relation to the male organ, it is so insofar as it designates the penis as lacking or potentially lacking. Returning to the little boy discovering feminine anatomy, Freud explains that it is not the penis as such that the boy ascribes to the girl, but the penis as having been cut off. The boy tells himself that her penis was once there but is now missing, and he now has to confront the possibility of his own castration. In 1908, Freud had maintained that the boy was not aware of a lack; in 1923 he bases the castration complex on the fact that the boy perceives the female genital as lack of a penis—that is, as a phallus. Unfortunately, he concludes, he does not have any data about the corresponding process in the girl.

Two years later, in "Some psychical consequences . . . ," he sets about to remedy this. The unique contribution of this paper is to set forth the way in which the primacy of the phallus is revealed for each of the two sexes. Although it is the same phallus that the boy and the girl respectively discover in the anatomically opposite sex, this discovery is inscribed in the register of *lack* for the boy and the register of *veil* for the girl. Entry into the problematics of castration occurs for both, but in different ways. Anatomy does not evoke the same response in the one as in the other, and each sex repudiates anatomical difference in its own fashion. The boy is irresolute, he doubts, he seeks further information; the girl understands everything instantly: "She has seen it and knows that she is without it and wants to have it" (Freud 1925, p. 253).

The moment of seeing the difference opens up for the boy an infinite time in which to understand, while for the girl it seems to coincide immediately with the moment of ending. The girl's masculinity complex stems from this instantaneous perception and develops along two lines, hope and denial: hope of one day obtaining a penis that will make her like a man, and denial in which she refuses to acknowledge that she is lacking anything; persists in the conviction that she does, after all, have a penis; and feels obliged to behave as a man does.

The difference between the boy's attitude and the girl's is thus a psychic result of the anatomical discovery and hence of the support (or lack of support) that perception furnishes for their mechanisms of thought. For the boy, feminine anatomy offers nothing to be perceived. He is confronted with the hole, that is, with that which cannot be thought without the concept of lack. The threat of castration now takes on its basic function, which is to provide the concept of the signifier of the phallus as a reference point for his mental effort. But, reference point though it be, this concept remains a swindle, a pretense: by naming as "lack" what is "hole," that is to say, nothing at all, he precludes the discovery of the female genital as such.

Granoff (1979) has astutely noted the importance of this process. Because the feminine does not confront the boy with an obvious fact, he has to make a mental effort to signify it— except that the only thing about it that can be signified is the phallus and not the female genital. This mechanism, Granoff observes, involves a definitive impairment that will mark all of the boy's thinking and investigation. As for the girl, she encounters an obvious fact from the outset. The anatomy of the other sex presents her with an unarguable *sign* that leads her right to the time of concluding without passing through the time for understanding to which the boy is condemned. She has seen, she knows, she wants: the issue is clear cut. Whereas the boy is inserted into the problematics of castration only by a *judgment*, the girl can spare herself this mental effort thanks to the visible evidence of the penis. Yet this evidence is not less deceptive than the absence of the sign encountered by the boy, since, for the girl, the sign of the penis serves as a screen hiding the nature of her own lack. This difference in the approach to castration for the boy and the girl can be better understood in terms of the distinction between the symbolic and the imaginary registers. The boy is introduced to it from the perspective of the symbolic: he brings into play the *signifier of lack* in the place where he encounters the most radical *lack of a signifier*. The girl, on the other hand, approaches the opposite sex through an imaginization: she accords the penis the function of the sign of the sexuated identification of which she feels deprived.

Having described the manner in which the girl and the boy enter into the castration complex, we now have to assess the consequences for their respective Oedipal structures. Here we find an asymmetry.

For the boy, the Oedipus is a primary formation, the first that we can recognize in him. This situation is easy to understand, since, in the Oedipus, the boy retains his attachment to the object he had invested from infancy, his mother. Is there a prehistory to the masculine Oedipus? Nothing is less certain. Freud mentions various hypotheses on this matter: a primary loving identification with the father, masturbation in infancy and the role played in it by enuresis, and finally archaic fantasies of the primal scene. But, he concludes, much remains unexplained, and we cannot speak of a prehistory for the boy's Oedipus as we can for the girl's. As for the future of the boy's Oedipus, however, the answer is clear: there is none. Here Freud takes up the argument proposed in "The waning of the Oedipus complex" (1924a), namely that, for the boy, the castration complex shatters the Oedipus complex. The latter is not simply repressed under pressure from the threat of castration, but, Freud says, in ideal cases it disappears altogether from the unconscious, replaced by the superego. This astonishing thesis suggests the ideal realization toward which the logic of the unconscious would lead, if neurosis and the symptom did not prevent us from following that path. Fortunately, one might say, ideal cases are less common than neurotic ones, since the ideal in question does not promise much besides the tyranny of the superego. Neurosis, however, serves to reserve a certain future for the Oedipus complex and hence for unconscious desire.

The situation for the girl is more complicated. Freud announces at the outset that, for the little girl, "the Oedipus complex raises one problem more than in boys" (1925, p. 251). The problem is to explain how and why, given that here too the mother was the first object, the girl comes to renounce her in favor of the father. It turns out that the Oedipus complex, primary for the boy, is secondary for the girl. The castration complex thus plays an asymmetrical role for the one and the other sex. It tends to make the boy's Oedipus disappear, but it is the origin of the girl's, that is, the origin of her giving up her mother and choosing her father. The prehistory of the feminine Oedipus overlaps with the castration complex in the relation of the girl to her mother. The penis envy that arises when the little girl sees the trait identifying her father's genital, and that leads to her masculinity complex, is not without consequences for the way she views her primary object, the mother, nor for the way she judges her own body. Freud lists four such consequences.

The first is a feeling of inferiority, of having a lesser value, that forms like a scar over a narcissistic injury. It is thus on the level of narcissism, of identificatory supports, that penis envy has its first effect. It is as though the girl was unable to support her sexuated identification on any distinctive genital trait. She therefore begins to share the scorn in which the female sex—the sex that "falls short"—is held by men, and in so doing she becomes similar to the boy with whose judgment she agrees. The paradox here is clear: by judging herself inferior, she becomes the man's equal by virtue of this very judgment. Freud adds an ironic footnote to the effect that "this fact represents the core of truth contained in Adler's theory" (p. 253, n. 4), that is, the theory of the masculine protest, which is based on the reaction of girls to their lack of a penis.

The second consequence of penis envy is the particular manner in which feminine jealousy is constituted. Here, too, we are in the register of narcissism, but this time from the perspective of the relation to the image of the other. Freud refers the reader to his analysis of the fantasy that "A child is being beaten" (1919a), especially to the first stage of this fantasy in which the father is beating the child of whom the girl is jealous. He now adds that "[t]he child which is being beaten (or caressed) may ultimately be nothing more nor less than the clitoris itself" (1925, p. 254).

This statement calls for some commentary. We may recall that in this female fantasy it is always boys who are being beaten, and that being beaten is equivalent to being loved. Consequently, the little girl identifies now with the person who is being beaten so that she can be in the position of the one who is loved, and now with the one who is doing the beating so that she can take revenge on the boy of whom she is jealous. But if the beaten child is identified with the clitoris, it is the clitoris that becomes worthy of love. That the clitoris is beaten/loved means that it is not necessary to be a boy equipped with a penis in order to be loved by the father; the clitoris, cut short as it is, will do. This fantasy, therefore, corresponds to the wish to see the clitoris elevated to the rank of the penis, that is, to the rank that attracts the father's recognition and love. This much-wished-for equivalence underlies the jealousy typical of women. One woman is jealous of another *as if the other woman were a boy*: she is jealous because the other possesses, or seems to possess, the special feature that makes her worthy of love. What makes a woman jealous is not so much that her lover desires other women as that he thinks of another woman as having "a little something" that makes her irresistible. This "little something," this index of a sign that will magically capture the desire of the other, is what women are constantly tracking down in other women.

A third consequence of the discovery of castration is what Freud calls "the loosening of the girl's relation with her mother as a love object" (p. 254). The girl holds her mother responsible for her lack of a penis, accusing her of having brought her into the world insufficiently equipped. This reproach can also be understood with reference to the category of the sign, in which the girl gives a function to the penis. The daughter thinks that her mother hasn't given her a true genital organ like that of a boy; she thus feels deprived of an unarguable sign of her own sexuated identity. The female genital always remains *unentdeckt*, undiscovered, as Freud says, in both the literal and the figurative senses of the term. This flaw in identity leaves only the mother available for a feminine identification. But maternity is not femininity, and, furthermore, the identification with the mother is fundamentally ambivalent because the mother is equally deprived of the penis and is thus essentially devalued by the girl.

Finally, penis envy arouses in the girl an intense reaction against clitoral masturbation, since this involves an unbearable narcissistic humiliation for her. In other words, she refuses to go on getting pleasure from this sub-penis that cannot even sustain her sexuated identity. Freud here begins a complex train of thought that relates the girl's masturbatory activity with the dialectic of activity and passivity. He concludes that the narcissistic humiliation that spoils masturbation and so leads to its abandonment is the motive behind the girl's final acceptance of femininity. We have here, to say the least, a paradox, the workings of which are clarified in "Femininity" (1933). Here the exclusive importance assigned to penis envy begins to reveal an impasse in Freud's reasoning. For Freud has to perform the feat of explaining feminine destiny on the sole basis of penis envy; that is, he must explain how it is the masculinity complex that leads the girl to become feminine!

This development of femininity, according to Freud, is supposed to occur in the second phase that begins after the establishment of the castration complex, that is, in the phase where, disappointed by her mother, the girl turns toward her father and enters into the Oedipus proper. This phase is ushered in by a metaphor. The father is substituted for the mother, and, consequently, the wish for a child comes to replace the wish for the penis. The father becomes the love object, the mother becomes the object of jealousy, and the girl "has turned into a little woman" (Freud 1925, p. 256). If we relate this upheaval to Lacan's formula for metaphor, and especially for the paternal metaphor, we may write it as follows:

1. the metaphor : $\dfrac{S}{S'} \cdot \dfrac{S'}{x} \longrightarrow S\left(\dfrac{I}{s}\right)$

2. the paternal metaphor (Lacan) : $\dfrac{\text{Name of the Father}}{\text{Desire of the mother}} \cdot \dfrac{\text{Desire of the mother}}{\text{signified to the subject}} \longrightarrow \text{N of F}\left(\dfrac{A}{\text{Phallus}}\right)$

3. the Freudian metaphor : $\dfrac{\text{Father}}{\text{Mother}} \cdot \dfrac{\text{Mother}}{\text{Penis}} \longrightarrow \text{Father}\left(\dfrac{A}{\text{child}}\right)$

From now on, Freud constantly comes up against the question of whether this passage from the first to the second phase of the feminine Oedipus does indeed involve something of the order of a metaphor. For, as he comes to see more and more clearly, the problematics of femininity ultimately have to do with the ineluctable return of the archaic relation to the mother. *It is as though, for the little girl, the father never entirely replaces the mother*, as though the latter always continues to act through the figure of the former. To put it another way, the issue is whether Freud's two-phase construction of the feminine Oedipus has to do with metaphor or with metonymy.

The question is all the more relevant because the connection between penis envy and the wished-for child from the father seems itself to be only a metonymy rather than a metaphor. In wishing to receive a child from her father, the girl, basically, does not at all renounce the penis. She simply seeks an equivalent for it. What could be better than a penis, if not a child? This passage from penis to child does not result in the production of a new signifier, the criterion of metaphor. Given the lack of a penis, that a child will constitute the sign of feminine identity is never anything but a hope, indeed, a denial: clinical psychoanalysis shows that motherhood, from this perspective, is often accompanied by depression or by a superficial contentment that speaks volumes. Freud himself encountered this failure in the elaboration of his theory. This is why he concluded, in "Analysis terminable and interminable" (1937), that penis envy in women is irreducible, implying that the return to the mother, with all its ambivalence, is an inevitable part of the girl's destiny. We shall see how Lacan enables us to find a way out of this impasse.

All this leads us to examine in detail what happens in the mother–daughter relationship. Now, on this crucial question, so decisive for feminine destiny, it is striking that the psychoanalytic literature contains nothing substantial, apart from the two papers of Freud's that we have just been discussing. Today, more than fifty years after its publication, we can still agree with Freud's statement in the paper on "Female sexuality":

> Everything in the sphere of this first attachment to the mother seemed to me so difficult to grasp in analysis— so grey with age and shadowy and almost impossible to revivify—that it was as if it had succumbed to an especially inexorable repression. But perhaps I gained this impression because the women who were in analysis with me were able to cling to the very attachment to the father in which they had taken refuge from the early phase that was in question. [1931, p. 226]

Thus the analyst himself makes matters more difficult: not only is this domain especially hard to explore, but its repression is reinforced by the analyst insofar as he takes the place of the paternal substitute—which was, as we know, admittedly Freud's inclination. The explorer is thus caught in his own trap. As a result, we can go no further with this question unless we reinterrogate and redefine the position of the analyst in the treatment of a woman, which does not mean, as one might conclude overhastily, that all the analyst needs to do in order to obviate the difficulty is to take the mother's position.

It is all the more necessary that the bond with the mother emerge in the analysis because, Freud says, there is a direct relation between the phase of that bond and the etiology of hysteria as well as the origin of paranoia. The preoedipal phase thus takes on such importance that Freud issues this revolutionary statement: "Since this phase allows room for all the fixations and repressions from which we trace the origin of the neuroses, it would seem as though we must retract the universality of the thesis that the Oedipus complex is the nucleus of the neuroses" (1931, p. 226). Freud had already administered an initial shock when, in 1925, he calmly suggested that, under the influence of the castration complex, the Oedipus complex could be erased from the unconscious. Now he goes even further in questioning the Oedipus: the neuroses, at any rate in girls, may well have their source elsewhere! This astonishing argument is immediately minimized by Freud, who declares that no one is obliged to follow him on this terrain.

How are we, today, to assess the term *preoedipal* that Freud uses to characterize the archaic relation to the mother? How can we better understand this relation than by seeing it as the child's connection to the first Other, the maternal Other, whom Lacan (1955–1956) presents as not yet divided by the place of the Law? Thus, in the girl, there persists a relation to the Other who is "normally" superseded by the intervention of the paternal metaphor. We must be careful, here, not to draw conclusions that are too general. We are not, of course, to think that girls are not subject to the paternal metaphor, which would amount to saying that women are psychotic. Nevertheless, something of this sort occurs. The father does not truly intervene as a metaphor in feminine destiny; or, more exactly, the girl does *not-all* submit to this metaphorical function. For her, the paternal agency does not cause the first, maternal Other to disappear into oblivion. It seems that the father finds his place in the feminine Oedipus as a figure always liable to be reduced to a metonymy for the mother. He thereby regains his original status: "[D]uring that phase a little girl's father is not much else for her than a troublesome rival, although her hostility towards him never reaches the pitch which is characteristic of boys" (1931, p. 226).

This limitation to the extent of the paternal metaphor for the girl can be explained. For, if the father's function is to introduce the subject to the law of the phallus, and if this signifier of the phallus fails, by definition, to signify the nature of femininity, then the signification brought about by the paternal metaphor is always incomplete, inadequate to assign to a subject her place as daughter. Phallic identification merely emphasizes the exclusion of the female being from representation. Thus the girl can only experience the limit of this metaphor, either rejecting it or exposing it as a masquerade. As a result, although the girl—if she is not psychotic—may subject herself as well as does the boy to the phallic law established by the paternal function, it is nonetheless the case that, for her, this law does not operate everywhere. The girl will be situated simultaneously within the law and partially outside-the-law. This uncomfortable situation has certain advantages, however. It is true that, in the case of the girl, there is a contradiction between the path shown her by the paternal metaphor and, on the other hand, the oedipal position strictly speaking, since it is when she rejects the mother as love object—at the moment, therefore, when she is most hostile toward the mother—that she must nevertheless identify with her in order to occupy her position vis-à-vis the father. Thus the difficulty inherent in the feminine Oedipus is that the girl must retain by way of identification the very element that she must abandon as a love object.

So it is hardly surprising that Freud was so eager to understand what determines the passage from the preoedipal relation to the mother to the oedipal relation to the father. Let us see how he undertakes this problem in "Female sexuality."

He begins by spelling out what is involved in the change from the first to the second phase of the Oedipus. The girl, he says, must change not only her love object but her sex organ. The sex change here is more significant than the change in sexuated identity that he had discussed in the case of the young homosexual woman. It is not only the identification that is at stake here, but also the *jouissance* that the subject gets from the genital organ. For the girl must not only abandon her mother as love object and turn to the father, she must at the same time abandon clitoral *jouissance* (which, for Freud, is masculine) in favor of vaginal *jouissance*. And this new argument introduces a new complication, as Freud is well aware. Just as the mother, abandoned as a love object, still remains present as an identificatory pole in the second phase, so the clitoris, too, continues to play its role in the later sex life of the woman. It is clear that, with regard to sexual *jouissance*, the substitution of the vagina for the clitoris is not complete, at any rate not as a metaphor. There are two distinct sexual zones, of which one (the clitoris) is bound up with the relation to the mother—the "first seducer"—and the other comes to the fore in the relation to the father. But vaginal *jouissance* does not exactly supplant the *jouissance* derived from the clitoris; it is added to it or is connected to it.

Once again, we have the impression that this is a metonymic, as opposed to metaphoric, connection. And this is something that has been known in all times; we need only consult any treatise on sex, be it from ancient China, from India, or from present-day California, to find that this split in feminine sexuality has always been dealt with by an attempt to link, to place in continuity, the two female sex organs, which implies that they are thought of as being connected metonymically. A recent example, vivid and tragic, is that of Freud's pupil Marie Bonaparte, who suffered from frigidity and therefore underwent an operation to bring her clitoris closer to the vaginal opening.

Thus the two changes meant to bring about the feminine Oedipus seem quite problematic. And women's romantic choices and marital life bear witness to these difficulties. Freud notes that many women repeat with their husbands not so much their father–daughter relational patterns as the troubled relations they had had with their mothers. The paternal object is, as it were, given credit for the affective ties the girl had with her mother. But what is the cause of this transfer? What justifies the abandoning of the mother who had been loved so exclusively? Why is the mother felt to deserve the real hatred that the girl aims at her at the same time as she continues to love her?

To answer these questions, Freud lists a variety of factors, some unique to the little girl's sex life, others applicable to the little boy as well. The first is infantile jealousy toward rivals for the mother's love, among them the father. Next, Freud mentions the very nature of infantile love, which, being without measure and not directed toward a specific aim, is bound to be disappointed. But one of the most important factors is the role of the castration complex for the girl. As he had done earlier (1925), Freud lists as consequences of the feminine castration complex the following: the girl renounces all sexual activity (a reaction that, in the adult, will take the form of depression); or she enters the masculinity complex and maintains, through denial or hope, her wish for a penis like the boy's; or she follows the path that Freud considers to be that of true femininity and turns to the father in the hope of receiving from him a child that symbolizes what the mother was unable to give her.

In each case, the little girl can only devalue the female genital and feel contempt for women in general and her mother in particular. The narcissistic injury is increased by the discovery that the mother, too, lacks a penis.

A fourth reason for hating the mother stems from the ban on masturbation that the mother imposes on her daughter. This interdiction is all the more unwelcome because it is most often through the mother herself, or her surrogate, that the little girl discovered clitoral pleasure when her bodily needs were being attended to. The girl understandably resents the fact that the woman who initiated her into pleasure is now the one who forbids it, and this resentment resurfaces later on, each time the mother presents herself as the guardian of the daughter's chastity and the opponent of her free sexual activity. Finally, a fifth motive for hostility toward the mother, and perhaps the main one, is that the mother has not given the daughter a real genital organ, that is, that she allowed her to be born a woman.

But to all these previously discussed motives Freud now adds another, one that he sees as a more adequate reason for the girl's hostility toward her mother. This is the ambivalence

that marks the beginning stages of love; thus, from the outset, the little girl's tie to her mother involved hate as much as
love. It might be objected that the little boy will likewise experience this initial ambivalence toward his mother. Yes, Freud
replies, but the difference is that the boy can empty out all
his hate onto the person of the father, retaining for the mother
only the loving part of his original feelings. As we can see,
this last explanation has to do neither with the effects of the
castration complex nor with the disappointment of the little
girl's demand, but instead with a characteristic feature of the
daughter's love for her mother.

What is the basis of this love/hate that the girl feels toward the mother? Can we account for it solely by reference
to the ongoing imaginary, erotic/aggressive relation between
mother and daughter? Let us recall that, for the girl, the
mother represents both a love object (the Other) and a pole
of identification (an other). Like the lady adored by Freud's
young homosexual patient, she has a double nature. And
while, for the boy, this twofold status can be divided up by
the father's entry onto the scene—identification shifting to
him while the mother remains the love object—for the girl
identification with the mother seems to be what is supposed
to make it possible not to love her anymore. A total paradox.

But this paradox does not explain everything. Something
beside the imaginary relation is in play in the ambivalence
toward the mother, as Freud goes on to say. In the third
section of this paper, he reconstructs the archaic mother–
daughter relation in terms of the dialectic of activity and passivity. At the time of the exclusive tie to the mother, the girl's
sexual aims are both active and passive. But these two poles
are in conflict, since all children try to perform actively what
they had previously experienced passively; there is a funda-

mental human tendency to repudiate passivity in a desire for separation. In our present context of the relation to the first Other, this means that the dialectic of activity and passivity involves an oscillation between *being the mother's object* and *taking the mother as an object*. There is a struggle around the object from the place of the object as subjective positions are sorted out. We can inscribe the terms of this conflict in a diagram that locates the object at the intersection of the fields of the subject and the Other:

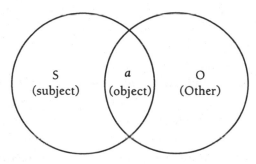

This diagram shows what is at stake in the revolt against passivity. For it is only by removing herself from the position of the Other's (the mother's) object that the girl can secure her position as subject and take this Other as her object.

But Freud's text teaches us that this struggle leads to a new impasse, a new paradox of feminine destiny. In detaching herself from the mother in order to move from a passive position as *objet a* to an active position in which it is the mother who is the object, the girl must leave the path of her destiny, since, according to Freud, activity is equivalent to masculinity. In short, in order to become a subject, the girl must become masculine! Freud illustrates this with examples of little girl's favorite games: playing doctor, playing mommy, or doll play in which the active side of femininity reflects an exclusive tie to the mother and indifference to the paternal object. All these pastimes, he says, come down to the relation with the mother and the struggle there around the pole of *jouissance*. The girl has to eat the mother who fed her, Freud notes aphoristically. This archaic relation to the mother is thus in no sense a fusion or communion. On the contrary, it is a harsh struggle whose ultimate stake is to determine who will devour whom.

Now, if this struggle is more problematical for the girl than for the boy, and if it always threatens to reappear in her subsequent relations with her father or, still later, with men, isn't this because, even as she separates from her mother and the passive position toward her, the girl must nonetheless retain a passive element in order to situate herself as a woman? This, at any rate, is what emerges from the logic of Freud's reflections on feminine destiny. Once again we find there an internal contradiction in the process of becoming a woman: the girl must abandon passivity in order to separate from the mother, but she must retain this passivity in order to attach herself to her father.

From whatever angle, preoedipal or oedipal, we approach the trajectory that the girl must follow, we come up against this same objection. Whether we consider this passage from the point of view of change of object, change of identification, change of genital zone, or change of the mode of *jouissance*, we always reach the conclusion that these changes are not so much *substitutions* as *divisions*. As a result, the characteristics of the preoedipal relation are never entirely eliminated and are always ready to gain the upper hand. The girl's destiny thus appears to be that of an impossible metaphor or a permanent struggle to escape from the register of metonymy to that of metaphor.

11

Becoming a Woman

We have been looking at the problematics of the mother–daughter relation in Freud's theory, a relation of which Lacan used the term "ravages" in view of the fact that it has all the features of a passion that can be escaped only through a violent break. The story of a girl and her mother seems to be one of an indefinitely postponed separation, and, to follow Freud, this is because of the double role of the mother in the girl's structure: she is at once love object and pole of identification, so that the moment when the girl most hates her mother is also the moment when she must identify with her. We have added, as an additional justification, the issue of the metaphorical function of the paternal agency in the case of the girl, for the substitution of the father for the mother in the feminine Oedipus does not result in the production of the hoped-for new signifier, the sign of a feminine identity proper. Given this failure—or partial failure—of the paternal metaphor, the girl must choose among three solutions: either she accepts her flawed identity and adopts the phallic masquerade to which the law of the signifier invites her, or she refuses what she considers to be a defeat and persists in a demand of the hysterical type, or she returns to the previous phase and barricades herself in an entirely masculine position like that of the lesbian.

Shortly after the paper "Female sexuality," Freud returns to the problem of female destiny in a lecture entitled simply "Femininity" (1933). He begins by giving femininity its status in speculative thought—that is, in speculative thought structured in the masculine mode. Femininity, he tells his audience, is an enigma "to those of you who are men; to those of you who are women this will not apply—you are yourselves the problem" (p. 113). Thus, on the one hand, femininity is an ungraspable object of thought, and, on the other hand, for women themselves it belongs to the register of ineffable being that has no need to be thought about in order to exist. The enigma of femininity thus has a double role, depending on the sexes: it motivates men to speak and women to keep silent. This does not prevent Freud from paying tribute, a few pages further on, to the work of some women colleagues (Mack Brunswick, Lampl-de Groot, Deutsch) on this topic.

If femininity seems enigmatic to Freud, this is because it is not a primary given, at least on the level of the unconscious and its representations: "When you meet a human being, the first distinction you make is 'male or female?' and you are accustomed to make the distinction with unhesitating certainty" (p. 113). In fact, nothing is less certain. Anatomy may distinguish two sexes, but it is mute when it comes to determining virility or femininity. As for psychology, Freud continues, it uses the terms *masculine* and *feminine* for the distinction between activity and passivity, but this analogy cannot be a criterion on the level of the sexual life of human beings. Thus "a mother is active in every sense toward her child;

the act of lactation itself may equally be described as the mother suckling the baby or as her being sucked by it" (p. 115). Here Freud is putting in question what he had up to now held to be the equation between activity and masculinity on the one hand, passivity and femininity on the other. This dualism does not adequately express sexual difference on the psychic level. Nor can we characterize femininity "as giving preference to passive aims. This is not, of course, the same thing as passivity; to achieve a passive aim may call for a large amount of activity" (p. 115). This is the very enigma of femininity. Consequently, the task of psychoanalysis is not to describe what a woman *is*, for this is impossible, but to investigate how the little girl *becomes* a woman, that is, "how a woman develops out of a child with a bisexual disposition" (p. 115).

Femininity is thus a matter of becoming, not being. We cannot overestimate the revolutionary scope of this thesis that, if it were to hold true, would be scandalous even today. What it means is that, for Freud, a certain number of girls never become women but, on the psychic level are or remain, quite simply, men. A woman must be manufactured, as it were, through an extended psychic effort. One of Freud's closest disciples, Ernest Jones, disagreed when, in 1935, in response to the question of whether women are "born" or "made," he said that it is impossible to conclude that half of humanity could be "made." This repudiation of the Freudian discovery also led him to a complete revision of the theory of the feminine phallic phase in a direction that Lacan has rightly criticized. As for Freud, he does not mince words when he establishes as the point of origin for becoming a woman a phase in which we must acknowledge "that the little girl is a little man" (1932, p. 118). For example, she is in entire agreement with the little boy's notion of the female genital organ, seeing it not as another genital but as the site of a castration, of a penis that has been shortened or cut off. Here Freud condenses the results of his thinking in a well-known formula: "It seems that ... the truly feminine vagina is still undiscovered by both sexes" (p. 118). This does not, of course, mean that the *material* existence of the vagina is disregarded, but that it is not known as anything other than a hollow phallus.

If the little girl is at first a little man, it is easy to see why her development is more complicated than the boy's. In order to become a woman, she must overcome two obstacles that have no counterpart for the boy: she must, as Freud had already noted in "Female sexuality" (1931), change her love object (moving from the mother to the father) and her sex organ (substituting the vagina for the clitoris). Now, this transformation has nothing "natural" about it. There is no automatic attraction to the opposite sex to guide the girl toward loving her father. We are not dealing, here, with an animal instinct in charge of sexual destiny but instead with an artifice, an unconscious psychic mechanism—in short, with a fact not of nature but of culture. Thus what impels the little girl toward the father is not attraction to a man but hate for the mother. We are by now familiar with Freud's analysis of this hate, and in the present lecture he repeats its essential points, stressing the fact that the relations of the girl to her mother are "libidinal relations" (p. 119), active and passive, in which the mother plays a major role as initiator. For it is she who, in caring for the child's body, evoked the first sensations of pleasure in the genital area. The fantasy of seduction by the father, reported by the girl later on, must therefore be brought back to its basis in a primary seduction by the mother.

Thus, for the little girl and the little boy alike, we must start out from *the desire of the mother* in both senses of the genitive: the mother's desire for the child, and the child's desire for the mother. In his seminar on *The Formations of the Unconscious* (1957–1958), Lacan emphasized that there is only one way to desire, regardless of one's sex: the way that emerges in the relation to the mother. The active and passive aspects of this desire correspond to the two senses in which the desire *of* the mother can be understood,

In the desire of the mother for her daughter, the child at first occupies the position of what plugs the lack that causes desire: she makes her mother into a "full," or fulfilled, woman. In this phase, the child—girl or boy—is still only a part of the mother's body; even after delivery, we can say that the child has not yet been "brought into the world" as a subject. But this phase is not, as has sometimes been imagined, one of heavenly fusion, for already in this early stage the mother–child relation is pregnant with conflict, even if these are conflicts within the mother. Thus we commonly find a discord in the mother between the place and function of the *real* child and those of the child as *imaginary* in her fantasy during pregnancy. The distress of young mothers when faced with the little being who awakens them from their dream is well known. The child may seem to be an alien object, frightening and unapproachable, of whom they feel unable to take care when he seems too real, that is, too foreign to the imaginary realization they were expecting. Without going so far as to mention the extreme cases of postpartum psychosis or those in which the new mother is "inexplicably" uninterested in her infant, we need only think of the alarm aroused in certain women by the slightest imperfection in their babies, or of the more or less severe depressions regularly observed in mothers during the days following delivery.

The desire of the mother for the child thus has as its condition that the child, as *objet a,* be covered over by something of the imaginary that allows the mother to misrecognize him and, at the same time, to maintain him in this position of object. What this amounts to, after all, is nothing but the alliance between object libido and ego libido that Freud established at the end of his study "On narcissism" (1914): in order to be invested, the object must conform to the ego—in other words, wrapped in a narcissistic image. This image, on its own, already involves an opening onto a "beyond" of the status as the mother's object, since it is a derivative of all the lacks that have led the mother toward one or the other feature of her narcissism. It thus constitutes an initial fulcrum for the revolt against passivity in which the child will seek his own reference point in his mother's desire for him. We can see that, at this elementary level, the mother–child relation is triangular from the start, composed of the mother as all-powerful Other, the child as real object delivered over to maternal *jouissance*, and, in contrast to this real position, the imaginary child as repository of maternal narcissism, that is, the child who is supposed to veil the lack felt by the mother:[1]

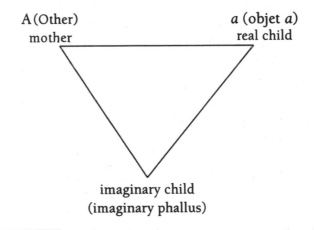

A (Other)
mother

a (objet *a*)
real child

imaginary child
(imaginary phallus)

---

1. Translator's note: I have retained the use of the symbols A and *a* (for *Autre* and *autre*) in view of the fact that Lacan's symbolic notation is widely used even in translated texts. These symbols correspond to O and o (*Other* and *other*, respectively) in some English translations.

This third pole of the relation will entail an extensive development. For if the child wants to identify with the imaginary child who corresponds to the mother's lack, he must situate the mother as lacking that which he is responsible for supplying; as a result, he cannot help making a breach in the idea of the Other's omnipotence. Through this breach in the maternal Other, the paternal agency can find its function as stopping point and reference point of the lack inscribed in the mother's desire. For it is from the father that the phallus, solely imaginary in the mother–child relation, can receive its symbolic grounding. As far as the girl is concerned, this development, while presenting a way out of dependence on the mother, arouses a deep discontent: everything that is signified for her here as a reference point is situated in the phallic register and sheds no light on her femininity.

We can try to inscribe in this triangle the basic struggles that mark the preoedipal relation of the girl to her mother. Between A and *a*, the mother and the real child, is the register of the drives, in which there takes place the battle between the subject and the Other around the object of *jouissance*. The feeding situation, with its many conflicts, offers an example: take or receive the breast, devour or be fed, swallow or spit, and so forth. Between the real child and the imaginary child is the entire register of identifications. Here is where we have to locate, for example, the little girl's doll play, the aim of which is to stabilize an image of the mother and a corresponding image of herself—an ambivalent relation like all specular relations. Finally, between the mother and the imaginary child we have the opening to the problematics of castration, an opening that is more or less marked depending on whether the mother's unconscious desire is more or less determined by penis envy, that is, whether her own castration has been more or less accepted.

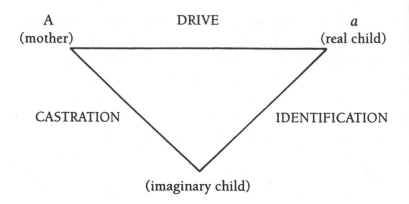

As we noted in the previous chapter, the crucial point in this construction is to determine why the separation from the mother is such a difficult task for the girl. After all, the boy, too, must pass this way and find, through his father, an outlet, the bit of air that will enable him to breathe, that is, to detach himself from the identification with the imaginary phallus in which his mother's desire has bound him. But, in so doing, the boy finds in his father a support for the virile identification corresponding to his sex. For the girl, the problem is more complex. Lacan has taught us that an imaginary identification is consolidated as a gathering-together of the subject only when it has the support of a symbolic trait—the "unary trait," as he calls it—a sort of minimal signifier that the subject draws from the Other to fix his identity. Now, the mother can never furnish her daughter with a unary trait to support her identity as a girl, because the signifier of feminine identity does not exist. It is this radical lack in the Other that the girl must confront, and the deficiency somehow doubles feminine castration and makes it into a bottomless lack with regard to masculine castration. It is the lack of an "absence word," of a "hole word."

All that the mother can provide in the way of a symbolic trait in support of identification is the phallus. Whether she has it (as the child first thinks) or does not have it (as will turn out to be the case), she is referring her daughter to a guidepost that she can signify to her but that she does not herself possess. This is surely the radical explanation for the fact that feminine sexual life is strongly oriented to love and the demand for love, that is, to the demand that the Other give her what she does not have. The mother's lack with regard to her daughter is thus twofold: the lack of the signifier of a feminine identity and the lack of the phallus.

Such a doubling of the deficiency of the Other is experienced by the girl as an actual injury (cf. Freud 1914), and this lends her castration complex its tone of violent hostility toward the mother. The complex, for her, is essentially different from the boy's. While the boy is afraid of losing the sign of his sexuated identity, and thus of no longer being able to be a man, the girl discovers that she never received, and never will receive, such a sign. In the former case, the complex unfolds under the sign of threat, in the latter, under the sign of envy and jealousy. Once this discovery has been made, the girl can take one of three paths: the first is that of neurosis and sexual inhibition, the second that of the "character disorder" of the masculinity complex, and the third, finally, that of femininity,

The path of neurosis begins by an abandonment of phallic sexuality, that is, of clitoral masturbation, the clitoris having been devalued with regard to the male penis. Furthermore, the mother and, in general, all women are affected indirectly by the scorn in the little girl's mind. This means—an essential detail—that the girl's preoedipal love for her mother is love for the *phallic mother*. Once the mother is known to be castrated, this idyll vanishes. The love for her mother was directed at an Other without flaw, an Other who is not barred, as Lacan puts it. We find an almost pure expression of such infantile love and the catastrophe of its disappointment in the first psychoanalytic paper of Lou Andreas-Salomé (1980; cf. 1964). She describes the discovery of maternal castration in the form of an allegory of the disappearance, or the non-response, of God. But, as Freud (1933) subtly observes, this depreciation of the mother and of women in general does not prevent the girl from nevertheless identifying with her. For, in abandoning or repressing masturbation, "the girl, as it were, herself takes over the role of her deposed mother and gives expression to her entire dissatisfaction with her inferior clitoris in her efforts against obtaining satisfaction from it" (p. 127). Moreover, when she gives up masturbation, the little girl also partially gives up active sexuality: "Passivity now has the upper hand, and the girl's turning to her father is accomplished with the help of passive instinctual impulses" (p. 128). Does this mean, for Freud, that such a development favors femininity to some extent, and hence that neurosis is the path to femininity? A restriction is imposed here, but its vagueness is quite awkward: femininity can find a support in this renunciation of masturbation only if "too much is not lost in the course of it through repression" (p. 128).

Here we have one of the ambiguities of Freud's position. The girl must lose her phallic activity, but not entirely; she must also keep it in part, just enough to sustain the demand she will go on to address to the father. For, Freud writes,

> [t]he wish with which the girl turns to her father is no
> doubt originally the wish for the penis which her mother
> has refused her and which she now expects from her fa-

ther. The feminine situation is only established, however, if the wish for a penis is replaced by one for a baby, if, that is, a baby takes the place of a penis in accordance with an ancient symbolic equivalence. . . . It has not escaped us that the girl has wished for a baby earlier, in the undisturbed phallic phase: that, of course, was the meaning of her playing with dolls. But that play was not in fact an expression of her femininity; it served as an identification with her mother with the intention of substituting activity for passivity. *She* was playing the part of her mother and the doll was herself: now she could do with the baby everything that her mother used to do with her. Not until the emergence of a wish for a penis does the doll-baby become a baby from the girl's father, and thereafter the aim of the most powerful feminine wish. [p. 128]

This passage clearly shows how, in Freud's thought, it is ultimately penis envy that enables the girl to become feminine by turning her from the mother to the father—a paradoxical view that justifies Freud in considering the wish for a penis "as being *par excellence* a feminine one" (p. 129).

A further weakness in Freud's reasoning is that, in relying on maternal identification (even if this oscillates, from the first to the second phase, from the pole of the phallic mother to that of the castrated mother) to guide the girl toward the realization of her femininity, he reduces femininity to the desire for motherhood. *Becoming a woman is confused with becoming a mother.* The wish for a child that is supposed to realize symbolically the wish for a penis ultimately shows that, for lack of another sign, Freud symbolically accords the baby the role of the signifier of feminine identity. This argument does not stand up to the test of clinical psychoanalysis. Moreover, doesn't the case of Freud's young homosexual patient demonstrate that, once she has achieved the oedipal position with regard to her father, the girl can easily find herself cast back into a preoedipal relation if the child she had expected symbolically from the father is really given by him to another woman? This position vis-à-vis the father seems quite precarious. Freud seems to be aware of this, since, in discussing the masculinity complex, he himself notes that the fixation on the father is liable to come undone; furthermore, at the end of this lecture he speaks of the multiple problems that the woman encounters in her sex life once she moves from her fixation on her father to the love of other men, problems in which we see the constant resurgence of the archaic fixation on the mother.

The second path of reaction to the discovery of maternal castration is the formation of what Freud describes as the masculinity complex. In contrast to the preceding path, the little girl emphasizes her masculinity, clings to masturbatory activity, and takes refuge in an identification with the phallic mother or with the father. This attitude influences the girl's object choice in the direction of overt homosexuality, although this, to be sure, does not stem directly from infantile masculinity (it is a regression, later on, due to a disappointment inflicted by the father).

On this point, a remarkable paper by Karen Horney explains a number of difficult points in Freud's conception of the masculinity complex. Entitled "On the genesis of the castration complex in women," this paper is all the more exciting because it dates from 1924; it is thus later than the analysis of the young homosexual woman but earlier than the papers in which Freud develops his arguments on the prehistory of the feminine Oedipus. Thus Horney is the first to emphasize the archaic relation to the mother, and the reversals of love objects and identifications, that occur in the course of the feminine castration complex. She is addressing the issue of whether the masculinity complex encountered in certain women—and not just lesbians—must be attributed exclusively to the influence of penis envy and the resulting discontent. Horney shows that this is not the case, that the masculinity complex actually stems from disappointment in the father and is thus later than the girl's turn from her mother to her father—in short, that it constitutes a deviation and a regression in the girl's Oedipus complex proper.

Horney states that women with a strong masculinity complex originally identified with the mother and hence took the father as love object. As Freud was surprised to discover at the end of "A child is being beaten" (1919a), the masculinity complex and the fixation on the father are not mutually exclusive. In fact, the masculinity complex is the emergence of an archaic relation to the mother at the very center of the relation to the father. Horney cites the case of a woman patient who had numerous rape fantasies in which the rapists all represented her father; these fantasies, she says, like rape fantasies in other patients, show how the girl constructs a fantasy of rape by the father on the basis of an identification, loving or hostile, with the mother.

Such fantasies are bound to be disappointed in reality: it is the mother who benefits from the father's sexual desire and gets babies. This gives rise to a feeling of disappointment in the father, and jealousy toward the mother, on the part of the girl. The disappointment can lead the girl to give up not only her erotic claim with regard to the father but also her desire for a child. Thus she regresses to penis envy, and this, Horney says, is the masculinity complex strictly speaking. But she goes on to add that the renunciation of the father as love object is accompanied by an identification with him. Here, then, we have the model of the situation in which the love relation becomes an identification when the demand for love is thwarted (a pattern we noticed in the case of the young homosexual woman). This identification with the father is not to be confused with the desire to be a man: it is the desire to play the father's role. The girl will take on a number of his traits, choosing the same profession, behaving similarly toward the mother, coughing like him, and so on, but without necessarily making a complete homosexual object choice; this is the crucial shade of difference between the case of Dora and that of the young homosexual woman.

By demonstrating that the masculinity complex is motivated not by penis envy (since the latter has the effect of guiding the girl from the mother to the father) but by the girl's disappointment in her father, Horney minimizes the role, which Freud considers central, of the girl's hatred of her mother, whether this is the aggressive hate of the phallic rival, at the stage when the little girl still thinks of herself as a little man, or the contemptuous hate for the castrated woman, at the stage when she has discovered castration and turns to the father. But this approach to the masculinity complex does not resolve the paradox of feminine destiny in which it is penis envy that impels the girl toward becoming a woman. Far from shifting this envy onto the father, the girl can only encounter a disappointment such as we saw in the case of Elisabeth von R. How, then, can she escape the masculinity complex?

Freud himself seems to have gotten no further in resolving this problem, as we see in the last pages of "Femininity" (1933). He must agree that the establishment of femininity always remains vulnerable to a resurgence of the girl's archaic masculinity: "Some portion of what we men call 'the enigma of women' may perhaps be derived from this expression of bisexuality in women's lives" (p. 131). This oscillation between the two phases of the Oedipus, and hence between the two love objects and the two identifications that they entail, will be a permanent feature of the woman's sex life. The woman's romantic choice is, like the man's, subject to a split between anaclitic and narcissistic objects, and this split is further complicated by the oscillation between masculinity and femininity. Thus a woman will choose a man either according to the paternal model (the anaclitic choice) or according to the narcissistic model (narcissistic choice). In the latter case—the more frequent one, Freud says—the man she chooses will be similar to the one the little girl would have liked to become in her preoedipal period. But if the choice is made on the paternal model, it soon reveals the mother behind the father: "The woman's husband, who to begin with inherited from her father, becomes after a time the mother's heir as well" (p. 133) and thus receives all the hostility that the girl had formerly felt toward her mother.

This resurgence of the relation to the mother at the heart of the woman's love life is, however, the necessary condition for marital happiness; its success, Freud tells us, depends only on a correct redistribution of identifications. If the woman is inclined to find a mother in the person of her husband, even if he was originally chosen on the paternal model, the couple must, as it were, exchange roles so that the husband occupies the place of the child and the wife that of the mother. The birth of the first child, Freud says, can bring about this change in identification. But, fundamentally, "a marriage is not made secure until the wife has succeeded in making her husband her child as well and in acting as a mother to him" (pp. 133–134).

At this final stage of Freud's reasoning, it is strange to find a sort of hypothetical convergence between the respective Oedipus complexes of the boy and the girl, in the sense that the completion of the former and the incompletion of the latter ultimately link the man and the woman in the celebration of the mother. In identifying with the mother, the woman "acquires her attractiveness to a man, whose Oedipus attachment to his mother it kindles into passion" (p. 134). But Freud expresses a reservation concerning this reconciliation (a reconciliation that one may guess will be stormy). Most often, he says, "it is only his son who obtains what [the husband] himself aspired to!" (p. 134). Freud's text leaves us with the impression that there is an irremediable distance between the man's love and the woman's.

The elaboration of Freud's theory of femininity thus ends in an impasse, and a twofold one at that: the impasse of becoming a woman and the resulting one of the couple, in which becoming a mother elevates the mother–son relation above that of the wife to her husband. This foundering of the feminine problematic on the notion of motherhood as the symbolic realization of the wish for a penis will lead to the near-delusional speculations of Helene Deutsch (1925), for one, who will make motherhood the fulfillment of a woman and childbirth the model of a specifically feminine *jouissance*. It is true that such vagaries are encouraged by the fact that Freud leaves unresolved the issue of feminine sexuality as such. For, although he notes several features of a woman's romantic object choice, of the division of the female sexual organ, and of drive satisfaction, Freud does not manage to articulate the specificity of feminine sexuality (nor, though he notes its frequency in women, to shed light on the symptom of sexual frigidity). These obscurities account for the fact that Freud's theory of femininity and the clinical practice strictly based on it encounter two forms of bedrock in the analysis of women: penis envy and the demand for love.

It may well be because Freud says little or nothing about desire and *jouissance* in women that their flawed identity looms so large in his thought. In maintaining that there is a single libido in service of both female and male sexuality, Freud preserves an ancient doctrine, to be sure, but he simply shifts the problem when he adds that this libido has aims—modes of satisfaction—that are active and passive. Although there is no specifically feminine libido, there is nevertheless a more distinctively feminine mode of satisfaction, or at least a preference for such a mode. The pair activity/passivity, whose importance we have highlighted in Freud's earliest work, thus reappears forty years later. But, we may note, it does so without having become the slightest bit clearer in terms of content and dialectic; its meaning remains just as obscure. Freud himself seems to recognize this imprecision in his paper "Female sexuality" (1931), where he agrees that there is a problem with the notion of passive libidinal tendencies. But he goes no further in examining the issue. Likewise, in the lecture on "Femininity" (1933), he confines himself to saying that the connection between feminine sexuality and passive satisfaction is to be found in biology, the reproductive aim being dependent on masculine aggression and thus more or less independent of the woman's consent.[2]

Moreover, the fact that women have two distinct genital organs remains highly problematic for Freud. We have seen

---

2. [sic] Nowadays, of course, developments in contraception and reproductive technology tend to prove that "masculine aggression" is increasingly irrelevant when it comes to reproduction.

the weakness of the idea that one of these organs, the vagina, is substituted for the other, the clitoris, at the same time as, in the development of Freud's thought, the vagina as a genital remains unknown. Why should women somehow sacrifice the clitoris to the vagina, unless this is because Freud could not conceptualize becoming-woman otherwise than as becoming-*entirely*-woman, that is, as a complete elimination of phallic sexuality? This project clearly verges on the ideal, in the sense not of an aim but of a dream, an ideal that is no doubt an aspect of Freud's own problematic, the nature of his desire as far as woman is concerned. With regard to this problematic, which marks the origin and expansion of psychoanalysis, it is difficult to say anything that is more than a hypothesis. But we may remember that, at the outset of his work, Freud had admitted that his desire was to subject the power of the female sex to law and reason (see Chapters 2 and 3). The desire for domination and *Aufklärung* thus rested on a postulate that reappears at the beginning of the lecture on "Femininity": femininity is an *enigma*. Such a claim inevitably recalls Oedipus—not as Jocasta's husband but as the solver of the riddle, the one who confronts the female figure of the Sphinx.

Did Freud perhaps need to preserve this figure of the Sphinx in order to sustain his desire to decipher a riddle? Did he perhaps love her as an enigma (while hating her for the same reason)? Several passages in his work suggest this interpretation, from the poem to Fliess that we have already discussed to the allusions to mother goddesses in *Moses and Monotheism* (1939), in addition to the dream of the Three Fates (in 1900), "The theme of the three caskets" (1913), and the study on *Gradiva* (1907). All these texts show that, although Freud kept on denouncing the mysterious, irrational, even dangerous side of femininity, especially in connection with the mother, he also kept on maintaining the woman in her state of enigma and obscurity. From this point of view, we may say that Freud's desire is structurally akin to the hysterical desire of Dora when confronted with Frau K.'s body: adoring, subjugated, and searching through the dictionary in a quest for knowledge. Indeed, we may wonder whether, ultimately, there is any desire other than the hysterical sort.

Perhaps we can find a key, or at least a clue, to the solution of this problem in the famous letter that Freud sends in 1936 to Romain Rolland, describing a difficulty he had had some thirty years earlier when visiting the Acropolis. Freud reports that, when he finally fulfilled his longstanding desire to see the Acropolis, he found himself in front of something too beautiful to be true, to the point where he became preoccupied with the thought that what he was seeing was not real. *Do we have to believe in the reality of what we see?* This is exactly the dilemma of the little boy when he discovers the female genital area, as Freud himself has told us. In any case, in order to believe it, the little boy is obliged to go through the detour of a long elaboration: the infantile sexual theories that blend truth and falsehood, light and shadow. This half-saying of the truth that the man elaborates and the woman embodies is our only approach to the real. And there is no reason to think that psychoanalytic theory itself can escape from this rule. This implies that psychoanalysis must get to the point of interrogating its own truths (or the concepts that seem to function as truths). It is especially important to reexamine the entire theory of castration.

The rereading of Freud to which Lacan invites us suggests that the theory of castration is in itself a half-saying, one that has a certain function. Is it not, ultimately, the theory of castration and its basis in the primacy of the phallus that locate and protect the woman as mystery? The theory both masks and reveals the object that it defines.

As a result, if we want to progress beyond Freud on the issue of femininity, we must first of all ask what it is that makes woman an enigma and impels us to cultivate that enigma instead of resolving it. The life of the speaking being is, perhaps, invested in not lifting the veil from this mystery. So, at least, we are led to believe from what both women and men say about what a woman *is* and what a woman *wants*. A woman's desire always remains a question, but this benefits each of the partners, since the lack of an answer is a stimulus to desire. Likewise, the fact that her *jouissance* can never be fastened to a definite and unambiguous sign guarantees that it is demanded over and over again. In this fool's bargain, neither the offer nor the demand risks being extinguished, for it is not so much sexual pleasure that is negotiated as its excess (*plus-de-jouir*).

What happens when, in the name of a more reality-based truth, the partners want to give up the pretense? Consider the man who is in the habit of complaining that women don't show their desire, that they conceal from him the essence of their *jouissance* and even lie about its existence or its intensity. If, in response, a woman leaves her hiding-place and shows him her desire directly or speaks of her *jouissance* in unveiled terms, this man will flee, overcome with panic or disgust. Here is where the prostitute finds her universal function. Because she is conventionally assigned the role of the woman who pretends to desire and to experience orgasm, everyone is sure that she is lying. It would be a catastrophe if she were not to lie, if she were really to get an orgasm from the penis that she encounters in passing. This is why we can regard the prostitute as the authentic guardian of the feminine mystery and understand why she is held in universal respect.

This cult of the woman as the locus of a hiding-place has been admirably set forth by Granoff and Perrier (1979) in their paper on female perversion. This remarkable text emphasizes the extent to which the male mind conceives of woman as a hollow object, a hollowed-out phallus, similar to the finger of a glove turned inside out. For it is surely insofar as she is taken to be the very incarnation of the phallus that a woman is mysterious and cannot be unveiled. We are dealing here with a true interdiction, as Lacan writes in "The signification of the phallus" (1958a) with reference to the frescoes in the Villa of the Mysteries in Pompeii: "That is why the demon of *Aidos* (*Scham*, shame) arises at the very moment when, in the ancient mysteries, the phallus is unveiled" (p. 288). And we have clinical evidence of what happens when this ban is lifted: there occurs an attack of mania. For the manic subject the veil has been torn; for him, the phallus is no longer an open-ended question but a knowledge bequeathed him by Oedipal failure—a poisonous knowledge, since it is knowledge of the void camouflaged by the masquerade of the "human comedy." He knows that the phallus is a mere pretense, and for that very reason he is the victim of an excess of knowledge that excludes him from the community. All he can do is become the spokesman for this derision, for this void modestly covered by the phallus, showing by his speech and acts that, when it comes to women, there is absolutely nothing to respect.

Between the misrecognition that transfixes the women into an enigma and the excess knowledge that makes the manic a non-dupe condemned to wandering, a question therefore arises: is it our job, as analysts, to lift the veil from the mystery of femininity? Or should we be content to understand why it is that the subject maintains that veil? This question concerns the ethics of psychoanalysis before it becomes a matter of psychoanalytic technique. Can the end of an analysis be identified as a revelation, a "masks off!"? The clinical treatment of mania, which we have touched on, suggests caution. And didn't Lacan himself draw attention to the frequency of manic-depressive effects at the end of some analyses? If, then, there is something like a revelation at the end of an analysis, we must specify that it can bear only on what Lacan called the *half-saying* of truth. What analysis must reveal to the subject is that the truth can never be *all* told.

12

Jouissances

We have shown how the logic of Freud's theory of femininity leads to an impasse: the feminine Oedipus complex seems to allow for no outcome other than a regression to the preoedipal relation with the mother. So we must examine the question again from a different angle, and this is what Lacan undertakes to do in his 1972–1973 Seminar *Encore*. His project rests on two observations. Lacan notes, first of all, that for both Freud and his disciples the question of feminine sexuality—and in particular of the woman's sexual *jouissance*—remains practically untouched, which leaves the field open to the most salacious debates about clitoral as opposed to vaginal *jouissance*. And then, taking note of Freud's failure to base the process of becoming a woman on the structure of the feminine Oedipus complex, he denounces the commonly held notion that the girl in the Oedipus is like a fish in water, arguing instead that femininity is the problematic of a being who cannot entirely subject herself to the Oedipus complex and the law of castration. With this aim in mind, he places the accent less on the question of feminine *identity* than on that of feminine *jouissance*, less on castration and the claim to which it leads than on the *division* that the primacy of the phallus creates in the girl.

In order to acquaint ourselves with these new propositions, however, we should first determine how they were announced, anticipated by advances in Lacan's teaching, in the years leading up to *Encore*. For it was in the course of work in progress, as Lacan was developing his theory, that the question of femininity arose for him. As the years went by, this task shifted the center of gravity of his inquiry from the register of desire to that of *jouissance*. In the "Guiding Remarks for a Congress on Feminine Sexuality" (1958c), Lacan had not gone beyond an admission of failure and an enumeration of the problems that would have to be cleared up in addressing feminine sexuality. Paragraph V of the text is especially incisive. Under the heading "The obscurity concerning the vaginal organ," he denounces the impotence of psychoanalysis when it comes to shedding light on the nature of feminine *jouissance*, even though, given its fundamental reference to sexuality, psychoanalysis would seem to promise to undo all the secrecy surrounding this topic. "The vaginal orgasm has kept the darkness of its nature inviolate," he observes (p. 89), going on to note the failure of women analysts to have contributed anything of substance on this issue. In conclusion, he writes, "a congress on female sexuality is not about to hold over us the threat of the fate of Tiresias" (pp. 89–90, translation modified).

It would be fifteen years before Lacan ventured a reply to the questions he set forth here. By 1972–1973, he had reached a point where he could formulate several theses, which I shall set forth in a general and preliminary way here before looking at them in greater depth:

1. Femininity is characterized by a twofold division of *jouissance*, a division that cannot simply be reduced to the vagina/clitoris opposition. It is this process of division, and not castration alone, that is the driving force behind the problematic of femininity.

2. We therefore have to reconsider Freud's notion that there is only one libido, since a woman's sexuality is not structured in the same way as a man's.

3. If there is anything mysterious about femininity, it is to the extent that Woman is supposed to make up for the nonexistence of the Other on the level of sex. The enigma thus serves to cloud over the absence of a sexual relation.

4. The problematic of femininity stems from the modalities according to which the phallic function operates, on the level of the unconscious, as a signifying function, and from the manner in which subjects acknowledge their subjection to this law.

The articulation of these theses and their underpinnings presupposes a knowledge of the theoretical context in which *Encore* developed. This Seminar is presented as a detailed study connecting two a priori opposing terms: on the one hand the *signifier* and its effect as signified (hence the phallic function), and on the other hand *jouissance*. It is at the intersection of these two fields that the question of femininity arises, precisely insofar as it reveals the ways in which the two fields overlap or diverge. By 1972 these concepts, signifier and *jouissance*, already had a long history in Lacan's discourse. In order to define them accurately, we must situate them in certain earlier writings, especially in the two fundamental texts "The signification of the phallus" (1958a) and "The subversion of the subject and the dialectic of desire in the Freudian unconscious" (1960).

The first words of *Encore* involve what might be called *an ethical engagement*. It is useful to recall it here, since it opens the debate by drawing the boundaries of the terrain on which femininity will be interrogated. Referring to his Seminar on *The Ethics of Psychoanalysis* (1959–1960), Lacan announces that he has a little more to say on this subject, having come to see that his earlier approach was on the order of "I don't want to know anything about it" (p. 1). What did he not want to know about? About *jouissance*. The Seminar on *The Ethics,* which revolves around the notions of pleasure, satisfaction, and the sovereign good, is therefore worth reviewing and re-formulating in terms of *jouissance. It is jouissance that bars the way to knowledge* and is at the root of the "I don't want to know anything about it." Which brings up a question: Is it possible to know anything about *jouissance* ?

But what *jouissance* are we talking about, and what knowledge? Right from the first lesson, Lacan distinguishes *jouissance* from both the Freudian *Lust* ("pleasure" or "desire") and the concept of satisfaction. *Jouissance*, he says, is what the law speaks of; to enjoy [*jouir*] something is to be able to use it to the point of abusing it—the abuse being precisely that which the law seeks to delimit. The notion of usufruct, for example, linking *usage* and *fruit*, signifies that the use we may make of a possession is circumscribed: we may consume the product—the interest—but not the capital. The law thus regulates enjoyment by keeping it within the bounds of utility. *Jouissance* is defined *a contrario* as that which is opposed to utility; it is, Lacan says, *that which is of no use. Jouissance* is thus posited as a negative agency that cannot be reduced to the laws of the pleasure principle, concern for self-preservation, or the need to discharge excitation. This is a very broad concept, within which we are justified in situating the more restricted notion of sexual *jouissance*. For Lacan's idea is that *sexual* jouissance is in itself a limitation on *jouissance* in general. Sexual *jouissance* imposes a limit because it depends on the signifier, for it is the signifier that introduces the dimension of the sexual for the human being, namely the phallic organization and the focus it entails on one organ that the signifier isolates from the rest of the body.

The dialectic between *jouissance* in general and sexual (or phallic) *jouissance* corresponds to the relation between *being* and *the signifier* that Lacan discusses by contrasting Aristotle and Bentham, that is, a philosophy of being and one of fiction (p. 3). We can appreciate the full scope of this distinction by looking at the way Lacan reverses the relationship of these two terms. Being, he maintains, does not pre-exist the signifier but is produced by it. Language should not be considered a superstructure that comes to be stuck onto being, onto the real; it is the tool that fashions and determines that being. This reversal of the relations between real and symbolic, and hence between *jouissance* and sexual *jouissance*, is the backbone of the entire Seminar. To grasp its importance, we must go back to 1960, when Lacan first began to develop his theory of *jouissance* in "The subversion of the subject and the dialectic of desire."

One of the central issues in this text is knowing how the human being derives *jouissance* from sex and how analysis can provide access to this sexual *jouissance* even though, according to Freud, castration poses an obstacle. But is it castration that debars us from *jouissance*? Lacan thinks not, and in "Subversion of the subject" he shows that, on the contrary, it is thanks to castration that the register of sexual *jouissance* is open to us. He thereby corrects the trend of thought based on Freud's *Totem and Taboo* (1912a). What Freud's myth seemed to suggest was that only the one who is not castrated, the primal father, is able to enjoy, in the sense that he is able to possess all the women, while the sons are torn between the wish to enjoy like the father and fear of being castrated by him. As we know, they finally decide to kill the father in the belief that this will resolve their ambivalence. But after doing so they actually enjoy less than before, since by establishing the incest taboo they interdict for themselves, even more harshly, the coveted *jouissance*. For Freud, then, it is the Oedipus complex and the attendant castration complex that are the obstacles to *jouissance*, the threat of castration becoming the bedrock, the insuperable barrier to the achievement of the analytic aim. But Lacan finds that the way to get around this impasse lies in a more complex notion of *jouissance*.

Accordingly, in "Subversion of the subject" he states that we must distinguish between two types of *jouissance* and that the *jouissance* Freud attributes to the primal father is not sexual *jouissance* in the strict sense of the term. The latter is in effect a cut performed in the field of the *jouissance* that, originally, pertains to being as such. We are severed from this *jouissance* of being by language, and especially by the phallic signifier. Through this cut, language opens up for us the realm of a new *jouissance* linked not, as before, to being, but rather to *seeming*. One type of *jouissance* corresponds to being, that being which remains lacking with regard to the signifier and to the mode of existence of the subject of the signifying chain. This *jouissance* supports the "I am," insofar as "I am" is not entirely symbolized in "I think." It serves as proof that there is being and that being persists; it is the reply to the question, "Why is there being rather than nothing?" The universe has no reason to exist, and to continue in existence, except *jouissance*: "What am I? I am in the place from which it is shouted

out that 'the universe is a defect in the purity of Non-Being.'
And rightly so, for in protecting itself this place makes Being
itself languish. It is called *Jouissance*, and this is the thing for
lack of which the universe would be in vain" (p. 317).[1] That
kind of *jouissance* is, of course, virtually inaccessible; since it
does not correspond to any desire on the part of the subject,
it resists any attempt to grasp it and any reasoning through
the signifier. The masses, reproducing themselves, have no
notion of their *jouissance* in being, which, moreover, is most
often manifested in the form of suffering.

But this *jouissance* of being is not sexual *jouissance*. And,
in a word, sexual *jouissance* has the effect of interdicting it. We
enter into sexual *jouissance* not through our being, but through
the signifier. Now, it is the distinctive feature of the organization of signifiers—and this is the basis of Freud's castration
theory—that there is one signifier missing: the one that would
account for the feminine sex as such. There is only one signifier
of sexuation, the phallus, and, as a result, on the level of unconscious discourse a relation between two opposite sexes cannot be formulated. For the unconscious, the sexuated Other
does not exist, and Woman is not granted any foundation for
her being. Because sexual *jouissance* is connected to the phallic signifier, it therefore precludes enjoyment of a feminine
being as such. This interdiction is to be understood etymologically: inter-dict.[2] The *jouissance* of being—especially of the
feminine being, of the sexuated Other as such—cannot be spoken. It is thrown back into what persists, between the words
that are spoken, as the unsayable, the outside-of-language:

1. Translator's note: This translation uses "defect" and "lack" where
the French has the single word *défaut*.
2. Translator's note: Latin *inter* "[coming] between" and *dict*, "say"
or "speak."

"What we must hold to is that *jouissance* is interdicted to any speaker as such, although it cannot be said except between the lines for whoever is a subject of the Law, since the Law is grounded in this very interdiction" (p. 319).

The phallic signifier thus brings about a division of *jouissance*. In so doing, it reveals a twofold function; on the one hand, it interdicts *jouissance*, while on the other, it permits it. Lacan sums this up in the incisive formulation with which the text concludes: "Castration means that *jouissance* must be refused so that it can be reached on the inverted ladder of the Law of desire" (p. 324). The *jouissance* interdicted by the signifier is infinite *jouissance*, the kind that Freud ascribed to the primal father and whose basic tenet is: any man may enjoy any woman. The primacy of the phallus entails, in effect, the impossibility of the relation of one sex to the other, of a "male being" to a "female being,"[3] sanctioning the relation only in the register of semblance: "It is the only indication of this *jouissance* in its infinitude that includes the mark of its interdiction, and, in order to constitute this mark, entails a sacrifice: the sacrifice that is made in one and the same act with the choice of its symbol, the phallus" (p. 319, translation modified).

This also means that the phallic signifier argues against our being able to speak of a *sexual instinct* in a human being, in the sense of an automatic attraction of any man to any woman and vice versa. Freud's discovery consisted precisely in specifying that it is for lack of such an instinct that sexuality takes on unusual importance for the human being; with a unified concept of sexuality he contrasts its dispersal into a series of partial drives, of which none is by nature genital.

---

3. Translator's note: This may also be translated as "of a 'being male' to a 'being female.'"

This brief commentary sheds light on the level of the graph that Lacan constructs in "Subversion of the subject" (pp. 303–315):

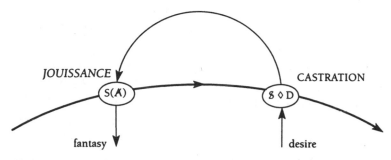

where S◊D = the series of partial drives, and S(Ⱥ) = the signifier of a lack in the Other.[4]

To interpret this level of the graph, we must set it parallel to the one beneath it, in which Lacan formulates the relation of the signifier to the signified and to signification:

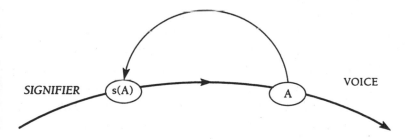

where A = the locus of the treasury of signifiers, and s(A) = the punctuation where signification is constituted in the unwinding thread of the signifying chain.

---

4. Translator's note: Here and below, A (barred or unbarred) stands for *Autre*, "Other."

From this perspective, the upper level of the graph takes on the following meaning: the signification resulting from the play of partial drives is lacking. In other words, nothing unifies these drives into one overall sexual drive that could account for the relation of one sex to the Other sex, since the latter is not represented by any signifier.

This dialectic between two *jouissances*, first undertaken in 1960, is fully developed in the Seminar *Encore*, where it serves as the basis for establishing the problematics of femininity. The phallic signifier reappears here in its double value of *final* cause for the *jouissance* of being (or *jouissance* of the Other, as Lacan designates it from now on), and *original* cause for sexual, or phallic, *jouissance*. The *jouissance* of the Other is referred to as a para-sexual *jouissance*, outside of language, that supports being or the body as such, that is to say as living rather than dead. We have no notion of it, since it escapes the influence of the signifier; we can only postulate it, either because we imagine it from contemplating the spectacle presented by certain animals, or because we deduce it logically from the hollows of certain discourses, such as those of psychotics or some mystics. We shall see how it is this *jouissance* of the Other that Lacan will, with many nuances, reintroduce in connection with femininity.

In contrast to it is *phallic or sexual jouissance*, which, being dependent on the phallic signifier, is completely determined by language to the point where Lacan, at times, calls it a "semiotic" *jouissance*. This kind of *jouissance* starts out from lack-of-being instead of from being and is located outside the body; it is attached to the body only by the slender thread of the sexual organ or the phallicized image of the bodily form. Moreover, it has to do not with the body as a whole, but only with certain parts capable of functioning as equivalents of the genital organ.

The relation of the speaking being to *jouissance* is, therefore, fundamentally insecure. For the *jouissance* he can derive from the sexual relation is never the kind he needs, in the sense that it always bears witness to the disjunction of the body and the genitals and constantly poses an obstacle to the establishment of a true sexual relation between one sex and the other.

We can thus trace a continuous path from the distinction of types of *jouissance* that Lacan introduced in 1960 to its reformulation in 1972, but there is nevertheless a break between these two conceptualizations. For a major modification is introduced in *Encore* with regard to the meaning of the interdiction imposed by phallic *jouissance* on the *jouissance* of the Other. This modification is all the more important because it allows Lacan to resituate feminine *jouissance* in its proper place relative to the problematic of castration. In 1960, Lacan seemed to posit being and the infinite *jouissance* it supports as antecedent to the signifier and to the phallic *jouissance* that the signifier brings into existence. In this approach, the phallic signifier somehow comes to colonize a pre-existing being on which it imposes its limits. But in the 1970s, Lacan reverses the relation between being and the signifier and hence the relation between the two *jouissances*. Being, now, is no longer conceived as antecedent to the signifier but instead as produced by it. In other words, without the signifier nothing would exist, not even being. And so, after noting that language makes us presuppose, willy-nilly, a "near side" and a "beyond" of itself, Lacan, in the fourth lesson of *Encore*, spells out his argument:

> Positing a "near side"—we're well aware that what we have there is only an intuitive reference. And yet we can't do away with this supposition, because language, in its effect as signified, is always only on the side of the refer-

ent. From this perspective, isn't it true that language imposes being on us, and, as such, obliges us to admit that we never have anything of this being?

What we have to get broken into is replacing this elusive being with *para-being*: being *para*, being alongside. [p. 44][5]

In other words, being, in which an entire philosophical movement believed it could discern fundamental reality, is merely a signified brought about by the signifier, if only by the verb "to be."[6] But the real itself, the referent, must be situated on the side of this signifier (it is here that Lacan places *objet a*). It follows that the notion of a prediscursive reality is only a dream: "There is no prediscursive reality," Lacan states. "Each reality is based on and defined by a discourse" (p. 32, translation modified). More precisely, being is a meaning-effect in the master discourse, that form of discourse in which the signifier assumes the function of a commandment. Lacan plays on this term, emphasizing that the hidden dimension of the master discourse [*discours du maître*] is that of the signifier *m'être*, ["being myself"],[7] the signifier that claims to give me a being.

What we might call the *jouissance* of being is thus a completely ambiguous notion. In any case, it would be futile to try to make it a category antecedent to the signifier or independent of its determinations. Evoking the *Nichomachean Ethics*, Lacan argues against Aristotle and in favor of Bentham: "What Aristotle is looking for (and that is what opened the way for everything he later brought in his wake) is what the

---

5. Translator's note: I have modified the translation considerably. On *par-être*, see Fink's note 19, Lacan 1972–1973, pp. 44–45.

6. Translator's note: The verb "to be" and the gerund "being" are the same in French: *être*.

7. Translator's note: *Maître* and *m'être* are homonyms.

jouissance of being is. . . . The being—if I absolutely have to use that term—the being with which I contrast that . . . is the being of signifierness" (pp. 70–71).

If being is thus produced by, and not antecedent to, signification, if the presumed near side of language turns out to be its far side, we must reconsider the relation of the two *jouissances*. When all is said and done, isn't the *jouissance* of being, of the Other as such, produced by sexual *jouissance*, by the phallic function, as its "beyond"? Doesn't the "inter-diction" of *jouissance* consist, not in the exclusion of a primal *jouissance*, but in the evocation, between the spoken words, of the hope of an Other *jouissance*, more complete, more bodily—an Other *jouissance* especially ascribed to women? This is the central question that Lacan investigates throughout this Seminar.

That we can thus consider situating feminine sexuality, at least partly, in a "beyond" of the phallic function, and as corresponding to a *jouissance* Other than so-called sexual *jouissance*, is also due to the way in which Lacan reinterprets the Freudian notion of bisexuality, in this Seminar, in order to reformulate the difference between the masculine and feminine positions with regard to sex. As is his habit, Lacan gathers the ideas he has worked out on this point into a few "mathematized" formulas arranged in a table known as the "quantum schemata of sexuation" (p. 78):

MAN (THE ONE)	WOMAN (THE OTHER)
$\exists x . \overline{\Phi x}$ $\forall x . \Phi x$	$\overline{\exists x} . \overline{\Phi x}$ $\overline{\forall x} . \Phi x$
$\begin{matrix} \text{\Cancel{S}} \longrightarrow \\ \\ \Phi \end{matrix}$	$\begin{matrix} S(\cancel{A}) \\ \quad\uparrow \\ a \quad \mid \\ \text{The} \end{matrix}$

The left-hand column describes the structure of the so-called masculine position in sexuality, a position whose major signifier, as we shall see, is the signifier of the One; the right-hand column gives an account of the so-called feminine position, whose key signifier is that of the Other. Let us be clear right from the start that this division in no way corresponds to the anatomical difference between the sexes. Instead, it indicates a division of the subject into two halves, the choice of subjective position being determined in the very discourse of the subject, sometimes contrary to his or her anatomy. In each of the columns, there is a series of notations all of which deal with a single function, Φx, which states that what pertains to sexuality depends on the phallic function (Φ), on whatever side it is located. The difference in position or sexuated identification is established in speakingbeings [*parlêtres*], male or female, only through the way in which they are inserted as subjects into this function. Thus it is not the function Φx, the phallic law, that in itself makes them different, but rather the subjective position in which they declare themselves subjected to it.

The formulas that describe these diverse forms of insertion into the Law involve two types of signs, two types of "quantifiers": the existential quantifiers $\exists x$ and $\overline{\exists x}$ (read, respectively, as "there is an x such that . . ." and "there is no x such that . . ."), and the universal quantifiers, $\forall x$ and $\overline{\forall x}$ (read, respectively, as "for all x . . ." and "for not-all x . . ."). The lower-case "x" in each formula denotes the subject.

Thus the masculine side, in the upper left quadrant, is defined by two formulas:

$\exists x, \overline{\Phi x}$: there exists a subject for whom the function Φx is not operative; in other words, there exists a man who disproves the validity of castration;

∀x, Φ x: for every subject, it is true that Φ x is operative;
in other words, all men are subject to castration.

The contradiction between these two formulas is only an apparent one. Their relation is one not of contradiction but of rule and exception: the exception not only confirms the rule but, even more radically, provides the basis for it.[8] This twofold definition accounts for the Oedipus myth in Freud's *Totem and Taboo*. The exception, the supermale, the only one to escape castration, recalls the primal father who can enjoy all women (or the all-woman), in consequence of which all the others, those defined as sons, are stricken by castration.

This "at-least-one" (*au-moins-un*)—Lacan sometimes writes "*hommoinsun*"[9] —who escapes castration is most often encountered in what is said by women, especially hysterics, for whom he embodies this wish: he is the only one who could substantiate[10] the existence of a sexual relation, the only one who would be capable of desiring and enjoying any woman, hence the only one to establish, from the male point of view, the corresponding identity of the feminine sex. In the face of this ideal of the "real man," all males cut a more or less sorry figure. Not one among them truly loves women, as our lesbian analysands remind us every day. Yet it is from this constitutive impotence that males receive their identity as men. For what Freud's myth tells us is that from the fact of the exception of the founding father, the clan—that is, the group of castrated sons—comes into being. Castration, therefore,

---

8. Early on, from the time of his unpublished Seminar on Identification (1961–1962), Lacan referred in this context to the logic of Peirce.

9. Translator's note: The two French terms are pronounced nearly alike; the neologism *hommoinsun* suggests "man minus one."

10. Translator's note: The French is *donner corps à*, "to give body to."

serves visibly as a limit and assurance of the masculine position. It is the price one must pay in order to be able to call
oneself a man and be recognized as such, with, on the horizon, the necessity that at-least-one can escape castration, or,
for each individual man, that he can, at least once, overcome
this impotence.

This dialectic between $\exists x,\ \overline{\Phi x}$ and $\forall x,\ \Phi x$ explains the
success, attested to by women as much as by men, of the myth
of Don Juan. Who is Don Juan, if not the very incarnation of
the feminine wish as well as the masculine identification—
the man who quivers at the sight or the scent of every woman?
We may note, by the way, that in several versions of this myth
the Don Juan character mocks the father and derogates the
paternal law all the more because he claims to be a law unto
himself.

On the side of the diagram representing the feminine
position, we likewise have, in the upper right quadrant, two
formulas:

$\overline{\exists x},\ \overline{\Phi x}$: there is no subject for whom the function Φx is
inoperative; in other words, there is no woman who is not
subject to castration.

$\overline{\forall x},\ \Phi x$: for not-all subjects it is true that Φx is operative;
in other words, woman is not-all subject to castration.

The first of these notations indicates that, on the feminine side, there is no figure who founds a group of women:
no woman constitutes an exception to the rule by challeng-
ing the validity of castration. We have here a void, a lack,
echoed in the signifier S($\cancel{A}$), the signifier of the hole in the
Other. No woman, no "superwoman," is equal to founding
the existence of a non-phallic sex. Think of the classic fig-

ures of woman in our cultures: they are all phallic figures (and it is also in this way, as delusional metaphors of the phallus, that they reappear in the thought processes of psychotic subjects). The figure of the Virgin, for example, cannot adequately sustain a feminine group (cf. the fantasy of the Amazons), nor can that of the Mother, the Sister, the Prostitute, or the Star. Lacan here provides a logical formulation of the conclusions to be drawn from Freud's work on the absence of a feminine identity and the non-discovery of the vagina as a genital that is not phallic.

Since no woman challenges the validity of castration, since there is no exception to the rule, the rule, too, is lacking: there is no clan of women, no closed set that imposes on itself a common law on this side of the diagram. The subjects who line up on this side have, as a result, to choose between two paths. Either they reject this lack of foundation, or they accept it. If they reject it, they can only line up on the other side, the side of $\forall x$, Φx, to find the shelter of an identity. This is the path of penis envy when it develops into a masculinity complex. What this means is that in order to define themselves as members of a closed set, to form a body, women have no recourse but to declare themselves castrated like men.[11]

The other path is a new one: it is Lacan's proposal for a way out of the impasse of the feminine Oedipus complex, the impasse to which Freud's doctrine led. This path starts from the established fact that The Woman does not exist, and infers from this the conclusion that women are only an open

---

11. This is surely what outrages feminist movements, which, however, have no rallying cry—of despair and acknowledgment all at once—except "castration."

set and should thus be counted one by one. They do not make One, in the sense of men's gathering together, but remain in their infinitude. Moreover, each "one" is inscribed only partially, not-all, in the phallic function and hence in the sexual function as it is set in place by the signifier. Here again there is no true contradiction between the two formulas that define the position of the subject. The first ($\overline{\exists x}$, $\overline{\Phi x}$) says that no woman escapes castration; the second ($\forall x$, Φx) specifies that, although she cannot escape it, she is nevertheless only partially subjected to it. Femininity is revealed in a division with regard to castration: a woman is split, instead of unified, under the signifier "woman." This is represented, in the lower part of the table, by the fact that the woman—which should be written with the "the" barred because "the" Woman does not exist—has a relation, in her sexuality, to the phallic signifier that a man may embody for her, as well as to the signifier of the Other, the Other that does not exist on the level of *jouissance*.[12]

This division of the feminine position is determinative not only on the level of the subject's identity but also on the level of *jouissance*. The phallus' effect of severing, instead of unifying, the feminine position also holds true for so-called phallic *jouissance*. In this position, a woman experiences one part of herself as being caught up in phallic *jouissance*, while the other is located in what Lacan calls *jouissance* of the Other or *jouissance* of the body. And that is where to find—more reliably than in the clitoris/vagina conflict—the famous feminine *jouissance* that has caused so much ink to flow! But we must not leap to hasty conclusions, because Lacan's thinking on this matter is exceptionally complex and subtle. Needless

---

12. Translator's note: On the matter of the bar, see Fink's note 29, in Lacan 1972–1973, pp. 72–73.

to say, there is no question of his adopting this perspective in order to rehabilitate a feminine essence, since he constantly states that nothing of the sort exists. Nor is he concerned to make this Other *jouissance* the feminine characteristic par excellence, which would amount to re-establishing two closed sets: phallic *jouissance* for men on the one side, and the *jouissance* of the body for women on the other.

About this *jouissance* that is other than phallic we know nothing. We can, therefore, only postulate it. Certain women—not all—say that they have actually experienced it, and certain female mystics have offered evidence suggesting that there is a *jouissance* beyond the phallic kind. But perhaps this is merely an idea, an imaginary production. Be that as it may, the fact that this Other *jouissance* is located outside of language means that it cannot be described in words and thus is in danger of having to remain in the register of belief. It does indeed seem that we must take this as our point of departure if we are to approach the question. Let us set out from the belief in an Other *jouissance* and ask ourselves what supports it. Let us even ask whether it is possible *not* to believe in it.

Now, there is no doubt that the enigma a woman represents for a man comes in large part from his supposing that her *jouissance* is of another sort than his, although he cannot define it. What we have to do is not believe in it, deconstruct the process of this belief; yet, indisputably, there is a tendency militating against this dismissal. Where does this tendency come from? Isn't it that, basically, we are all dissatisfied with phallic *jouissance*? It is clear that it is not appropriate for the sexual relation, that in itself it is an obstacle to the *jouissance* of the Other's body.

It is doubtless this hypothetical character of the *jouissance* of the Other that leads Lacan to employ especially complex formulas, as in the following passage that is crucial to the articulation of what we are trying to grasp:

> *Jouissance*, then—how are we going to express what wouldn't be needed with regard to it, if not this way: if there were a *jouissance* other than the phallic kind, it wouldn't need to be that one. . . .
>
> If there were another one, it wouldn't need to be that one. What does it refer to, *that one*? Does it refer to what, in the sentence, is the other, or to the *jouissance* we set out from in order to designate this other kind as other? What I'm saying here is tenable on the level of material implication, because the first part refers to something false. *If there were another*; but there is no *jouissance* other than the phallic kind—except the kind about which woman doesn't breathe a word, perhaps because she doesn't know that *jouissance*, the kind that makes her not-all. It is false that there is another one, which doesn't prevent what follows from being true, namely that it wouldn't need to be that one. . . .
>
> Suppose that there were another kind—but there just isn't. [1972–1973, pp. 59–60, translation modified]

The key to our mystery lies in this relationship of material implication. If there were another . . . but what leads us to suppose any such thing? It is phallic *jouissance*, as being partial, outside-the-body, that makes us think of a beyond, of a "more" or a "something other." After all, isn't it a fundamental property of the signifier, insofar as the signifier is a cut, a delimitation of a border, to evoke something other than what it says and thereby to produce, literally, its beyond? Isn't it a fundamental property of the phallic signifier—which, in language, designates meaning-effects—to act as a veil, and hence to make us believe in a beyond of the veil, in a hidden presence on the order of being?

The presupposition of an Other *jouissance* thus appears to be an effect, indeed the most radical effect, of the phallic signifier. This is, I think, the solution to which Lacan inclines when he explains that this Other, extralinguistic *jouissance*, is, in relation to phallic *jouissance*, not *complementary* but *supplementary*. We can evoke and locate it only on the basis of castration. Thus there can be no question of a *jouissance* of the Other's body except through sexual *jouissance* limited by the organ. There can be no question of a non-phallic *jouissance* except through the phallic function: "It isn't because she is not-all in the phallic function that she is not at all in it. She's *not* not at all in it. She's fully in it. But there's something in addition" (p. 74, translation modified). This "in addition" appears only as castration's margin: we have to go through castration so that a boundary can be drawn beyond which a place is hollowed out for a beyond. But this product of castration is empty, insubstantial, except when given an imaginary substance.

This hypothesis sheds light on a certain homosexuality that may well be considered a structural part of the feminine position. The lower section of the diagram we're examining shows that, on the side of The woman, the division of *jouissance* is played out between two poles, that of the phallus (Φ) that the man can embody for her, and that of S($\cancel{A}$), that which is lacking as a signifier in the Other, in other words the feminine sex itself, a pole that is obviously located on the feminine side. That a woman does not derive all her *jouissance* from her male partner, but, in addition, receives part of it from her own sex inasmuch as this sex is not-all phallic, confers a special status on female homosexuality. (In truth, it's incorrect to speak of homosexuality on this level; this so-called homosexuality seems, rather, to be the most radical heterosexuality, in that it is the heterogeneity of woman to the phallus that is interrogated by the relation (The → S(Ⱥ))). That the specifically feminine part of *jouissance* is articulated at S(Ⱥ), beyond the phallic contribution made by her partner, means that a woman takes pleasure in herself as Other to herself. The male partner, of course, can only feel deprived of that *jouissance*, since from his position as male he has no access to that gap wherein a woman occupies the place of the missing Other.

For the man, the relation to his female partner amounts only to fantasy. By writing the structure of fantasy as ($ ◊ a), Lacan indicates that, for the man, a woman ultimately has value only as *objet a*, that is, as part-object with regard to what the body of the Other would be. The man derives *jouissance* from a gaze, a voice, a skin, from more or less fetishized bodily extremities, and never (unless he assumes the feminine position) from the feminine body as such in its radical alterity. It's no wonder that his satisfaction is always mingled with a certain anxiety: even if he has had sexual pleasure and given it to his partner, he can never be sure of having possessed her, that is to say, of having participated in the *jouissance* that is *hers*.

As a paradigm of this situation Lacan evokes Zeno's famous paradox: "Achilles and the tortoise: that's the system of experiencing *jouissance* on one pole of the sexed being. When Achilles has taken his step, gotten it on with Briseis, she, like the tortoise, has gone a bit ahead because she is *not-all*, not all his. There's some left over. And Achilles has to take the second step, and so forth" (p. 8, translation modified). This dragging on forever of the man's relationship to the woman-as-all has as a frequent consequence a certain misogyny. If the man tends to conceive of femininity as a secret, and sees this secret evading his grasp, he has only to put this secret down to a lie: femininity, to his mind, is no longer the half-saying of the truth but a lie; it is not double but duplicitous.

The film Luis Buñuel based on Pierre Louÿs' novel *That Obscure Object of Desire* is an excellent illustration of this dialectic and the panic and resentment it causes. It shows the feminine division, seen from the viewpoint of the male hero, as being the duplicity of a someone who at times craves sexual *jouissance* and at other times denies herself completely to the man. The latter grows all the more enraged because he can't manage to get rid of his object; the young woman in question follows him everywhere, without, however, being any more at his mercy. Should he go along with the suggestion of his male servant, who gives him advice in the form of an aphorism: "Woman is a bag of excrement," and take on this poisonous burden, making it his symptom?

The final explosion with which Buñuel concludes his lesson, after the man has signaled his fascinated interest in the work of a woman who is sewing up a rip in a bridal gown stained with blood, leaves us with the thought that the most radical cause of terrorism might be, after all, only the impotent rage of men in the face of the impossibility of the sexual relation. The bomb would thus be just a desperate means of bringing into existence the hole that the man cannot manage to conceptualize. This hypothesis will turn out to be less fantastic than it seems, if the reader will recall how Freud himself (1908a) noted that one of the first games of the little boy, at the time when he is confronted by the enigma of sexuality, consists in making holes in the objects around him.

13

Otherness of the Body

Lacan's debate with Freud in the Seminar *Encore* (1972–1973) offers a way out of the blind alley into which Freud led the problematics of femininity when he reduced it to the impossibility of gratifying penis envy. In basing the feminine position on a division more radical than castration (since castration is one of its two branches), Lacan manages to get around the obstacle that castration represents in Freudian theory. For him, castration is no longer the rock on which woman must run aground; on the contrary, it becomes a path to its own transcendence. To understand this formulation, we have to look at Chapter V of *Encore*, where Lacan maintains a dialogue not only with Freud but with Aristotle as well.

This lesson begins with a sentence that immediately places the debate in the context of *jouissance*, the *jouissance* of a being defined as speaking—a speakingbeing [*parlêtre*], as Lacan sometimes calls him—who, by virtue of this very *jouissance*, says that he *has* a body: "All the needs of speaking beings are contaminated by the fact of being involved in an other satisfaction . . . that those needs may not live up to" (p. 51). This other satisfaction is the one based on language, a satisfaction not of the organism's need but of speech, of what is said and what is not said. We have already noted that the need for food, for example, is completely subverted in human beings by the *jouissance* of eating that comes from the signifier: the mere announcement of the menu causes us to desire, opens up an appetite beyond appetence. The other satisfaction arises in the transformation of the object of need into an object/cause of desire; the mother's breast, big with milk, becomes the empty space around which the mouth begins to call out. This effect is clear in sexuality. Some hysterical women, for example, can tolerate sexual relations only with men who declare their love. Such women thereby show that sexuality is something other than a need for discharge, that it becomes something specifically human only in the dimension beyond need.

Lacan is quick to find a source for this other satisfaction in Aristotle's *Ethics*, a work he had already emphasized in the first lesson of *Encore*. If we can be lacking, that is, put ourselves in default, with respect to this other satisfaction, this is so because the latter assumes so much importance only for lack of another *jouissance*, one that does not depend on speech. In these few words, Lacan shows himself to be in agreement with the approach of the *Nichomachean Ethics*. Although this work attempts to determine the nature of *jouissance* and the way in which the honest man must conduct himself with regard to it, it leaves unclear just how Aristotle himself, as he was writing it, revealed a certain position with regard to *jouissance*. What pleasure did he indulge, or deny himself, in writing the *Nichomachean Ethics*? Page after page, as he tries to find out what the *jouissance* of being is, Aristotle inevitably slips into another satisfaction: to speak of *jouissance* is necessarily to displace *jouissance* into speech, to give oneself over to a *jouissance* that consists in the very articulation of signifiers.

This example allows us to define a tripartite stratification: satisfaction of needs, the *jouissance* of speech, the *jouissance* of being.

A certain *lack* persists from one level to the next. The satisfaction of needs is lacking in comparison with the *jouissance* of speech, which, for its part, is lacking as compared to the *jouissance* of being. This lack is unavoidable; it is inherent in speech, in the mechanism of the signifier, where the signifier always falls short with regard to its referent. The *jouissance* of speech—which is our only device for approaching reality—is thus affected by a central flaw: it is what stands in the way of there being any sexual relation. The *jouissance* of speech, in other words, involves the failure of another *jouissance*. Lacan makes this explicit when he says that "the universe is the place where, so to speak, everything succeeds," adding immediately, ". . . succeeds in making the sexual relation fail, in the male way" (p. 56, translation modified). And so the *jouissance* that Aristotle experiences in articulating the signifier in the discourse of the *Nichomachean Ethics* is the very reason for his impotence in defining the *jouissance* of being by means of these same signifiers.

The division that has been introduced here is at the heart of our examination of femininity. What Lacan does is to distinguish between two ways of causing the sexual relation to fail: one way is male, and then there is another that is developed out of the not-all (and not out of the universe, the all),[1]

---

1. Translator's note: the original is "*et non pas de l'univers, du tout,*" which can also be read: "and not out of the universe, not at all."

and that he will explore in interrogating the relation of the woman to God.

The male way to fail in the sexual relation, and hence to be in default with respect to the *jouissance* of the Other or of the body as such, comes from the fact that, in the enjoyment of his right to speech,[2] the male can produce only a phallicized object as a sexual partner, the *objet a*, and not a sexed Other, which does not exist on the level of the signifier. "The failure is the object," Lacan observes (p. 58). This amounts to saying that, for the man, the phallic function Φx is condensed with the function of fantasy. That is why, for him, phallic *jouissance* is at one and the same time the *jouissance* that must be (as a signifying imperative) and must not be (as a lack with regard to another *jouissance*). The register of "necessity" is condensed with that of "falling short,"[3] and thus the principle of phallic *jouissance* is to keep the woman beyond the man's reach. However, as we saw in the previous chapter, this Other *jouissance* that would not depend on the function of speech is a pure supposition: there is no other kind, says Lacan. As a result, the relation between these two registers, as far as the man is concerned, is organized as follows: it is *false* that there could be another *jouissance*, and so, *failing* this other kind, there *must unfailingly* be phallic *jouissance*[4] —this "must" taking on the tone of a superego injunction.

---

2. Translator's note: *L'exercice de la parole dont jouit le mâle*: there is a play on *jouir*, which, in addition to referring to sexual pleasure, can be used in the sense of "enjoy a right," or "enjoy the profit from the possession of something."

3. Translator's note: The French text has *falloir* and *faillir*, the condensation being facilitated by the similarity of these words to the eye and to the ear.

4. Translator's note: Continuing the play on these words (note 3 above), the French text has *faux, faute,* and *faut*.

The fact that Lacan bases this phallic *jouissance* on the *jouissance* of speech shows that sexual *jouissance* is not so easy to define as one might think. It is actually misrecognized systematically, above all in the sex act. Lacan even goes as far as to suggest that the sex act is just a misunderstanding with regard to *jouissance*!—which, we must admit, is a sensational point of view in this age of sexology:

> It's the speaking body in that it can't succeed in reproducing itself except through a misunderstanding of its *jouissance*. That is to say, it reproduces only thanks to a failure of what it means,[5] because what it means—namely, as the French language puts it so well, its sense—is its actual *jouissance*. And it's in failing at it that it reproduces itself—that is, in fucking (up). When all's said and done, that's precisely what it doesn't want to do. The proof is that when it's left alone, it sublimates the whole time as hard as it can . . . . [pp. 120–121, translation modified]

Phallic *jouissance*, then, should not be confused with what goes on between lovers in bed—or at any rate we can't restrict it to that. One of the major revelations of analytic experience is this recentering of so-called sexual *jouissance*: its domain is not so much the *bed* as the *said*. This is why it is repressed and misrecognized by the subject—it's not even enough to enable him to encounter his partner appropriately in bed! Quite the contrary; it's what makes things go wrong in bed: "Repression occurs only to prove in all acts of saying, in the very least act of saying, the implications of my act of say-

---

5. Translator's note: *Ce qu'il veut dire* literally, "what it/he wants to say."

ing of a moment ago, that *jouissance* isn't appropriate—*non decet*[6]—to the sexual relation. Because the aforesaid *jouissance* speaks, the sexual relation doesn't exist" (p. 61).

This absence of a sexual relation leaves the woman as unsatisfied as the man. But, for her, something other than the fantasy-object makes up for the lack. What is it, then, that takes the place of what Lacan in his diagram of sexuation designates as S(Ⱥ)? It's God, he suggests. We still have to grasp what he understands by this term, which obviously cannot be reduced to the God of Christianity. "God," here, refers to the Other, by nature incapable of being signified in speech, who is concerned in what Lacan calls *jouissance* of the Other. For the Other who is in question in this *jouissance* is not the Other of speech (which would be a way of situating phallic *jouissance*), but the Other insofar as it would—in the conditional—have *real* substance beyond its linguistic dimension. Feminine *jouissance*—or at least the kind women are presumed to have—is thus connected with another facet of the Other, one where the Other doesn't exist on the level of the signifier, the facet of the sexuated Other.[7]

This is, therefore, a real turnabout that Lacan is proposing when he identifies God with this facet of the Other as Other sex:

> For me, it seems evident that the Other, put forth at the time of "The agency of the letter" as the locus of speech, was a way—I can't say of secularizing, but of exorcising good old God. . . . Maybe instead I'll show you in what way he *does* exist, this good old God. His way of existing

---

6. Translator's note: *non decet* = "it isn't fitting/proper."
7. Translator's note: I have translated as "facet" the word *face*, which is less abstract, more personal.

may not please everyone, especially not theologians, who, as I've often said, are much better than I am in doing without his existence. . . . This Other, if there is only a single one, surely must have some relation to what appears of the other sex. [pp. 68–69, translation modified]

At this point in the text, Lacan is indirectly alluding to his Seminar on *The Ethics* (1959–1960) and to what he said there about courtly love. Now, in this connection, what was the lesson of that Seminar, if not that the knight or the poet establishes a very special status for the Lady? The Lady of courtly love is elevated, beyond her function as object, to the rank of what Lacan at that time called "the Thing" in an initial approach to what he would later designate as S($Å$). In other words, courtly love raises the Lady to the level of the absolute real Other, inaccessible in itself, but we must note that at the same time this Other is perfectly empty, devoid of substance. It occupies the place of what would be the whole (not partial) object, the missing object that would enable one to speak of a complete sexual drive (as opposed to several partial drives). The construction of this figure of the absolute Lady, of Woman, is possible only at the cost of leaving her empty of any specific attributes. Here we have again the idea of "being of significance" that Lacan contrasts with the being that is already there, prior to the signifier, in which an entire branch of philosophy believed, with Aristotle at the head. The signifier begets being, as the courtly poet begets the Lady, and as the feminine position in sexuation begets "God."

This model of procreation, not a model of antinomy, will be the one we shall follow in trying to resolve the issue that concerns us here, the relation between phallic *jouissance* and feminine *jouissance*, or between the Other as locus of speech and the Other as Other sex. Lacan's train of reasoning is as follows: from the fact that there exists in the Other, as locus of speech, a signifier S($\cancel{A}$) that says that there is a hole, we can assume that this hole is real and marked out as such. For example, it is because language includes words like "unsayable" or "unnamable" that a place is hollowed out where something unsayable or unnamable can *really* exist. That is why Lacan conceives of feminine *jouissance* as *supplementary* with regard to phallic *jouissance*, to the *jouissance* of speech.

The complexity of this relation of an Other (as symbolic locus) to the Other (as real assumed on the basis of the symbolic) is difficult to conceptualize, since it also remains the case that there is no Other of the Other. Lacan does not evade this difficulty, one that can only lend new energy to the fundamental inquiry into the nature of the signifier. Thus he concludes:

> Since all this comes about thanks to the being of significance, and since this being has no locus other than the locus of the Other (Autre) that I designate with a capital A, we see the short-sightedness of what's going on. And since that's also where the function of the father is inscribed, insofar as castration is related to this function, we can see that this doesn't make God two, but it doesn't make only a single one either. [p. 77, translation modified]

The development of this entire line of thought, then, rests on the ambiguity of the status of the Other and on the status of femininity in relation to this Other. The ambiguity is due to the fact that, as locus of the signifier, the Other contains a signifier, S($\cancel{A}$), that signifies that it does not contain all, that all cannot be said. Does this imply that there actually is some other thing? That's the whole question. Now, femininity is presumably defined by this very relation to S($\bar{A}$), this hole in the symbolic Other, which leads us to think that it can be Other than what the unconscious says, Other than what can be named by the signifying chain organized in A by the law of the phallus and castration. This is what situates The Woman on the level of the radical Other, the real sexuated Other, about which the unconscious can say nothing except with regard to its lack. And so we don't have two Others, because only a single one exists—but not nothing more than a single one, because the symbolic nonexistence of the second is just as important as the existence of the first.

If "God" gets involved, Lacan says, this is because the ambiguous status of femininity is fraught with an appeal to being, to a being that would have its foundation elsewhere than in the locus of speech and would thus have a substance other than that of the being of significance. In short, femininity inevitably poses the question of the Other. How can this empty appeal be maintained? How can a woman rest content with insubstantiality? For surely in her *jouissance*, or at least in the part of it that goes beyond the phallic reference, a woman must want as partner a being who places himself beyond the law of the phallus. This wish leads her to slip from her position of castrated *not-all* toward a goal where there would be a partner who was *not at all* castrated, ($\exists x, \overline{\Phi x}$), the place where the man would become God and, as a result, a woman would become The Woman. It is by way of the dream of a supreme Being who would make her all Woman that a woman tends to respond to the hole that opens up in S($\bar{A}$), just as the man, for his part, responds to it through his fantasy object.

This tug of war between Woman and the Other, as we shall try to show, can be explained as that of the relation of a subject to the body. For in the subject's apprehension of the body we see the same two polarities we found in regard to the Other: a locus where the signifier is inscribed and is therefore existent and ascertainable as the being of significance, and, on the other hand, a real sexuated substance and as such unnamable. The disjunction between the Other of desire, who exists, and the Other of *jouissance*, who does not, is thus reproduced on the level of the body.

And no wonder, if we observe that, in the final analysis, the Other (in all senses of the term) of whom Lacan speaks is, for the subject, basically the body. This formulation may come as a surprise to those who were under the impression that, for Lacan, the Other was the unconscious. But Lacan never said this; he said that the Other is *the locus* of the unconscious and spoke of *the locus of the Other*. This is no mere turn of phrase, no gratuitous affectation of what is held to be an inflated style. Lacan's affectations are no more gratuitous than those of the *Précieuses*:[8] they have their full weight. What is the meaning of the statement that the Other is a locus, and only a locus? And what is this locus?

This question brings us back to the very basis of man's dependence on the signifier, and to the effects of the signifier on his being. It is clear that the human being's captivity in language entails a loss as far as the body is concerned—both his body as well as that of the Other. This takes the form of a *loss of being* of which language bears the trace: we don't say that man *is* a body, but instead that he *has* one. By virtue of

---

8. Translator's note: On the *Précieuses* see Lacan 1955–1956, pp. 114–118.

the fact that he speaks, the human being is no longer a body. A disjunction appears between the subject and his body, the latter becoming an external entity from which the subject feels more or less separate. The subject, brought into existence by the effect of language, is, as subject, distinct from his body. He therefore has the burden of inhabiting it or of reaching the body of the Other. But he can do this only through the signifier, because it is the signifier, to begin with, that tells us that we have a body; indeed, it leads us into the illusion of a primal body, a body-being [*un corps-être*] prior to language. Language constantly intervenes between the subject and the body, constituting at the same time a means of access and a barrier: access to the body insofar as it is symbolized, and a barrier to the body insofar as it is real.

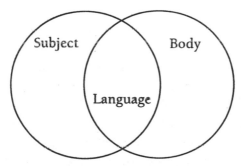

The bodily being of the human animal thus becomes inaccessible, or at any rate beyond direct, unmediated access. We have no idea of the way the body "enjoys itself," except indirectly through our imaginary projections onto animals or plants, or through logical deduction based on language. We can grasp what a body is only to the extent that we cut it up and organize it with the signifier—a mechanism that hysterical conversion pushes to the point of caricature. This does not mean that the body has no reality. The real body continues to exist, of course, but we have to face the fact that we aren't truly *inside* it. On the contrary: for the most part we collide with this real of the body as if it were a solid wall outside us: we bump into an obstacle, we hurt ourselves, we fall, we go for a doctor's examination and find out that we have an illness we hadn't suspected, and so on. It is only these isolated encounters that reveal to us that our bodies, too, are organisms alien to the idea we have of them.

This disjunction has its effect. If language causes an emptying out of the body's being, the body thereby becomes a locus devoid of substance, where there occurs a series of signifying inscriptions. Clinical psychoanalysis makes it clear that there is at all times a principle at work in culture: the notion of the erogenous zone, the process of a conversion symptom, or psychosomatic illness join up, in their singularity, with the generality of symbolic practices such as circumcision, tattooing, and the like. To this extent, we may propose the theory that Lacan's Other coincides with the body insofar as the body is a locus of inscription, a web of signifiers on the one hand, while on the other hand, insofar as it is real, the body remains beyond the reach of what can be named or symbolized.

This distinction between the two aspects of the body is consistent with the dialectic of *jouissances*. It isn't because the Other or the body doesn't *exist* as real that it can be eliminated: its signifying non-existence constitutes a singularly irreducible mode of being. In fact, the subject and the body as such have no relation that can be formulated; the body is always a remainder over and beyond what can be said of it. The relation between the subject and the body therefore seems to be analogous to that of Achilles and the tortoise, which Lacan mentions at the beginning of the Seminar.

So a strict parallel is established among three sets of two terms each: man and woman, the subject and the Other, the subject and the body, all three relations being illustrated by Zeno's paradox. That Achilles will never catch up with the tortoise, nor the subject with the body, does not mean that the tortoise and the body aren't there. They are quite real, but they are situated in another dimension than the one in which Achilles is moving: beyond the step [*pas*], beyond the ever-more-meticulous signifying journey by which he tries to join up with them. What is this dimension, other than that of the step? It is what recalls the notion of the real number, namely the limit: "A number has a limit, and it is to that extent that it is infinite. Achilles, obviously, can only overtake the tortoise; he can't catch up with her. He catches up with her only in infinitude" (p. 8, translation modified).

This limit is exactly what Lacan designates as S(Ⱥ) in bringing together the signifiers of the Other as symbolic locus. S(Ⱥ) indicates that there is something unnamable, some hole, some outside-of-language, in short, some radical alterity. This signifier thus counterbalances another key signifier that Lacan mentions several times in *Encore* and to which he devoted almost all of the preceding year's Seminar (1971–1972), the signifier "One." These two terms, S(Ⱥ) and One, are the two poles between which a relation cannot be written, the two points irremediably separate in meaning that ground the impossibility of the sexual relation.

Why does Achilles run after the tortoise, why does man tirelessly seek Woman, why does the subject struggle to join up with his body? Because the meaning they depend on offers them the signifier "One," this signifier that has no signified other than "There's such a thing as One" [*"Y'a d'l'Un"*], as Lacan enigmatically puts it.[9] While S($\cancel{A}$), the signifier of the unnamable, allows for the existence of the outside-of-language, the signifier One, for its part, suggests to the subject that he could *become one* with this outside-of-language, that he could, indeed must (the commanding effect of the master-signifier) become one with the woman or with the body. This bipolarity fosters a relentless conflict inherent in the symbolic order. The speaking being is necessarily torn between these two vanishing points of language, the signifier of division and the signifier of unity. One part of being inevitably escapes him, and yet the subject finds himself ordered to merge with being. And so what can Achilles do, then, with his tortoise, the man with the woman, the subject with the body? Put to the test of division, the wish for unity can only be diffracted in accordance with the ambiguities that play on the One. Unable to become One with the woman, the man has to take women one by one like Don Juan (the universe scattered in an infinity of units), or else identify with a woman, that is, make himself uniform with her, like the parakeet that was in love with Picasso's jacket (p. 6): union transformed into imaginary uniform-ity.

The heterogeneity of the two *jouissances* overlaps with that of the subject and the body. If a woman can incarnate the body to which the subject vainly seeks to be united, this is because woman, or woman's body, serves as a metaphor of the Other to whom there is no signifiable relation. Like the Other, woman has been made incomplete, not-all subject to

---

9. Translator's note: on the possible meanings of this difficult term, see Fink's note 12 in Lacan 1972–1973, p. 5.

the signifying law.[10] But—and this must be emphasized once again—the idea of a *jouissance* of the body as such, or of a specifically feminine *jouissance*, remains *an idea*, that is, an effect of the signifier. The body is a product of language; bodily *jouissance* is a product of speech. Nature, in short, does not pre-exist culture: cells, atoms, proteins, lipids are undoubtedly there before language, but they don't form a *body* except through language, that is, from the moment that the signified of a body, as an entity, comes to be formulated. If the signifier interdicts[11] access to the body as such, if it banishes it outside the field of what we as subjects can enjoy, it is nonetheless at the root of this body and of the *jouissance* that is attributed to it; in a word, the signifier creates the body at the same time as it interdicts it. This contradiction stems from the conflict, intrinsic to the symbolic order, between the One and the Other, between the requirement of unity and the requirement of alterity. We should become One with the Other —but if we succeed, there will no longer be an Other, and if we don't, unity collapses.

This principle of irreducible heterogeneity entails the fundamental failure of the sexual act. Lacan had already given quite a radical definition of this act in his Seminar on "The Logic of Fantasy": "In sum, sexuality as it is experienced and as it functions can be fundamentally presented through what we discern

---

10. We may note that this thesis was already apparent between the lines of the "Seminar on the Purloined Letter," well before *Encore*; see *Écrits* (Lacan 1966, pp. 11–61).

11. Translator's note: Lacan calls attention to the etymology of this word: *interdicere*, literally to prevent (or come between so as to prevent) by speaking. I have therefore been using it where "prohibit" or "forbid" would be more idiomatic.

in analysis as 'defending oneself' against following up on this truth that there is no Other of the Other" (1966–1967, session of January 12, 1967). If men and women sleep together, it is because they "still" (*encore*) want to unite with the real Other, even if they presumably know that it is out of reach.

For the full scope of *jouissance* is to enjoy the Other, the body of the Other as such. So-called sexual *jouissance* is an obstacle to this, a defense against the *jouissance* of the Other or of the body, in that the sexual is derived, and takes on its phallic determination, from language. This determination is laminated onto the real body, regardless of that body's anatomy, for better or worse. What we call the sexual organ, that is to say the phallus, must be identified as outside-the-body, because of its nature as signifier: it is a signifier that is inscribed on the body from without. It thus forms a barrier to our wish for enjoyment of the Other's body as such. A body, says Lacan, "can't enjoy itself unless it is bodified [*corporisé*] in a signifying manner" (1972–1973, p. 23, translation modified). The *jouissance* of the signifier that intervenes between the subject and the Other's body bars his access to it: that is the law of castration, the function Φx to which every subject must submit. From then on, the sexual act of coitus takes the form of an eternally failed act in which the absence of a sexual relation, the failure to unite the subject and the Other as body, is confirmed time and again. The satisfaction obtained from it can best be defined as lack of the *jouissance* of the body and return to the *jouissance* of the organ. Lacan has a nice name for this: idiot's *jouissance*, with "idiot" being understood in accordance with its Greek root, namely *jouissance* that does without the Other.[12]

---

12. Translator's note: In Greek, *idios* means "separate, private, one's own."

As the saying goes, *post coitum omne animal triste*.[13] But the saying is wrong in the sense that only the speaking being has a fundamental reason to feel sad, for he alone finds meaning in having aimed toward the Other and having failed to reach it. Language, in short, doesn't keep its promises. It leads us to believe in the Other and at the same time withholds it from us; it conjures up the vast scope of a bodily *jouissance* but prevents us from getting there. Sexual *jouissance* is inevitably tinged with dissatisfaction. The pleasure we get from it along the way certainly isn't negligible, but we still[14] have to acknowledge its paradox: it is also what interdicts true satisfaction for us. The *jouissance* of the Other's body thus remains beyond the boundary of the sex act. We can enjoy that *jouissance* only "in our minds," says Lacan (1971–1972, session of March 8, 1972).

And yet this Other, this body that flees like Achilles' tortoise, is definitely there and definitely real! Let's take up our questions again from a different angle, starting out not from the subject, but from the Other. In this displacement of the question the term "feminine *jouissance*" can find its only reality. Achilles, of course, doesn't catch up with his tortoise; he just gets closer to her, little step by little step, into infinitude. The subject cannot become one with the body but just enters it signifier by signifier: the man, in the end, doesn't get to enjoy the body of the woman he can't take in her entirety. He never catches hold of her except one by one, and, with each one, piece by piece, body part by body part. The One of

---

13. Translator's note: "All animals are sad after intercourse."

14. Translator's note: Here too the word is *encore*. The ambiguity of this word ("more/again" and "however") conveys the paradox being described.

Oneness, the All-One, must dissolve into the One of difference, the singular One.

But meanwhile what's happening with the tortoise? While her partner is wearing himself out trying to join her, what is the woman's body experiencing? If the subject cannot enjoy the Other, might the Other, for its part, be enjoying a *jouissance* that the partner can't manage to get for himself? Put in these terms, our question plays on the ambiguity of the expression "*jouissance* 'of' the Other." Up to now we have understood it as an objective genitive; now let's take it in its subjective sense, where it's the Other who is doing the enjoying.

Perversion offers the most convenient way to approach this question: does the thing we use for our enjoyment also enjoy, and with a greater *jouissance*? Perversion, with its aim of corrupting the Other, constantly articulates and confirms the assumption that true *jouissance* is to be found in the position of being enjoyed, not in that of actively taking one's pleasure. Rereading Sade, we see that the high point of his work is his reference to the *jouissance* of the victim and not that of the tormentor, who is conspicuous for his strange apathy. A passage from Pierre Klossowski's fine book *Sade my Neighbor* (1967) sheds light on the pervert's position in a way that can be generalized. Klossowski sees it as an attempt at *subjectivation of the Other*:

> The mental representation of having a body whose state is not that of one's own body is clearly specific to perversion. Although he is aware of the alterity of the alien body, what the pervert feels most of all is that others' bodies are his own and that the body that is normatively and officially his is really *alien to him*, that is, alien to the rebelliousness that defines him. If he is to have an idea of the

effect his own violence has on others, he *must first inhabit another*. In the reactions of another person's body he confirms this strangeness: the irruption of an alien force within "himself." He is at the same time inside and outside. [p. 47, translation modified]

In other words, the *jouissance* of the Sadean tormentor lies less in the final discharge in which "the situation is disrupted" than in the moment when, during the torture, he seeks to put himself in the victim's place. The purpose of the scenario is, to be sure, to allow the sadist to enjoy the body of the person being tortured, but in the *subjective* sense of the expression. The inference is that underlying the sadistic act is a masochistic fantasy.

This subjectivation of the Other is even more evident in the case of masochism. The man who gets himself humiliated, insulted, whipped by his confederate is really seeking to take her place as the woman. He offers himself as object in a typical masculine fantasy scenario only in order to experience the remaining *jouissance* not mastered by that fantasy. The question that the masochist puts to the test of his practice involves knowing what the experience is of the body that the other enjoys under the lash of the whip or of the signifier: Does this body also enjoy? And does it enjoy beyond what it gets from the instrument that leaves its mark on it? Yes, answers the masochist. But this *jouissance* to which he bears witness can obviously not be transmitted to his partner, since she occupies the position usually assigned to the man, that is, the position of Achilles vis-à-vis the tortoise. The *jouissance* "of" the Other, if it is sustained from a *subjective* point of view, therefore remains impossible from the objective standpoint: the sexual non-relation is thereby confirmed.

It may seem paradoxical that we have been approaching the domain of feminine *jouissance* by way of masculine perversion. But this detour is made necessary by the fact that, when it comes to the *jouissance* of the body (subjective genitive), women tell us nothing, as Lacan keeps on emphasizing with ill-concealed resentment. Having no revelations coming from women themselves, we can only turn to the discourse of perverts, who offer us a kind of mimetic caricature of feminine *jouissance*. Moreover, we may note that, the first time Lacan (1966–1967) dealt with this question of the *jouissance* of the body, he framed it in terms of the *jouissance* of the slave. And in *Télévision* (1974) he makes a statement of principle to the effect that if the man wants *The* woman, he can attain her only by failing in the domain of perversion. If the man reaches The woman, this contact remains a failure because it is limited to a mere exchange of positions. The masochist may take the part of the Other, or of the Woman, but he still hasn't established a sexual relation.[15]

This kinship between the aim of the perverse position—especially that of the masochist—and the subjective feminine position in *jouissance* explains why post-Freudian psychoanalysis has misunderstood the notion of a *specifically feminine masochism*. As if women particularly liked to suffer and be humiliated! This idea, commonly accepted by a goodly number of analysts, can in no way be attributed to Freud him-

---

15. An example of this failure of the perverse position can be found in Philippe Sollers' *Women* (1990). The hero, in the belief that by pretending as women do he will be able to pass among the other sex, constantly finds himself reduced to the *jouissance* of the idiot. His only recourse is to declare that the Other is death and the rest only imposture, or, alternatively, to believe in God. This is a way of retorting to women that the truth about femininity is just as deceptive as belief in God.

self. To be sure, he speaks of "feminine masochism" as one of the three forms of masochism, but we must understand this in the context of the argument in which it appears. According to Freud, masochism appears "as a condition imposed on sexual excitation, as an expression of the feminine nature, and as a norm of behaviour. We may, accordingly, distinguish an *erotogenic*, a *feminine*, and a *moral* masochism" (1924b, p. 161). But it must be noted that, as in "A child is being beaten" (1919a), Freud is referring to the analysis of perverse fantasy. It is in the masochist's perverse scenario that he locates an "expression of woman's being"; he does not find in woman's behavior an expression of the masochist's being. The subjective position of the masochist in his fantasy is in effect a position characteristic of femininity, Freud says, and this is why he called this form of masochism "feminine." For Freud, then, it is not a question of maintaining that women take pleasure in suffering—an idea that would be developed by Helene Deutsch (1925) and Jeanne Lampl-de Groot (1983)—but, instead, of discerning the way in which the masochistic man exhibits something on the order of a feminine position: it is his subject position that is feminine, not the intermixture of pain in pleasure. The meaning of the phrase "feminine masochism" is not that women are masochistic, but that the masochist is a woman or is trying hard to be so.

Now that the notion has been restored to its proper context, how can we distinguish between the two forms of splitting respectively entailed by the perverse and the feminine positions? In both cases the subject is divided: on one side, castration is acknowledged and subjectivized; on the other side it is neither. But how does the non-acknowledgment (the denial) of castration by a pervert differ from its non-subjectivation (the not-all) by a woman? This brings us back to the issue of knowing what *logical* distinction separates the two parts of Lacan's table of sexuation.

The table shows that on the one side there is a split between subjection to castration ($\forall x$, Φx) and negation of castration ($\exists x$, $\overline{\Phi x}$), while on the other the split occurs between the assertion of a partial non-subjectivation ($\overline{\forall x}$, Φx) and the negation of the negation of castration ($\overline{\exists x}$, $\overline{\Phi x}$). The masochistic position, whatever aim it may share with the feminine position, must therefore be distinguished from it; it is merely its caricature. This difference is clearer if we note that the pervert believes in the Other, in the subjective *jouissance* of the Other, whereas a woman has no need to believe in it—she is simply in the place where the question of the Other is posed. For the masochist, the bar is never truly inscribed on the Other, and as a result he must endlessly replay the scenario in which the Other receives this mark from his partner. But what a woman attests to is the irremovable nature of this bar, the *impossible subjectivation of the body as Other*. The pervert seems to be able to slip into the skin of this Other body like a hand into a glove; but as for women, they constantly say that this body doesn't fit them like a glove, that for them, too, it is Other, and that the *jouissance* that can occur there remains alien to them and unable to be subjectivized. Hence the anxiety of depersonalization—or, to use what seems to be an apt term here, of *desubjectivation*—that overcomes a woman when she happens, we don't know why, to experience this *jouissance*. For as a *subject* she can speak of and subjectivate only her relation to Φ, and not to the body as such.

The mystical discourse of St. Teresa of Avila (cf. 1975), when she describes herself as having been "carried away," "ravished," "seized" irresistibly, is no doubt just as much of a caricature as the masochistic scenario. Driven to this point of desubjectivation, a woman can orient herself only by appealing to God, the supreme Being located beyond Φx. This appeal to God—which, in the case of St. Teresa, is answered—enables us to understand the formulation in *Télévision* to the effect that, if the man attains The Woman only by getting stranded in perversion, a woman encounters The man only in psychosis. Applied to St. Teresa, this statement emphasizes the role religion played for her: that of a symptom allowing her to contain, rather successfully, the psychosis of which she shows all the signs. But here we must consider in its entirety the passage from *Télévision* in which this formulation is introduced:

> [A] woman encounters The man only in psychosis. Let us assert this axiom, not that Man does not ex-sist, as is the case with Woman, but that a woman interdicts him to herself, not because he's the Other, but because "there is no Other of the Other," as I've said. So the universal of what women desire is madness: all women are crazy, as the saying goes. That's even why they aren't all [*toutes*], that is, not crazy-at-all but instead accommodating: to the point where there is no limit to the concessions each one of them makes for *a* man: with her body, her soul, her fortune.[16]

To the appeal arising in $S(\cancel{A})$—or the appeal to a partner for *jouissance* of the body—a woman, as a rule, refrains from answering. Except in the case of psychosis, a woman encounters neither God nor the superman: she interdicts him to her-

---

16. *Télévision*, p, 63. I have translated as "not crazy-at-all" the phrase *pas folles-du-tout*, which can also mean that their madness is not caused or characterized by "the all."

self, Lacan says; she renounces the idea that there is an Other of the Other that she herself embodies.

This interdiction placed on Man had already been identified by Freud (1912c) as the key element of a woman's love life. If women thus renounce Man, with a capital "M," it is in order to preserve their position as subject, in order to avoid the slippery slope of desubjectivation (what Freud marks out as sexual *subjection*).[17] They will do anything so that their man will remain "a" man and will not be "The Man." In the end, this leads them to support male fantasy and to espouse[18] its phallic domination. Hence the continuation of the passage from *Télévision*: "She falls in with the perversion that I consider to be that of The Man ["L'Homme"]. Which leads her to the masquerade that we know and that isn't the lie that some ungrateful people, clinging to The Man, impute to her" (p. 64).

What are the implications of this turnabout of the feminine position? It means that if sexual *jouissance* causes the failure of the *jouissance* of the Other's body, women are in a good position to know that matters would be even worse if it did not fail. Sexual *jouissance*, because it is above all *jouissance* of the signifier, no doubt entails a painful disjunction between the subject and the body, but at least the subject finds a place there that the *jouissance* of the body might well abolish. It is normal for a woman to be intent on preserving her division, and, correspondingly, for her to be intent on the man's castration, since this is the condition of her subjectivity as a woman. In so doing, she falls in with the masquerade, pre-

---

17. Literature offers an example of a woman who does not make this renunciation and as a result becomes monstrously crazy: Kleist's Penthesilea.

18. Translator's note: *épouser*, literally, "to marry."

tends to be the Other who doesn't exist, and allows the man to misconstrue the object of his fantasy. And so "pretending to be the Other" would best define the feminine position, just as "pretending to be a man" specifies the hysterical position. Finally, we expect a woman to collaborate in making sure that there is no sexual relation except in pretense, because she, as a woman, knows that if men were not castrated and women not divided, if the sexual relation could be established, there would be a subjective catastrophe.

14

Love and the Woman

In the foregoing discussion of the dialectic of the *jouis-sance* of the signifier and the *jouissance* of the body, a term was left in abeyance, and it is one that now must be set in place, particularly since it is essential to the argument of the Seminar *Encore* (1972–1973). That term is *love*. What is the place, the function, the nature of love in the subject's unsteady relation to sexuality? How does it fit in with the terms we have been examining: desire, *jouissance*, pleasure? And, finally, why (if we are to believe Freud) does love have a privileged status in the problematics of femininity? Let us start with this last question.

If the division of *jouissance* into *jouissance* of the signifier (or of the phallus) and *jouissance* of the body (or of the Other) corresponds to the difference that language establishes between the subject and the body, and if, on the other hand, the feminine position consists in being not-all bound by the phallic law and hence not-all determined by the *jouissance* of the signifier, it follows that a woman's destiny is to be *not-all a subject*. Not-all a subject means that a woman is not wholly determined by her unconscious. How far we can take this conclusion? Should the analyst—like Meister Eckhart, who believed that women do not have souls—be led by Lacan to say that a woman does not have an unconscious? Let us say, not that she does not have it, but that she lacks it, and, as an immediate result, wants it back.

The fact that, as we have argued, the *jouissance* of the Other (in the subjective sense of the genitive) cannot be subjectivized sheds new light on the feminine demand that Freud interpreted as penis envy. What a woman wants is to subjectivize that unsubjectivizable part of herself that is her body. And of whom should she ask this, if not the psycho-analyst, since his job is to form a partnership with the sub-ject, the subject of the unconscious? Because, ultimately, what a woman wants is to get a supplementary unconscious, a supplement that will allow her to exist as a subject in the place where she is just a body in *jouissance*. That is, it seems to me, to be the correct reading of the following, rather enigmatic, passage in *Encore*:

> [I]f libido is only masculine, it is only from the place where the dear woman is *all*, that is, from the place where the man sees her, and only from there, that the dear woman can have an unconscious.
>
> And what good does that do her? It serves, as every-one knows, to make the speaking being, who is reduced here to the man, speak, that is to say—I don't know whether you've noticed this in analytic theory—exist only as a mother. She has unconsciousness-effects, but as for her own unconscious—at the boundary where she is not responsible for everyone's unconscious, that is, at the point at which the Other she is dealing with, the Other

with a capital O, works in such a way that she knows
nothing, because it, the Other, knows even less that it's
very hard to maintain its existence—this unconscious,
what can we say about it, if not to hold, with Freud, that
it doesn't make matters easy for her? [pp. 98–99, translation modified]

A woman has no unconscious except "from the place
where she is all," and only from there, and hence only insofar as she lines up with the formula of the all, of the masculine universe in which ∀x, Φx: for every subject, the law of
castration is operative. Thus women are subjects of an unconscious only to the extent that they define themselves as
castrated, that is, see themselves in the position in which
men place them. We may conclude that the feminine division—which Lacan notates by means of a bar on T̶h̶e̶ woman
—constitutes a different split from that of the subject of the
unconscious, $. The T̶h̶e̶ indicates that a woman is divided
between what she is as a subject, $, on the one hand, and
what she is as a non-subject, indeed as non-subjectivizable.
    Now, psychoanalysis can address only the subject of the
unconscious. It follows logically that a woman turns out to
be not-all analyzable, since she is not-all a subject. This as-
sessment is all the more distressing because, unless she is a
hysteric—in which case she acts as though she were a man—
a woman wants precisely to be recognized as a woman, that
is, to have the existence of the feminine subject acknowledged.
We can see the subtlety that is called for in the analysis of a
woman. For what can be the analyst's response to the feminine demand? It cannot simply be to invite her to let "the
speaking being" speak, in other words, to elicit speech from
the man, or at least the phallic, in her. Is the only possible

existence with which analysis can leave a woman—and note that this means existence as the subject of an unconscious—that of a man or a mother?

We would have to resign ourselves to that, if Lacan did not indicate, by means of the notation S(Ⱥ), that the unconscious itself is not-all, and that, as a result, the analyst's response cannot be *all* phallic. To be sure, the subject is affiliated with the unconscious only insofar as he is represented by the metaphor of the phallus. But the signifier S(Ⱥ) that Lacan introduces to inscribe the not-all that divides the feminine position, is not, like the phallus, the signifier representing the subject (S1). It represents the other (S2), the signifying other of the formula "a signifier is that which represents a subject for another signifier" (1964, p. 207). S(Ⱥ) is the signifier *for which* all other signifiers represent the subject.

In this "for which" is the dimension that Freud called "becoming a woman." But how to understand it? For this "other" signifier can only be in perpetual flight from the first one and thus always on the horizon of the chain in which the primacy of the phallus is operative. And the dialogue between analyst and analysand is in danger of replicating the race of Achilles and the tortoise. Each time Achilles/the analyst acts, each time interpretation brings the subject into existence, the tortoise/analysand takes a little step [*pas*] that, in a play on words, signifies a not-all [*pas-tout*]. Each time she is recognized, the "dear woman," as Lacan says, escapes. This is why the analysis of a woman entails, in a very special way, questions about the end of the analysis: the more the analytic set-up functions, the "more" [*encore*] of it she wants. This is also why the transference regularly takes a sharp turn, particularly when the patient is a woman and the analyst a man. For in this situation the love relation that forms in analysis absolutely requires that the transference be seen as a revelation of the truth of love.

To understand the place and the role Lacan accords to love, we must note that the Seminar *Encore*, in its overall development, involves the distinction between two registers, that of *jouissance* and the signifier, and that of love and pretense. These are two separate aspects, yet they are indissolubly linked. Lacan thus indicates, from the very first lesson of this Seminar, that it is from the rift that marks the register of *jouissance*, that is, from the non-existence of the sexuated Other as such, that there arises the demand for love. And he immediately adds that "[l]ove, of course, constitutes a sign [*fait signe*] and is always mutual" (p. 4). This statement is all we need to discern the separation between the two registers and to see how love seeks to realize the encounter that, in terms of *jouissance*, turns out to be impossible. Whereas *jouissance* is attached to the *signifier*, love depends on the *sign*.

This essential distinction leads Lacan, throughout the Seminar, to examine the nature of the signifier and, more precisely, to ask what, in the register of the signifier, can be, or give, a sign. Hence his many reflections on the function of the master-signifier and on the relations of the signifier and the letter that mark its development. Love, on the other hand, is said to be reciprocal, in contrast to *jouissance*, which, as we have seen, is by definition non-reciprocal: the two possible senses of the genitive in the expression "*jouissance* of the Other" do not overlap. Does this mean that the relation established in love might make up for the absence of the sexual relation in *jouissance*? As we shall see, although love actually tries to make up for what is missing in the sexual relation, the relation that it creates is not a "sexual" one. There are two reasons for this. The first is that the love relationship does not bind a subject to a body but rather a subject to another subject; the second is that love is fundamentally a-sexuated; as Lacan says, when one is in love, sex is not involved.

It is surprising that *Encore* does not make reference to Plato's *Phaedrus*, since a parallel reading of this text provides an excellent commentary on Lacan's reflections. For what, after all, is the *Phaedrus* if not a study of the conjunction of love and discourse (in its two aspects of speech and writing), of love and semblance, the alliance of these two terms finding its justification in an ethic of speaking well. The notion of love that Socrates presents here is, to be sure, different from Lacan's, but its exposition is similar in a number of respects. The basic argument of this Platonic dialogue is that if we want to know what love is about, we have to speak well. What is the aim of speaking well? To position the subject in speech, Socrates answers. If the subject is not present as subject in his discourse, he will inevitably fail to get at the nature of love; this failure leads to lies and deception and becomes a fault for which one must bear the guilt.

Plato's exposition has four phases. The first may be called the phase of false discourse. Phaedrus has challenged Socrates to make a better speech than the renowned orator Lysias, who has praised the overcoming of desire, maintaining that one should grant one's favors to someone one doesn't love instead of to someone one does. Socrates thereupon starts to make a speech in which he develops the idea that a man who is in love is more ill, and thus more sensitive, than a man who is not in love. But he is not able to finish this speech. He breaks off right in the middle, saying that he is ashamed of his words and wants to flee. A voice stops him, prevents him from leaving, and orders him to do penance for this bad speech.

This is the beginning of the second phase, that of the expiation of the fault. Socrates discovers that his feeling of guilt stems from a fault with regard to the speech he had been making, and he is obliged to retract what he said with a palinode in praise of love. He has misspoken and will now try to speak well, which first of all involves giving up the illusion of mastery that Lysias extends from the composition of the speech to the love relationship itself.

In the third phase, Socrates undertakes to make a new speech about love, one whose argument is the opposite of the one with which he had begun. We shall not stop to analyze this speech, although it deserves commentary, especially in regard to Socrates' conception of truth (he thinks it can be spoken in its entirety) or to the privileged role of Beauty as a stimulus to desire. Let us simply note that the speech finishes with the praise of narcissistic love, the lover seeing himself in the beloved as in a mirror. Socrates argues that only by speaking well can one arrive at the truth about love, and that it is therefore necessary to know what it means to speak or write well and to formulate the conditions for a speech whose goal is to say not what is plausible but what is true, not to persuade but to lead to the discovery of knowledge.

This is the aim of the fourth phase of the dialogue, in which Socrates, who speaks of himself as having a divine sort of love, introduces a new development. Setting out to reveal the true nature of the love he had mentioned in his second speech, he now locates it beyond the narcissistic relation between the lovers, since it is *the love of speech itself*. There follows a discussion on the difference between rhetoric and dialectic, and it turns out that, for Socrates, there is no valid rhetoric—none, that is, that sustains a relation to truth—

without dialectic. In other words, there is no speaking well that is not based on knowledge of the *object* of discourse. We have here the two Lacanian notions of the signifier and the object.

The *Phaedrus* enables us to explain and put in order the reflections on love that Lacan scatters throughout *Encore*. For the three perspectives on love that Socrates discerns are in direct relation to the registers that Lacan distinguishes in his approach, or rather his approaches, to the issue. As imaginary, love appears in the form of narcissistic love, a specular relation in which the lover loves the image of himself that the other sends back to him like a mirror, a relation that is itself governed by the connection of the lover to the gods and the world of ideas. On the symbolic level, the love of beautiful speeches has two subdivisions. On one side there is the love of discourse as practiced by the sophists or the logographers. This is merely the love of the master signifier, that is, of the signifier as the demand for unity; placed in the master position, the signifier in this case orders that opposites be unified, rendered similar. On the other side is the love of speech that Socrates invokes. This is not love for the signifier except insofar as the signifier enables one to define an object, a reality, that escapes the assimilations and confoundings put in effect by the master signifier. In this way we can see a real function of love, in which the One at which it is aimed is not the "one" of unification dear to the sophists, but instead the One of difference, of the unity to which the status of the object is resolved.

This triple distinction is also found in *Encore*. From the three perspectives of the imaginary of identification, the symbolic of the master signifier, and the real of the object Lacan tries to situate love and the semblance that regulates its process. For in each of these three registers, love is directed toward the Other but reaches only a semblance of it to which it attempts to give substance. Love seeks to discern the being of the Other, whose defect has been revealed by the division of *jouissance*. By this claim on the part of being, love is connected to ontology, Lacan observes (pp. 31, 39–40). But, in fact, love never realizes anything but a semblance of being.

It is on the imaginary level that this movement is most obvious, for here love and identification with a similar person are confused. And, as Lacan illustrates with the story of Picasso's amorous bird, this identification holds only insofar as "clothes promise debauchery" (p. 6), that is, insofar as the image of the other leads us to hope that the other harbors a consistent content. As fashion designers know, we assume a beautiful body, and, why not, a good mind when a woman is well dressed. But what is this content, this being that makes the image hold up? Analysis shows that it amounts to *objet a*, for example, to a gaze, or a voice, or a body part. The image of the other, *i(a)*, merely overlaps *a*, with which there is no possible union, at any rate no sexual union, since the object is by nature a-sexuated.

On the symbolic level, speaking of love also aims to grasp the being of the Other. This speech is essentially "you are . . ." or "be . . . ," and is linked to the functioning of what Lacan calls the master signifier, that is, the signifier that ostensibly gives substance to the subject. Thus Lacan writes:

> [L]ove aims at being, namely at what slips away most in language—being that, a moment later, was going to be, or being that, precisely because it was, led to surprise. And

> I was also able to add that being is perhaps very close to
> the signifier *m'être*,[1] is perhaps being in command, . . .
> and that we have there the strangest of illusions (*leurres*).
> Isn't that also the case in order to command us to ques-
> tion in what sense the sign can be distinguished from the
> signifier? [p. 39, translation modified]

On the symbolic level, then, the master signifier plays
the same role of semblance as the clothing on the imaginary
level. The speech of love isolates a signifier that is supposed
to designate the being of the beloved, the being that the beloved would be before all discourse in which he is alienated
as a subject. But to believe that a signifier can give substance
to a prediscursive being amounts precisely to being the victim of the illusion produced by the master signifier and to
failing to recognize the fact that the suggestion that being
exists is a property of the signifier. This misrecognition is
based on a confusion: the signifier (which merely represents
a subject for another signifier) is taken for a sign (which, as
the sign of something, supports a being). Being flees the signifier that has only the effects of the signified. Hence the paradox inherent in the speaking being's fundamental question:
"Who or what am I?" Any answer to this question, woven from
the signifier, can only increase my non-being and make even
more imperative the question of my being. It is necessary that
I be [*m'être*], but, in the place where I speak, I am not.

The claim of the speech of love is thus itself condemned
to infinitude, since it can only fall indefinitely short of the
Other's being. In this failure, however, something comes to

---

1. Translator's note: *m'être* ("to be me" or "being me") is homony-
mous with *maître* ("master").

light that is neither a thing nor a being, but a subject. The psychoanalytic experience of transference love reveals another truth of love than that of the aim of being. If love fills in for what is missing in the sexual relation, this is not, ultimately, by the establishment of a relation to the being of the Other, as it might seem, but in posing a relation of subject to subject.

In this sense, the end of the fourth lesson of the Seminar *Encore* involves a redefinition of the nature of the master signifier on the basis of analytic experience. Lacan argues that it is mistaken to believe that the sign is simply a sign of *something*. Smoke is not only the sign of fire; it is also, and primarily, the sign of a smoker, in other words, the *sign of a subject*: "Thus, a sign is not the sign of some thing but of an effect that is what is presumed as such of a functioning of the signifier. That effect is what Freud teaches us about, and it is the starting point of analytic discourse, namely the subject" (pp. 49–50). As a result, love too must be redefined, no longer as aiming at being but as aiming at the subject: "In love what is aimed at is the subject, the subject as such, insofar as he is presumed in an articulated sentence, in some aspect of a whole life that is organized or can be organized" (p. 50, translation modified). It is transference love that imposes this division, since it demonstrates that the analysand falls in love with his analyst—and, on this point, neither Lacan nor Freud hesitates to say that this is really love—only because he presupposes a subject to the knowledge that concerns him.

Thus, by changing the terms of the relation, love makes up for the impossible conjunction of the subject and the body that is borne out in *jouissance*. The relation of subject to subject that it establishes has as a copula the knowledge that each ascribes to the other, knowledge about who I am when I speak to the other. This presumed reciprocity of love is the problem here. If each partner ascribes to the other an unconscious knowledge, and to this knowledge a subject, nothing says that these two knowledges and these two unconsciouses either overlap or make One. That can happen, but only in isolated cases (as in the well-known telepathy between lovers). The speech of love tends to make this contingency a necessity: because it may occasionally happen that the relation to the Other stops not being written, it must not stop being written, must be written again and again [*encore et encore*], forever. . . .

This dialectic of love, on the symbolic level, is especially perceptible to the subject who claims the feminine position in sexuation, because the relation of subject to subject, and of unconscious knowledge to unconscious knowledge, is likely to correspond to the feminine demand that we have characterized as getting herself endowed with a supplementary unconscious, a supplement that makes her a subject precisely in the place where she is not one. It is not surprising that women question love systematically, nor that they demand it of their interlocutor. One has to love them and tell them so, not so much because of a narcissistic need as because of this subjective defection with which they, as women, are marked. If they want to be loved, therefore, it is not because this wish is part of a passivity natural to femininity, as Freud thought, but because they want to be made subjects in the place where the signifier abandons them. The fact that, for some women, love is a necessary condition for the ability to reach orgasm with their partner can thus be understood in the sense that sexual *jouissance*, in contrast to the *jouissance* of the body, is precisely concerned with the subject.

But the movement of love does not produce its effects solely on the imaginary and symbolic levels. It is also found on the level of the real. On this third plane, it functions with regard to the fundamental antinomy that the unconscious creates between desire and *jouissance*. We may formulate this antinomy as follows: whereas desire is always desire of the Other, *jouissance* is never *jouissance* of the Other (except by accident). It must be noted once again that the same Other is not involved in both cases. Desire puts in play the relation of the subject to the symbolic Other, that is, to an Other without substance, a pure locus of the signifier in which the subject's speech finds its foundation, while in the case of *jouissance* it is the body of the real Other that is called on, and missed out on, the relation being reduced to the connection established by fantasy between the subject and *objet a*.

This oscillation of the subject between the existence of a purely symbolic Other that is not incarnated in desire, and, on the other hand, the non-existence of an Other as body in *jouissance*, creates a rift into which real love sinks. On this level love is actually addressed to being. It chooses a being in whom desire and *jouissance* are continuous, a being in regard to whom desire will no longer serve as a barrier to *jouissance*. But this being remains out of reach, in perpetual evasion. In this slippage through which being escapes, an obstacle imposes a limit to, and simultaneously a support for, the aims of love: it is what Lacan calls the (*a*) wall. This ambiguous term is a compound of *objet a* and the wall that this object sets up in front of the grasping of being. On the level of the real, love is thus unknowingly reduced to the relation to the fantasy object. This is, moreover, what makes love deadly and likely to turn to hate. For, as he bumps up against the (*a*) wall, the subject gets more and more frustrated, since he never gets anything of the being of the beloved other than a few signs or remains. How, then, could he do better in his attempt to grasp this being than to reduce it to a corpse or to devour it, to swallow it in a real way? How better to possess the beloved than by destroying that person? The two final lines of *Encore* open onto this dismal perspective in which love is allied to the death instinct, where that instinct is most destructive.

This conjunction of love and death is undoubtedly intrinsic to passion, which includes an impulse toward the partner that does not stop at the border of wanting what is best for him or her. On the contrary: at this level of the real, love goes all the way to the death of the partner, according to a formula that can be expressed as "having one's being, even this entails its no longer being." That is why we can contrast the real dialectic of love with its symbolic dialectic. Whereas the latter is expressed, in the speech of love, by the wish that it last forever, that it no longer cease to be written, the former, which is produced on the level of the real, has one sole aim: that it cease. This is why, in *Encore*, Lacan says that love is "yum yum" coming from the stomach.

These reflections give a brief overview of the complexity of what is named by single term, love, and of its role in sexuality. Its three goals, or the three forms of semblance on which it is focused—the image, the subject, and being—are located in different registers and are in no way continuous with one another. This dispersal leaves the field open to various kinds of love. Lacan argues, in *Encore*, that love has nothing to do with sex. This is not the same as saying that the sexuation, male or female, of the beloved is incidental to the movement of love. It seems to me—and this is confirmed by arguments that Lacan made subsequently—that we are to understand this statement in the broadest sense, as meaning that love in its essence involves *the failure of sex*. Love, in short, says no to sexuality as it is determined by the unconscious sexual direction. That the latter strictly precludes the possibility of a sexual relation is what love keeps on contesting. Such a contestation cannot stand the test of the real, at least in the long run, but this is secondary to the message it carries. As the failure of the unconscious,[2] love relies on an encounter, a successful encounter, to maintain that it is possible—and hence necessary—to thwart the unconscious desire whose law is the perpetual failure of the encounter. By nature, love tends to place itself beyond repetition: it claims to be that which does not fail. The experience of analysis, like the literary tradition, proves that this success is not necessarily what the subject desires, that it is sometimes more grueling than the failure imposed on us by the unconscious.

But does the law of the unconscious dictate everything? This question leads us to resume our reflections in the hope of verifying whether speaking well about love is possible. If we want to be rigorous, we will agree that speaking about love is the most difficult thing there is. Lacan himself, at the beginning of the second lesson of *Encore*, refuses to undertake such a project: "[W]hat I say about love is assuredly that we can't speak about it. 'Speak to me of love'—silly little song!" (p. 12, translation modified). Lacan accounts for this impossibility when, in the course of the Seminar, he sets forth two statements that are totally contradictory and yet are both true. For, although *love is addressed to knowledge*, it seems that,

---

2. This is an allusion to the title of one of Lacan's last Seminars, *L'insu-que-sait de l'Une-bévue s'aile à mourre* (1976–1977). Translator's note: this is a notoriously punning title. For our purposes, we may note that *insu-que-sait*, which means "the unknown that [someone] knows," is a homonym of *l'insu que c'est* ("the unknown that it is," where "it" may be *ça*, the id), and, relevant to the author's wording here, *l'insuccès* (the "unsuccess").

inversely, knowledge always fails to be addressed to love, which leads Lacan to say as well that *love has nothing to do with knowledge*. In trying to speak of love, we thus run the risk that we will wind up saying any old thing; the principle of non-contradiction seems not to hold true in this matter. And in fact, when we speak of love, we don't know what we're talking about, and the more we speak, the less we know about it. This is the first lesson to be drawn from Plato's *Symposium*. There is no reason to be silent about it, as Wittgenstein might advise, all the less so as, being psychoanalysts, we constantly offer ourselves to love.

As a phenomenon, love is obvious and at the same time ungraspable. It involves an indisputable certainty and an infinite doubt. Furthermore, at the very center of the field of psychoanalysis, it appears as the necessary condition for the experience and also as the fundamental resistance that threatens to render the experience impossible. How can we find a solution to these contradictions?

We must first distinguish two levels of questioning, following the example of Socrates in both the *Phaedrus* and the *Symposium*: when it comes to love, we have to determine not only what it is, but also what function it serves. If we can discover its role in the domain of sexuality, we will perhaps be better able to define what it is. Moreover, with regard to the nature of love, it is not out of place to recall the famous maxim according to which no one would experience love who hadn't already heard it spoken of. In other words, love is first a word, a *signifier*, that produces all sorts of *signified*-effects in a register that extends, I would say, from stupidity to horror. But does it have a *referent*? Nothing is less certain.

As we have seen, this referent would be precisely what language does not allow to be formulated, namely the sexual relation, whose impossibility is the umbilical point of unconscious discourse. But the fact that there is no sexual relation, as Lacan repeats, does not mean that the sexual relation does not exist ... sometimes. It is impossible, *in speech*, to posit the general statement: there is a sexual relation, that is, a relation in which one sex complements the other. Although the formula for this possibility is that the sexual relation "does not stop not being written," the exception proves the rule, and so it may happen, by chance, to "stop not being written." In accordance with the "I know, but nevertheless ... " that Octave Mannoni (1969) proposed as the paradigm of perversion, we may formulate the principle of love. We know that, for Freud, love can reestablish between lovers' perversions, or desires and perverse behaviors, that are otherwise repressed. Is this more than a coincidence (and one that may be merely imagined)? It is, at any rate, the wish entailed by love and by the declaration of love: again (*encore*)! ... forever! In other words, let the exception become the rule! But here the *certitude* of the encounter returns to *belief*, mixing two heterogeneous aspects of time, moment, and duration. Nor does this imply that the wish always fails in the real, but just that, seeking to make law of what is by nature outside the law, it entails something of a *challenge*, and this, again opens a door to perversion.

As it happens, it is in connection with the notion of law that we find the most fertile ground for reflecting on love and its function in regard to the feminine position. A fashionable heroine, Bizet's Carmen, proclaims that love has never known any law. This truth, universally acknowledged, makes a strict distinction between love and friendship, since the latter flourishes in obedience to the law and is sustained by it. This theme was central as far back as Plato's famous *Symposium*, where it appears explicitly in the speech of Pausanias and implicitly in the entrance of Alcibiades onto the scene. The lover, Pausanias argues, is the only one with the privilege of transgressing two fundamental laws of Athenian society, the one governing slavery and the one that honors vows. Note that these are not just any laws; they are those that govern the condition of the subject and the faith placed in his words. In contrast, says Pausanias, those who are the objects of love (that is, young boys) are not just under the law but are also under the strict surveillance of their teachers. Hence we have the perverse development of a discourse whose logic is the following: since only teachers can approach young boys without hindrance, we, the lovers, should become teachers and persuade ourselves that it is out of the love of teaching that we come to them. And if, in so doing, lovers deceive the boys' desire to know, no one will be disturbed, since it is fine to be deceived for a noble cause. Pausanias' lover is thus an outlaw who makes use of the law to his own advantage.

As for Alcibiades, his startling entry into Agathon's house is in itself a kind of scandal, one that is later confirmed when he upsets the laws that up to then had governed the assembly of symposiasts, for Alcibiades is the only one in the group to speak words of love, not make a speech *about* love. The man in love speaks through him, and this position places him outside the law. This does not make him any less a slave, and this is why he is enraged at Socrates, whom he would like in turn to reduce to the slavery of amorous dependence.

It is clear that lovers' position outside the law does not free them from constraint. As everyone knows, if it is love, and not desire, that is the law between lovers, it is "a heart for a heart, a tooth for a tooth," in other words, the law of the talon, dual retaliation in pure form. This complex relation of love to the law—and especially to the law of desire associated with the prohibition of incest—is a constant theme in literature, the basis of the fatal nature of love. When, for example, we read *Tristan and Isolde*, *Romeo and Juliet*, or Kleist's *Penthesilea*, we find the same challenge and the same drama. Tristan and Isolde love one another although she is the wife of Tristan's adoptive father; the love-potion proves stronger than the prohibition of incest. As for Romeo and Juliet, their indissoluble bond is affirmed despite the legendary opposition of their clans, the Montagues and the Capulets. Finally, the divine law of the Amazons does not prevent their queen, Penthesilea from choosing Achilles on the basis of a maternal command. In each case, the fate of the lovers is the same: Tristan is exiled and Isolde given over to the lepers, Romeo is banished, Penthesilea placed outside the law and rejected by her tribe. All cross the boundary that Lacan calls "the between-two-deaths"—death, in the absence of the law, offering them the only place where they can be together again.

Shakespeare's Juliet describes in the most explicit terms this transgression of the law to which love aspires. She reveals that what love contests is nothing other than the law of the signifier as such and the central function of the Name of the Father in it:

O Romeo, Romeo, wherefore art thou Romeo?
Deny thy father and refuse thy name;
Or, if thou wilt not, be but sworn my love,
And I'll no longer be a Capulet.
. . . .
'Tis but thy name that is my enemy;
Thou art thyself, though not a Montague.
. . . .

> .... O, be some other name!
> What's in a name? That which we call a rose
> By any other name would smell as sweet.
> ....
> .... Romeo, doff thy name,
> And for that name which is no part of thee,
> Take all myself. [II. ii. 33–49]

There could be no better expression of the wish that love would make the rule in place of the law of castration: deny your father and take *all* myself in place of your name. The rejection of the law of castration is called for in the name of another law, one that is more strong, more real, since it is the being of Romeo that Juliet wants (like the perfume of the rose), and the sacrifice of his name. Reciprocally—love, Lacan says, is reciprocal—it would be Juliet's being-woman that Romeo would take. Love here serves as a denial of the *not-all* that characterizes the feminine position. In her love, Juliet wants *not to be not-all* subject to the signifying law of castration, that is, to be *not at all* subject to it; in other words, she wants, like Romeo, to be situated under the regime of the exception, of the only one—here, the only couple—to escape the Law: $\exists x, \overline{\Phi x}$.

But this function of love reveals its paradox. As we have seen, the exception that it calls for, far from opposing the Law, has the effect of truly founding it. Moreover, from the logical point of view, we cannot write $\exists x, \overline{\Phi x}$ unless Φx is given at the outset. In the myth of *Totem and Taboo* (Freud 1912a), it is the sons, united by their common castration, who designate the primal father as outside the law. In other words, we can imagine a position outside the law only with regard to the Law. It must therefore be acknowledged that the Law is the basis of love, just as the signifier is the basis of the idea of being. Thus love cannot object to castration and to the feminine not-all except insofar as it originates in our submission to this limit: it is the ordinariness of castration that makes love extraordinary.

In this sense, we may note that the private law that love would like to see prevail over the common law always bears a trace of the latter. The move to escape the law is no sooner declared than it inevitably tends to legalize itself. In the extreme cases of pure romantic passion presented by the works of literature we have cited, death performs the limiting function that normally falls to castration, or (as in some novels by Marguerite Duras) more or less blatant madness does so. But, most often, love eventually comes down to a contract, be it the sadomasochistic contract or that of marriage.

Let us now look at the question of love within the analytic experience, and at the ways its role there has been theorized. It is striking that Freud's work, in its development, can be analyzed as an attempt to "legalize" love, in particular transference love. What Freud does is to try to reduce it, through interpretation, to an expression of repressed sexual desire. But this attempt fails, although Freud, between 1904 and 1920, completely changed his view of the dialectic between the sexual drive and love. For, in the course of Freud's work, there are two successive, and diametrically opposed, theories of the relations between love and the drive.

In the *Three Essays* (1905a), the emphasis is on the disjunction between the partial drives and love. On the one side there are the sexual drives, partial and partializing, the object of which is merely an ersatz, in itself indifferent and interchangeable, and on the other side there is the current of love, defined by its global aim and its overvaluation of a determinate object. The key term in this initial construction is *autoerotism*. In the autoerotic phase, the object of the drive and the love object emerge as such, in the form of the lost breast for the drive and, for love, as the global representation of the forbidden mother. The split is evident in the papers devoted to the psychology of love (1910a, 1912c), where Freud posits the notion of a generalized psychic impotence. This notion implies, for both the register of sexual desire and that of love, the need for an unsatisfaction that the subject carefully maintains. Freud is, however, unable to shed further light on this discovery, insofar as he remains attached to the concept of the satisfaction of need, his model being the satiated baby falling asleep on its mother's breast. Not having discerned in this "unsatisfaction" the call to a beyond of satisfaction, that is, the register of what Lacan terms *jouissance*, he is unable to go further with his reflections.

The second Freudian theory of love and the drive appears in 1920, in the study *Beyond the Pleasure Principle*. It is diametrically opposed to the first theory, since, now, the notion of the sexual drive has been revised according to the model of love: the two terms, previously quite distinct, are combined in the concept of Eros. We can assess the contrast between the two approaches by tracing Freud's earlier use of the Platonic concept of Eros in the successive prefaces and in the introduction to Chapter 1 of the *Three Essays*: serving as a foil in 1905, it becomes the master reference in 1920. But before examining the nature of this new theory, we must look at its antecedents and at the causes of the radical change. What are the turning points in Freud's work between 1905 and 1920? Let us look at the introduction of the notion of narcissism (1914) and then at two highly contradictory texts on transference love (1912b, 1915b).

The notion of narcissism—promoting a new object, the ego—is not intended merely to clarify the problematics of paraphrenia. It also seeks to resolve the split between love and the sexual drive. The ego now becomes the mediator between the object of the sexual drive and the object of romantic choice, between the lost breast and the forbidden mother. It thus establishes, between the sexual drive and love, a sort of relation of connected vessels: it unifies drive fragmentation and absorbs the representation of the mother. This resolution becomes all the more important for Freud in that, when we read his two consecutive papers on transference, we sense how within his very practice as a psychoanalyst he finds himself increasingly confronted with a fundamental obstacle, the love that bursts forth in the transference.

In 1912, Freud still holds to a simple principle: transference love is an expression of repressed sexual desire, a repetition. In this conception, the transference can be resolved by analytic interpretation that eliminates the resistance. But in 1915 Freud has to agree that this principle of interpretation is ineffective and that transference love includes a measure of the real that is irreducible and uninterpretable. When we tell a patient that his love for us is merely the disguised repetition of a repressed sexual desire, we are not telling the entire truth. Transference love cannot, therefore, be reduced entirely to a process of the sexual drive. But Freud does not know what to do with this irreducible part that makes the love *not-all sexual*, since he wants to pursue the idea of a confusion of love and the drive, and the concept of the transference as a repetition.

In *Beyond the Pleasure Principle* his effort culminates in a theory that combines love and drive under the notion of Eros and that is based not on autoerotism but on narcissism. In this context, the sexual drive is redefined as a unificatory process (not a partializing one) opposed to the fragmentation of the death drive, in the same way as love is opposed to hate. As for transference love, its uninterpretable part is now relegated to the "negative therapeutic reaction" of primary masochism, indeed of a demonic orientation of life. We may note in addition that, in the same movement, the introduction of the notion of narcissism also has the effect of erasing the indecisive aspect of the term *overestimation*, initially used by Freud to characterize romantic object choice, and of substituting *idealization*; between these two terms the entire difference between a metaphor and an imaginary formation is consigned to oblivion.

The trajectory followed by Lacan, and its culmination in the form of non-culmination, once again invites us to restore the truth of the early Freud. Lacan also has two consecutive notions of the relation between transference love and the sexual drive, but this succession goes in the opposite direction to that of Freud. For Lacan began by identifying transference and repetition; then, with his Seminar on *Transference* (1960–1961), he made an increasingly sharp distinction between these terms, to the point where he gave a Seminar on *L'Insu-que sait de l'Une bévue* (1976–1977; see note 2 above). These two concepts do not have the same theoretical reference points. Whereas, in the former, the reference point is the phallus, and the formula for love is that love gives what it does not have, the latter takes into account the reflections in *Encore* on the feminine position and refers to the signifier of lack in the Other, $S(\cancel{A})$. The result is a new formula for love: love is poetry. This reference to poetry and the meaningless metaphor that characterizes it is a clear invitation to reexamine the entire problematics of interpretation in psychoanalysis. Lacan, for his part, never really ventured to do so, feeling that he was "not enough of a poat [*poâte*]." This lowercase *a* inserted in the function of the poet indicates that Lacan saw the future of interpretation as lying with *objet a* and the cut, instead of with poetry and the hole in meaning. In other words, when it came to love, Lacan thought that he had to emphasize the limit, the (*a*) wall, more than the gulf that evokes it, S($\cancel{A}$).

There is perhaps no better example of such an interpretation than that of Socrates to Alcibiades at the end of the *Symposium*. Socrates, too, was not enough of a "poat." While admiring Agathon's verbal skills, he himself is content to create a vacuum, that is, not to substantify the love object. He has Diotima say that love serves to fill a void; that is why he, Socrates, refuses to be a love object, a stop-gap—which does not imply that he refuses to love. Socrates' knowledge concerning love is this: he knows that there is literally nothing to know about love, and that anything that pretends to fill this void is mere deception. Thus, when Alcibiades wants to force him to produce the *agalma*, that miracle that he thinks he has found within Socrates, and that, for him, is the very mark of the power of love, Socrates can only decline his proposition. In offering me the beauty of your body in exchange for the improbable beauty that you have discerned in me, he says to him in effect, you are suggesting a fools' exchange, the exchange of copper for gold. Yet the real dupe here is Alcibiades. For, in trying to dupe Socrates, he fails to recognize his own illusion, an illusion that impels him to this attempt at seduction. For he truly thinks that Socrates has something to give him, that *agalma*-fetish whose omnipotence he expects, the very root of the knowledge he ascribes to Socrates. But,

Socrates replies, "You must look more carefully, my good man, lest I remain hidden from you, I who am nothing" (219a, translation modified). At this point, Socrates is in some sense referring to the (*a*) wall: he renders himself absent, a mere hollow, having no power or function except that of resonating with the desire of his interlocutor.

As for the object, Socrates separates himself from it, referring Alcibiades to Agathon as the source of the *agalma* that Alcibiades had tried to take from him. The meaning of the name "Agathon" in Greek catches our attention.[3] Socrates is thereby indicating to Alcibiades that the object of his fantasy, the object that caused his seductive speech, is just a "treasure" in the most banal sense of the term: it is not only the treasure of Socrates, to the extent that Agathon is the latter's sweetheart, but it is also the treasure whose name means "riches". Socrates' final message is thus the following: that which makes you desire and sets a limit to the span of your love is wealth, the plenum, and not poverty, the void that I am. Very well! If you want wealth, here it is at my side. With these words, Socrates unlinks the *objet a* to which the fantasy gives substance from the void of S($\cancel{A}$) that this object tries to fill—that void that, for Socrates, constitutes the true cause of love and of love-talk, and that he strives to incarnate by rendering himself absent.

---

3. Translator's note : the name means "good" in Greek. In the following sentence, "treasure" is a somewhat loose translation of the Greek word here transliterated as *agalma*.

15

From the Masquerade to Poetry

The feminine position that we have outlined in the preceding chapters serves as a metaphor of the Other insofar as the latter is impossible to connect with. A woman thus remains, as woman, radically beyond the reach of the subject, including the subject who lines up with the feminine position. To put it more precisely, femininity cannot be reached or designated except as a semblance. To be a woman is, whether one wants to or not, to pretend to be a woman. This relation to semblance is not, as one might too quickly conclude, coquetry or a lie. It is first and foremost a matter of structure, since it is language that situates woman outside of what can be said. How can a woman accommodate herself to this position that, having no signifiable essence, can be affirmed only in artifice? How can femininity be made recognizable through a semblance that, in itself, is not feminine?

A woman is thus bound to realize that "[i]t is for that which she is not that she wishes to be desired as well as loved" (Lacan 1958a, p. 290). On this point, as before on the question of the *jouissance* of the Other, it is once again the examination of a male perversion that will enlighten us. For looking at transvestism is the best way to explain the connection between femininity and semblance. To illustrate it, I have chosen the case of the Abbé de Choisy (1973; see also Reynes 1983), whose *Memoirs*, which have some literary merit, are of great interest for psychoanalysis.

A strange man, this Abbé François-Timoléon de Choisy, who lived from 1644 to 1724, in the age of Louis XIII and Louis XIV, leading with impunity (at least from the legal standpoint) the life of a priest disguised as a woman. He could claim that he was not an exception, in that he had as his sidekick and close friend the illustrious brother of Louis XIII, "Monsieur," the most effeminate man in the kingdom and one who liked nothing more than to go about dressed as a woman. As it happened, the mother of the Abbé had played a role in the upbringing—which was, to say the least, peculiar—of Monsieur, who, from earliest childhood, had been taught to act like a girl, with the result that he became completely feminized and easily surrendered the throne to Louis XIV. The project, conceived and organized by the boy's own mother and supported by Mazarin, was a complete success: Louis became King of France, while Philippe, Monsieur, was content to rule over an imaginary feminine kingdom.

Madame de Choisy was an active collaborator in this scenario and imparted the same habits to her son, so that he could be in a better position to woo Monsieur. This mother was a woman of importance. She had started out as one of the *précieuses*, going by the name of Clélie or Charite, later becoming a first-class schemer, although she eventually lost her influence at court. After taking part in the feminization of Monsieur, she got herself appointed as the private tutor of the young Louis XIV and participated in all the intrigues at court, where she was soon respected, feared, and betrayed. She kept up a regular correspondence with a number of kings, queens, and princesses in different European countries, even with the Sultana of Istambul. Living in high style and giving sumptuous parties, she was also the go-between for illicit love affairs at court. She herself does not seem to have had any liaisons, no doubt preferring, in the typical style of a hysteric, to love by proxy. In contrast, almost nothing is known of the father of François-Timoléon, except that he was absent. A high-level official in the service of the King, he was constantly called away on missions abroad or far from Paris. His brief sojourns in the conjugal home were nevertheless enough for him to give his wife two boys and five girls, all older than François-Timoléon by some years. The latter was, in fact, a late-coming child, his mother being over forty years old at the time of his birth.

Starting from when he was very young, Madame de Choisy dressed him as a girl. When he was five or six, she made him wear laced corsets to lift his chest and slim his waist; she also, among other things, applied lotions intended to keep facial hair from growing. The boy continued this way until adulthood, when, no doubt guided by the signifier more than by religious vocation, he decided to take the robe of priesthood. But a priest's robe could not content someone used to frills and flounces. The Abbé relates, in his *Memoirs*, how within a few months he gradually modified his austere garments to the point where he was dressed just like a woman, asking (and obtaining) permission to be called "Madame." His parish priest was among the first to adopt this usage. The Abbé's greatest pleasure was to hear himself called a beautiful woman and to be loved as one. The love that he wanted to evoke by his beauty was not different from the love of God that, as a priest, he was supposed to foster. It was, in effect, a true *adoration*, in which his attire was just the sign of his absolute alterity:

> When I was at a ball or the theatre, wearing my beautiful *robes de chambre*, diamonds, and patches, and heard people murmur near me, 'There is a lovely woman,' I experienced an inward glow of pleasure which is incomparable, it is so strong. Ambition, riches, even love do not equal it, because we always love ourselves more deeply than we love others. [p. 30]

So here we have him, now the Abbé at Saint Médard, dressed as a woman and performing the traditional woman's task of taking up the collection at Mass. He is very good at it. He relates his adventures with as much self-satisfaction as he must have experienced in appearing in the world. The many anecdotes he tells are striking for the meticulous insistence with which, for pages on end, he describes his clothing, his jewelry, his hairdo, and everything that he offers to the gaze of his male and female adorers. And he takes advantage of this, since he has an active love life in which he uses the affectionate familiarities deployed by women to seduce innocent girls and get into their beds without having to conquer them, thereby enjoying the twofold consent, as it were, of his mistresses. Thus the young Charlotte, one of his first lasting liaisons, confides: "I am not constrained, . . . as I would be with a man; all I see is a lovely woman, and why should I stop myself from loving her? What an advantage women's clothes give you! The heart of a man is there, which has its effect on us, and on the other hand the charms of femininity transport us and quite disarm us" (p. 36).

This kind of declaration can only reinforce our hero in his certainty that charm is all on the side of the "fair sex." For his part, he is less in love with his mistresses than he is with himself—or should we say "herself"? Freud (1914) would no doubt find here evidence for the especially active narcissism that he considers typical of femininity. We may note, however, that if the Abbé de Choisy loves himself more than he loves his girlfriends, the object of his love is valued only for the alterity that is ascribed to it: he loves himself insofar as this feminized "himself" is the Other. He is, in truth, the first to be seduced by the charm of the feminine image that he deploys.

But he pushes the fantasy even further, since, having obtained the love of the young Charlotte, he persuades her to adopt the hairstyle and clothing of a boy. "Thus," he tells us, "I had the delight of often having Charlotte dressed as a boy, and, as I was dressed as a woman, it was a true marriage" (p. 39, translation modified). In short, there is nothing more genuine than the mask, or rather the exchange of roles in which each of the partners becomes the Other. The logic of the Abbé de Choisy thus goes a bit further than that of a Chevalier d'Eon, for whom dressing as a woman is the necessary condition for proving that he is a man. Choisy wants to believe, and give others to believe, only what the eyes behold, namely the feminine appearance, while the Chevalier d'Eon wants to demonstrate that sex has nothing to do with what can be seen. For the former, appearance is the only genuine thing; for the latter, it is entirely deceptive, to the point where he rejects even the appearance of being a man. This difference is enough to justify us in attributing a feminine position to Choisy, who is a woman because outward appearance constitutes sexual difference, and a masculine position to the

Chevalier d'Eon, who is a man because he cannot believe what he sees.

Having thus exchanged clothes with his mistress Charlotte—clothes make the woman as well as the man—the Abbé de Choisy likes to be seen in bed with the woman he calls his dear husband. He even holds a private party in which he organizes a simulated marriage ceremony with his partner. Always playing on the fact that, for his public, he is supposed to be a trickster, he likes to assemble a group of people around his bedside. There, lying with his girlfriend, he pretends to kiss her the way a big sister would kiss her little sister, or a mother her daughter, while, under the blankets, he caresses her much more intimately. The gaze of the audience clearly multiplies his pleasure tenfold, especially the aspect of deceiving the public eye. His sexual enjoyment comes from seeing the other duped by The woman, a *jouissance* that, for him, is closely connected with a knowledge, since he has known all along that femininity is merely a *trompe l'oeil*.[1] And it is only by surprising the gaze of the other who is the victim of this *trompe l'oeil* that he can free himself from it, that is, not take himself completely for The woman as he would do if he would do if he were psychotic.

What is the Abbé de Choisy defying in this way? Is it the other, whom he is pushing to the point where he will unmask him as a man? Isn't it rather the real of femininity that he is provoking? He confides at one point that one would never guess that he is not a woman. This is the confession of his perversion at the most structural level. For it indicates that what matters for him is not to prove that he could not be

---

1. Translator's note: a *trompe l'oeil* is an optical illusion, literally something that "deceives the eye."

unmasked as the man he really is, but, more subtly, that it is impossible to unmask woman as such. Why? Because she is *only mask*, or at any rate this is what he is trying to show. A dialogue that takes place the first time he has people to dinner dressed as a woman reveals the immutability of the feminine mask for him.

> "From now on," Madame d'Usson said to me, "I shall call you 'Madame.'" She turned me round before the curé, saying to him: "Is this not a lovely woman?"
>
> "That is true," he said, "but she is in masquerade."
>
> "No, monsieur," I said to him, "no; in the future I shall not dress otherwise." [p. 29]

His disavowal is intended to affirm the identity between the mask and the being of a woman.

Thus Choisy, like the masochist, seeks to adopt the feminine position. The difference between them is that the masochist wants to take possession of the *jouissance*, that is, the *body*, that he ascribes to the woman, whereas the Abbé de Choisy wants to have ascribed to him the *love* that she inspires, that is, the *semblance* that gives rise to it. Femininity is loved only for its deceptive appearance: this is what he aims to prove. Thus he flaunts himself as a deceiver, the extreme point of his fantasy being that, were he unmasked—that is, recognized as a deceiver—the other would be all the more seduced and he himself all the more loved.

His novella *The Marquise-Marquis of Banneville* (in Choisy 1973, pp. 109–129) illustrates this project. This is the story of a boy dressed as a girl (the marquise), who falls in love, the way a woman does, with a young marquis who, on the wedding night, turns out to be a deceiver as well: he is a girl disguised as a boy. This motif of mutual deception, where the reciprocity is confessed at the moment when the masks are dropped, is obviously reminiscent of Allais' story of the lovers at the Opera ball, a story that Lacan especially valued. But while Allais' narrative ends in a cry of horror, the Abbé's novella makes the moment of the revelation of the protagonists' real sex one of happiness, a happiness that links up seamlessly with the masquerade that precedes it. This is not surprising, since the author's perverse logic intends literally to scotomize any discovery of castration.

Two episodes in the novella deserve to be singled out: the meeting of the false marquise and the false marquis, and the dialogue in which the marquise attempts to win the marquis' hand. In both cases, the dimension of deceit, foregrounded as such, is apparent. Thus, when the marquise (really a boy who has been dressed in women's clothes since childhood) sees the marquis for the first time during a play at the theater, she finds him all the more attractive as a boy because he is wearing a very pretty doublet, diamond earrings, and three or four artificial beauty spots on his face: "'Madame,' she said to the Comtesse, 'that is a handsome young man there.' 'That is true,' said the Comtesse, 'but he is a dandy, and that does not suit a man. Why does he not dress as a girl?'" (p. 116, translation modified). It turns out at the end of the story that this boy, so appealingly feminized, *is* really a girl in disguise. But the reality is basically unimportant, since it is the cross-dressing itself that arouses the desire of out two heroes. Choisy has the marquise say this explicitly in the scene in which the couple become engaged to marry. The marquis protests that his interlocutor knows him only by his outward appearance, which can be deceiving. The marquise immediately replies that that is just what she likes about it. Thus her love will not be disappointed when she finds out the extent of the deception that her friend admits indirectly here.

This praise of deception, to which Choisy devotes his life as well as his work, is typical of a perverse position. Femininity is its object but appears only as caricature. Here we must distinguish between two types of pretense: *trompe l'oeil*, illustrated by the Abbé de Choisy, and masquerade, in which femininity is recognized. Once again the perverse split differs from the division entailed by the feminine position. Though passing as a woman, or rather as a semblance of a woman, Choisy is not less a man; he simply cuts off communication between these two aspects of his subjectivity. His life is nothing but the realization of this divide. Thus he declares, at the beginning of his *Memoirs*, that his existence has consisted of a perpetual oscillation between play and disguise: either he was pretending to be a woman, or he was playing and became a man again, and this to the point of ruin. A fulfilled woman or a ruined man—these are the terms of his subjective split.

It is not without interest, in this regard, to note that the considerable fortune of the Choisy family came from Jean de Choisy, the grandfather of our Abbé, who had managed to seduce the finance minister of Henri III through a masquerade. Though he was a renowned chess player, he had let himself be beaten by this minister, who then took him to the royal court, where he began a brilliant career. Thus the good fortune of the Choisy name was associated with the deception of a man who let himself lose at play. But, inevitably, what had been won would be lost by succeeding generations; Madame de Choisy and her son, great gamblers both, devoted themselves to so doing.

The perverse split of the Abbé de Choisy, like that of the masochist we looked at above, is eminently subjective. It is a split internal to the subject, $, whereas the feminine division operates between $ and a non-subjectivizable "surplus." This difference orients two pursuits that do not overlap: the pervert reaches for this extra-subjective feminine element and fails, and the woman tries to escape this extra part and to subjectivize it.

Thus we may contrast with the logic of the transvestite the lessons to be learned from a famous, yet seldom read, paper by Joan Rivière on "Womanliness as a masquerade." This short article is absolutely sensational, all the more so because, published in 1929, it preceded Freud's two great contributions: "Female sexuality" (1931) and "Femininity" (1933). Rivière announces her thesis at the outset: "[W]omen who wish for masculinity may put on a mask of womanliness to avert anxiety and the retribution feared from men" (p. 303). Pretending to be a woman, or putting on the appearance of one, can be an indirect way of affirming one's masculinity. Now, this feminine masculinity, the author explains, cannot be understood as simply the bisexuality inherent in all men and women; it is not an innate tendency but the result of conflict, and especially of a reaction against anxiety. Is femininity, therefore, just a defense against anxiety, placed, like a veil, over a fundamental masculine monosexuality?

The author gives a case example of what she calls "a particular type of intellectual woman" (p. 303), that is, one of those women who seem to excel in all domains, presenting the image of consummate femininity: brilliant in their professions, good wives, excellent mothers, and perfect housekeepers all at the same time. The woman whose problems

Rivière sets forth has a thriving career as a militant propagandist while being equally successful in marriage and homemaking. Everything would be perfect, except that she suffers from a symptom that appears each time she has to speak in public, something her profession often obliges her to do. Despite her intellectual accomplishments and her ability as a public speaker and discussion leader, she is gripped by fear on the night after every lecture, worried about having committed a blunder, and urgently in need of reassurance. She therefore needs to seek compulsively for attention from men whom she meets at the end of meetings in which she has played the leading role. She is less interested in having these men compliment her on her presentation than on eliciting sexual desire from them. Her analysis, moreover, shows that she approaches a particular type of man, someone who serves as a substitute for her father, who is also an intellectual.

The analysis also reveals, in its initial phase of explanation, that the young woman identifies with her father through her work but at the same time is in competition with him. While giving her lectures, she feels superior to the men who represent the father, but she seeks their favors immediately afterwards. Rivière explains this ambivalence by positing that, in her lectures, the patient is exhibiting the phallus that she stole from her father, but later, fearing paternal vengeance, offers herself to him sexually in order to escape punishment. In short, she first brandishes the phallus and then disguises herself as a castrated woman. This interpretation is confirmed by the patient's fantasies from childhood and by dreams experienced in the course of the analysis. For this woman, then, femininity is worn as a mask in order to camouflage her masculinity and to avoid reprisal on the part of men who might feel robbed of their attributes. Her behavior is like that of "a thief [who] will turn out his pockets and ask to be searched to prove that he has not the stolen goods" (p. 306).

But here a question arises: if femininity can function as a mask concealing a male identification (the phallic position), how can we distinguish between true femininity and disguise? The author goes as far as to declare that no such difference exists, that "whether radical or superficial, they are the same thing" (p. 306). The patient's problem is thus not that her femininity is false but that she uses it as a defense against anxiety instead of as a primary way of achieving *jouissance*. Rivière cites other cases in support of her argument. She describes a very capable housewife who, though she is also skilled at more typically male endeavors, feels constrained to act stupid in her dealings with craftsmen, as if she did not know how the job should be done. Then there is the case of a female university lecturer, who, when she has to lecture to colleagues, dresses in an especially feminine way and adopts a "flippant and joking" tone that is not appreciated by her audience; Rivière notes that this patient "has to treat the situation of displaying her masculinity to men as a 'game,' as something *not real*, as a 'joke'" (p. 308).

The author then returns to the original case and adds several details that reveal the full extent of the notion of feminine masquerade. She reports that her patient's attitude toward other women is just as problematic as her relations with men, for she feels that she is constantly competing with women, especially when they are pretty or have intellectual pretensions. She is not comfortable unless she can feel superior. Thus her achievements as a homemaker and as a professional reflect her attempt to outdo her mother. This is the reverse side of her Oedipus complex: behind the relation to her father and other bearers of the phallus lies her relation to her mother with all its connotations of rivalry and hate. This opens up a new perspective on the case, one that entails a revision of the interpretation that the author has been offering up to this point.

For it appears that, if this woman wants to be recognized as possessing the paternal phallus and then to win forgiveness with a show of femininity, this is because she wants to be able to restore what she feels she has stolen—to restore it to her mother. She identifies with her father and takes on his male role and insignia only in order to put them at the disposal of her mother. Always ready to be of service to women weaker than herself, the patient gets "a lavish return in the form of gratitude and 'recognition'" (p. 310). Thus this woman's symptom goes beyond a need to avoid retribution from the men whose position she is taking; what she is seeking is recognition from her mother.

The mechanism underlying this symptom thus has two phases. The patient must first be recognized as possessing the phallus, in order then to be able to be separated from it. When reduced to its structure, does the process still deserve to be called a symptom? The question needs to be asked, since this structure seems to me to correspond to the demand that emanates from the feminine position as such. A twofold recognition is at issue, the first, recognition of the possession of the phallus, serving only to establish the second. The woman must have the phallus, or rather give the illusion of having it, so that she can then present herself as giving what she does not have and thereby win recognition as a woman. Between these two phases there occurs the period of anxiety, in which her fear is not so much that she will lose the phallus as that she will be perceived as the true possessor of it. This woman's ultimate goal is, therefore, to be recognized as not having the phallus. But she can achieve this goal only indirectly: in order to be recognized as not having it, she has to pass through a phase in which she pretends to have it. And, after all, this first phase is no less deceptive than what follows, since the phallus is, fundamentally, the mask *par excellence*, the veil thrown over the unnamable hole.

Here we have, in the form of two consecutive phases, what Lacan's table of sexuation notates as the two equations governing the feminine position: (1) $\overline{\exists x}$, $\overline{\Phi x}$; (2) $\forall x$, Φx.

The first phase: she does not exist if she does not have it; she does not exist as a woman if she does not subject herself to the phallic function. The second phase: but she is not-all subject to this function. The formation of the neurotic symptom in Joan Rivière's case study stems from the fact that the patient can see this "not-all" only as an injury inflicted on her by the other woman or as a gift that she can grant to men. Hence she has the idea that she can give back the phallus and in so doing win recognition of her femininity. She stages a conception of femininity as sacrifice. The anxiety she avoids in this way is more archaic than her fear of her father's vengeance, and Rivière is quite right to relate it to the patient's mother: "But the task of guarding herself against the woman's retribution is harder than with the man; her efforts to placate and make reparation by restoring and using the penis in the mother's service were never enough; this device was worked to death, and sometimes it even worked her to death" (p. 311).

The repetition loops back upon itself. Once she is acknowledged not to have the phallus, she has to give it to her mother and to other women, so that they do not seem to be castrated. Why does the mother have to be phallicized? Isn't it because, beyond castration, this patient's anxiety stems from the horror of woman, of that position in which a woman, starting with the mother, has to define herself outside of any reference to the phallus? Her only response to this fundamental anxiety is the desire to be castrated and recognized as such. Castration keeps her from having to confront a "purely feminine" position in which, absent castration, she would be quite simply impossible to recognize as a subject. The division that the masquerade produces between two polarities—non-castrated and castrated—seems to mask the fundamental division that Lacan designates in his formula of the not-all.

Having come to the end of our exploration of the problematics of femininity, we can now return to our initial question and look at the answers that analytic experience provides. What does a woman want? We have examined the three forms that a distinctively feminine wish can take: identity and the trait it fixes on, the Oedipus and the symbolic function of the paternal agency, and sexuality accompanied by the splitting of *jouissance*.

The first theme we discerned in Freud's reflections on femininity is that of a *defective identity*. The differentiation inscribed on the psychic level is anything but a differentiation between two sexes as such. Since the phallus functions as the sole reference point, femininity can posited not as a given but only as an uncertain process of becoming. We have seen that, for Freud, this becoming oscillates between becoming-mother and becoming-passive, and that it is conditioned by two essential polarities, penis envy and narcissism. Having no identity of her own to start with, a woman is constantly in danger of fetishizing the penis as the founding sign of the other's identity, or of developing identifications, both masculine and feminine, that teach her that a woman can grasp femininity only indirectly, through an artifice.

The feminine Oedipus complex is the second problematic that we find in Freud's work, which presents it as having an additional difficulty compared to the Oedipus of the boy. The question is to determine whether, for the girl, the relation to the father can really substitute for the initial relation to the mother. We have noted the extent to which the girl's passage from mother to father tends to be a metonymic juxtaposition as opposed to a metaphoric substitution. The problem of the feminine Oedipus thus becomes that of knowing whether there is a feminine unconscious and how far it extends. The status of the wish for a child that, according to Freud, must replace penis envy is equally uncertain and fluid: is this a metaphor or a metonymy?

Lacan, in defining the feminine position as not-all obedient to the law of the unconscious, sheds light on this uncertainty even as he confirms the fundamental ambiguity of femininity. This is the reason for the extreme ambivalence that marks the evident claim women assert with regard to the father. They demand "some of father," to be sure, and they want even more of it because there is never enough (or it is never metaphoric enough) to consign the mother to the oblivion of prehistory. Thus the hysteric is right to denounce the structural impotence of the father for his daughter; where she goes wrong is in wanting to repair it at all costs. No father will ever be enough of a father to satisfy this wish, although Freud, infatuated as he was with his belief in the all-powerful father, thought this could be expected. In fact, the destiny of femininity depends on the non-existence of this sublime father. Thus Lacan emphasizes that the feminine position is ultimately addressed to God, with the man as the fantasmatic pole. God is in no danger of descending from heaven. As for the man, it is customary for a woman to forbid herself access to him when she happens to encounter him.

Finally, a look at feminine sexuality properly speaking gives rise to a third problematic. Here, too, the development of Freud's thought ends in an impasse, and for the same reasons. The change of sexual organ (the substitution of the vagina for the clitoris) and the change in mode of satisfaction (the substitution of passivity for activity) that Freud wanted to raise to the status of metaphors seem not to go beyond metonymic connection. Lacan, in reframing this problematic as one not of metaphor but of supplement, opens out a beyond of phallic sexuality and thereby enables us to get out of the impasse. The division effected by this supplement does not take place between two organs (vagina and clitoris), nor between two drive-related grammars (activity and passivity). It has instead to do with the distinction between language and the body, the symbolic and the real. The place of an Other *jouissance* evoked by the feminine position nevertheless remains a pure conjecture for which there is only a negative formula: since woman is not-all in phallic *jouissance*, a part of her must be located elsewhere. But, being outside of language, the *jouissance* of the Other is unsubjectivizable, and hence it is the cause of an anxiety less easily mastered than castration anxiety.

Taking these three problematics together, it is clear that, if we are going to continue to examine femininity, we risk encountering, beyond the dialectic of the signifier and castration, something unsignifiable, unsubjectivizable, of which the only trace in the unconscious is in the form of the navel, the hole. Lacan's suggested notation for this hole is a veritable tour de force: S($\cancel{A}$), the signifier of the lack in the Other as locus of the symbolic, that is, the signifier of what the Other's does *not-all* say. But it is precisely this defect in symbolization that is the origin of the fear, indeed the horror, that femininity can arouse, for women as well as for men, even more than castration.

A term of Freud's, seldom used nowadays but worthy of being revived, is *anxiety neurosis*. The term takes on new meaning with regard to women because of this division that makes femininity an oscillation between castration and the hole in which no subject can be inscribed as a subject. With regard to this gap, it is clear that all the anxieties of castration and all phobic and hysteric anxieties are only barriers, protections against a more fundamental anxiety that, in itself, is not connected with either the law or castration.

Unsignifiable, unsubjectivizable, hole in the Other: all these expressions seek to define the problem of femininity as a radical lack of the unconscious, a lack of repression (since only the signifier can be repressed) and hence a defect in sexualization. It follows that if, like any speaking being, a woman wants to be recognized as a subject, she cannot fail to come up against this point of lack at which there is no longer a recognizable subject because there is no signifier to represent it. We may propose, then, that what a woman wants is for something to come in the place of this missing signifier, that a fulcrum be made available to her at precisely the point where the unconscious has left her in the lurch. This demand can take several paths.

The first is that of hysteria. The hysteric flees that which is unrepresentable in femininity. She takes refuge in the phallus and covers herself with it as with a carapace. She is, of course, quick to experience this phallic armor as a prison; at the same time, the phallic imperialism is never extensive enough, never sufficiently the master of the body, for her to be satisfied with it.

The masquerade, as described by Joan Rivière, is another path. Here the subject tends to accept herself as not phallic, but she can do so only in the form of a renunciation or surrender: she does not have it, or rather she no longer has it, because, though she had it, she voluntarily gave it up. The masquerade enacts an imaginary not-all, the representation of the castrated woman functioning there as a *sign* assuring protection against the absence of the *signifier* of femininity.

Some women seem to find in love a third possible way. The fact that these women are so eager to be loved, and, more precisely, to be told that they are loved, is explained by the subject-to-subject relation that the declaration of love tends to establish. Love evokes a subject, the subject presumed by the partner, in the place of the missing signifier of femininity. This substitution is all the easier because there is a structural identity between Woman and the Lacanian Subject. Neither, as such, exists as a signifier; they are only *represented* by a signifier for another signifier. What they *are* is never anything but the place left empty, inter-dicted, between two signifiers. The trouble is that love does not consist solely of this relation established by speech; it also includes its real aspect in which, as we have seen, it comes up against its limit. Hence there is a tendency, illustrated by courtly love, to keep to the symbolic side of love: "It [courtly love] is a highly refined way of making up for the absence of the sexual relation by pretending that *we* are the ones who are setting up an obstacle to it. . . . For the man whose lady was entirely, in the most servile sense, subject, courtly love is the only way to cope elegantly with the absence of the sexual relation" (Lacan 1972–1973, p. 69, translation modified).

There is yet another way, more difficult to discern with psychoanalytic concepts, and that is the way of creation, for creation is the production of a new signifier in the place of the one that is missing. Elsewhere (André 1985) I have proposed that all creativity is, in origin, an attempt to respond to the non-existence of The Woman. But what distinguishes this attempt is that the new signifier created by the artist does not try to fill the hole left agape by S($\cancel{A}$), but, on the contrary, to reveal it and let it operate as such. Lacan (1959–1960, p. 121) gives the example of the potter who turns a vase around the void that he hollows out in its center, just as the architect raises his walls around empty volumes. What the artist creates is perhaps less the wall, which he offers to us as a *trompe l'oeil*, than it is the void sculpted by the wall. Maurice Blanchot explores this problematic in the domain of literature.

The issue is especially important in regard to femininity: women, as everyone knows, have a special relation to creativity because they can give birth. It is if they alone had the power to create directly, without having to make the effort of sublimation. For why should we not consider giving birth an authentic creation? The man's role here is just that of an instrument, like the painter's brush (*pinceau*).[2] Must we really follow Freud when he asserts the equivalence, for a woman, of the baby and the penis? Isn't the baby first of all an attempt to produce a signifier to take the place of S($\cancel{A}$) before settling for its phallic signification? Be that as it may, it seems that we are dealing here with a failure at creation, in the sense that the new signifier that is brought to light represents not woman as *woman* but woman as *mother*.

---

2. In this context, it is delightful to note the etymology of the word *pinceau*. Translator's note: *pinceau* is etymologically related to "penis."

•

Now that these brushstrokes have painted the picture of the issue in question, what can we say about the role of psychoanalysis in exploring what a woman wants? We have already observed how this examination marks the origin of psychoanalysis as a clinical practice. Freud invented the psychoanalyst as a new signifier in response to the appeals addressed to him by his hysterics. *What does a woman want?— A psychoanalyst, replies Freud.* We must consider what this response implies and assess whether it is valid as a response, and under what conditions.

Up to now I have been arguing that the feminine position, since it is not-all obedient to the signifying law of castration, can be understood as that of a lack in the unconscious, and hence that what a woman wants above all is to receive a supplement to her unconscious. We could use these terms to analyze the situation in which Freud found himself with his first hysterics: Isn't the demand for interpretation that a woman submits to the analyst primarily a demand for an unconscious? The case of Emmy von N. can be reread in this light, since we found in this patient's discourse associative chains that all led to the navel, the unnamable. There can be no question that, in making himself a psychoanalyst and putting analytic interpretation into practice, Freud supplied an unconscious. Thus clinical psychoanalysis was born, and it has had brilliant results . . . up to a certain point. For it is clear that psychoanalysis has left untouched the core of hysteria and the enigma of feminine sexuality, as well as the nature of transference love.

This fact led Freud to conclude that, with his women patients, he had reached the bedrock of penis envy. But these patients retorted that it was he who was the obstacle, and perhaps they were not entirely wrong. The reply of Freud, as psychoanalyst, was to give the woman a partner who tried to reduce her discourse to repressed contents, to argue that this repressed material was sexual in nature, and then to regard this sexuality as structured by the phallus and the castration complex. Now, a hundred years later, we can examine the balance sheet of clinical psychoanalysis. The system of interpretation that I have just very broadly sketched does, to be sure, work, and gets definite results, but only in the context of repressed material. Once we leave this context, we come up against something that is impossible to interpret (and this is why Freud did not recommend psychoanalysis for psychotics).

Now, if femininity is such an enigma, and if Freud failed to penetrate its secret, isn't this precisely because it confronts us with something other than the repressed? And if The woman does not exist, to use Lacan's formula, if the signifier of femininity is missing, it follows that femininity is not part of the repressed; something about it is impossible to repress. To use the distinction made by Lacan in his Seminar on *The Four Fundamental Concepts of Psychoanalysis* (1964, p. 27), I would argue that femininity has to do not with repression but with censorship. Freud, ultimately, kept on *repressing femininity* and thereby in trying to sexualize it, in the phallic sense of this term. This bias led him, in 1931 and 1933, to come up against a veritable wall that he described as an unshakable feminine frigidity. But what if this frigidity was just a means, for certain women, to show that feminine sexuality contains an aspect of *jouissance* that stubbornly resists sexualization?

Lacan takes into account not only repression but also censorship. The signifier that he notates as $S(\cancel{A})$ indicates that the unconscious has a limit, that it does not say all—in other words, that all is not repressed or sexualized. Femininity, for Lacan, is not repressible unless it takes the path of masquerade. An examination of femininity entails consideration of something uninterpretable, at least in the Freudian sense of interpretation. But is there another mode of interpretation than that of sexual meaning?

On the basis of this hole that is written $S(\cancel{A})$, that is, the non-existence of a signifier of the female genital, the psychoanalyst's problem becomes that of his non-knowledge, or rather of the knowledge that makes him know that he does not know. When a woman asks for a supplement to her unconscious, he is obliged to know that there is no positive response to this wish, since the Other, as locus of the signifier, is not equipped for such a response. How can he proceed in such a way that this deficiency will not turn into an impasse? How can he bring into play the lack of a signifier as an outcome, not a standstill? Lacan himself, during the last years of his Seminar, struggled to come up with the *new signifier* that would remedy the void left by $S(\cancel{A})$ but had to admit that he was not getting anywhere: "It happens that I've had occasion to say, along with the famous painter, *I don't seek; I find.* At the point where I'm at now, I seek more than I find. In other words, I'm going around in circles" (1977, p. 7). Hence his scandalous suggestion that psychoanalysis is a *fraud.*

We have to take this word with a grain of salt, to be sure. It leads us back to the dialectic of semblance between deceit and masquerade. Lacan is trying to say that psychoanalysis can promise a meaning (the sexual one), but that, in the end, this meaning will not come full circle. The fraud is not so much on the part of the analyst as on the part of the signifier, of, as Lacan says, the S_1 that seems to promise S_2. If we apply this formula to our current concern, what we get is this phallic sex that seems to promise another sex. Thus ambiguity, the fundamental ability of the signifier to have a double meaning, is the root cause of our belief in femininity as the other sex.

The movement of the unconscious, the meaning it impresses on discourse, goes on its own in the direction of masquerade. The goal of analysis, therefore, would be less to grasp or localize femininity than to lead the subject to realize that this very wish to grasp and localize sustains the deception that the unconscious makes him undergo. The obscure problematic of the two sexes, of a masculine that seeks its guarantor in a feminine that is always elsewhere, is constructed on the basis of a sort of bluffing effect produced by the signifier. The phallus—the signifier designating signified-effects in general—is nothing but this message: there is something that is never so much there, symbolically, as when it is absent. One sex evokes another exactly to the extent that one signifier, S_1, by nature, always evokes another, S_2. But psychoanalysis does not have to give substance to this Other; that would be to give meaning to meaning, whereas the subject has to be made to understand that meaning is created in the signifying process itself, and that meaning has no meaning. The goal of psychoanalysis, in other words, is not to follow the movement of the unconscious, but to find a way out of that movement, that is, to cause it to change.[3]

When it comes to the production of meaning, femininity is, from this perspective, the signifier's major utopia. The analyst should not try to give it substance (whether phallic

---

3. Translator's note: In the original, *de faire en sorte que ça change*, *Ça* ("that," "it") is the French equivalent of Freud's *Es*, the id, or, more generally, the unconscious.

or extra-phallic) through interpretation; he must respond from the place where meaning has a chance to slip away. The analyst should situate the role of interpretation itself as an integral part of the signifying fraud that governs the functioning of the unconscious. But how to respond from S($\cancel{A}$) without plugging its gap? The question is all the more crucial because Freud believed absolutely in the meaning of unconscious discourse; he also believed that using his mode of interpretation will consolidate this meaning and eventually result in the impasses of femininity. How can a subject be led to realize that the request for a supplement to the unconscious presupposes a belief in and adherence to the meaning of the unconscious—the unconscious that, however does not say all?

In his Seminar of 1976–1977, Lacan suggests a way that psychoanalytic interpretation might find a way out of what I would not hesitate to call the nonsensical babbling of the unconscious. In contrast to the fraudulence of meaning, he says, there is poetry, which can accomplish the feat of making a meaning absent. He invites his audience to find in poetry what psychoanalytic interpretation can hope to be. Instead of looking for a new signifier to replace the hole left in the unconscious by the lack of S($\cancel{A}$), the analyst should respond with "an empty word," modeled on poetry, "that is a meaning-effect but also a hole-effect." Is it the case, then, that what cannot be interpreted in terms of castration might be part of the analyst's intervention in the form of a practice of non-sense? Let us leave this inquiry open, since this is nothing more than a suggestion on Lacan's part. But he immediately goes on to confide these rather moving words: "Only poetry, as I've said to you, permits interpretation. That's where, in my technique, I can no longer get it to hold. I'm not enough of a poat [*poâte*]."

So let us leave the final word to the poet. In one of his poems written in French, Rainer Maria Rilke evokes the void in which I have conjoined femininity and non-sense:

> Woman's face, closed on her sleep,
> one would say she is tasting
> some noise unlike any other
> that fills all of her.
> From her resonant sleeping body
> she draws *jouissance*
> of being one more [*encore*] murmur
> under the gaze of silence. [1972, p. 498]

References

Abraham, K. (1927). *Selected Papers*, trans. D. Bryan and A. Strachey. London: Hogarth.

Allais, A. Un drame bien parisien. *Ornicar?* 28:151–155.

André, S. (1982). La structure psychotique et l'écrit. *Quarto* 8:27–35.

——— (1985). Le symptôme et la création. *La Part de l'Oeil*, revue de l'Académie des Beaux-Arts de Bruxelles.

Andreas-Salomé, L. (1964). *The Freud Journal of Lou Andreas-Salomé*, trans. S. L. Leavy. New York: Basic Books.

——— (1980). *L'Amour du Narcissisme*. Paris: Gallimard.

Assoun, P-L. (1983). *Freud et la Femme*. Paris: Calmann-Lévy.

Bonaparte, M. (1952). *Female Sexuality*. London: Imago.

Breuer, J. and Freud, S. (1893–1895). Studies on hysteria. *Standard Edition* 2:1–306.

Choisy, F.-T., Abbé de. (1720). *The Transvestite Memoirs of the Abbé de Choisy and The Story of the Marquise–Marquis de Banneville*, trans. R.H.F. Scott. London: Owne, 1973.

Deutsch, H. (1925). The psychology of women in relation to the functions of reproduction. *International Journal of Psycho-Analysis* 6:405–418.

Dolto, F. (1983). *Sexualité Féminine*. Paris: Scarabée.

Ferenczi, S. (1952). *First Contributions to Psycho-Analysis*, trans. E. Jones. London: Hogarth.

Fliess, W. (1897). *Die Beziehungen zwischen Nase und weiblichen Geschlechtsorganen*. Leipzig and Vienna: Franz Deuticke.

Freud, S. (1887–1902). *The Origins of Psycho-Analysis. Letters to Wilhelm Fliess, Drafts, and Notes: 1887–1902*, ed. M. Bonaparte, A. Freud, and E. Kris, trans. E. Mosbacher and J. Strachey. New York: Basic Books, 1954.

———— (1893). Some points for a comparative study of organic and hysterical motor paralyses. *Standard Edition* 1:157–172.

———— (1894). The neuro-psychoses of defence. *Standard Edition* 3:43–61.

———— (1895). Project for a scientific psychology. *Standard Edition* 1:281–397.

———— (1896a). Heredity and the aetiology of the neuroses. *Standard Edition* 3:142–156.

———— (1896b). Further remarks on the neuro-psychoses of defence. *Standard Edition* 3:159–185.

———— (1896c). The aetiology of hysteria. *Standard Edition* 3:189–221.

———— (1898). Sexuality in the aetiology of the neuroses. *Standard Edition* 3:261–285.

———— (1899). Screen memories. *Standard Edition* 3:301–322.

———— (1900). The interpretation of dreams. *Standard Edition* 4–5:1–625.

———— (1905a). Three essays on the theory of sexuality. *Standard Edition* 7:125–243.

———— (1905b). Fragment of an analysis of a case of hysteria. *Standard Edition* 7:3–122.

———— (1905c). Jokes and their relation to the unconscious. *Standard Edition* 8:1–243.

———— (1907). Delusions and dreams in Jensen's *Gradiva*. *Standard Edition* 9:1–94.

——— (1908a). On the sexual theories of children. *Standard Edition* 9:207–226.

——— (1908b). Hysterican phantasies and their relation to bisexuality. *Standard Edition* 9:157–166.

——— (1909). Some general remarks on hysterical attacks. *Standard Edition* 9:227–234.

——— (1910a). A special type of choice of object made by men. *Standard Edition* 11:163–176.

——— (1910b). The psycho-analytic view of psychogenic disturbance of vision. *Standard Edition* 11:210–218.

——— (1911). Psycho-analytic notes on an autobiographical account of a case of paranoia (dementia paranoides). *Standard Edition* 12:3–79.

——— (1912a). Totem and taboo. *Standard Edition* 13:1–161.

——— (1912b). The dynamics of transference. *Standard Edition* 12:97–108.

——— (1912c). On the universal tendency to debasement in the sphere of love. *Standard Edition* 11:178–190.

——— (1913). The theme of the three caskets. *Standard Edition* 12:289–302.

——— (1914). On narcissism: an introduction. *Standard Edition* 14:69–102.

——— (1915a). Instincts and their vicissitudes. *Standard Edition* 14:111–140.

——— (1915b). Observations on transference-love. *Standard Edition* 12:157–170.

——— (1916–1917). Introductory lectures on psycho-analysis. *Standard Edition* 15–16:1–240.

——— (1918a). The taboo of virginity. *Standard Edition* 11:191–208.

——— (1918b). From the history of an infantile neurosis. *Standard Edition* 17:3–122.

——— (1919a). "A child is being beaten": a contribution to the study of the origin of sexual perversions. *Standard Edition* 17:177–204.

———— (1919b). The "uncanny." *Standard Edition* 17:217–250.

———— (1920a). The psychogenesis of a case of homosexuality in a woman. *Standard Edition* 18:146–172.

———— (1920b). Beyond the pleasure principle. *Standard Edition* 18:3–64.

———— (1922). Medusa's head. *Standard Edition* 18:273–274.

———— (1923). The infantile genital organization: an interpolation into the theory of sexuality. *Standard Edition* 19:141–148.

———— (1924a). The dissolution of the Oedipus complex. *Standard Edition* 19:173–182.

———— (1924b). The economic problem of masochism. *Standard Edition* 19:157–170.

———— (1925). Some psychical consequences of the anatomical distinction between the sexes. *Standard Edition* 19:243–258.

———— (1927). Fetishism. *Standard Edition* 21:147–158.

———— (1930). Civilisation and its discontents. *Standard Edition* 21:59–145.

———— (1931). Female sexuality. *Standard Edition* 21:223–243.

————(1933). Femininity. Lecture XXXIII, new introductory lectures. *Standard Edition* 22:112–135.

———— (1936). A disturbance of memory on the Acropolis. *Standard Edition* 22:239–250.

———— (1937). Analysis terminable and interminable. *Standard Edition* 23:211–253.

———— (1938a). Splitting of the ego in the process of defence. *Standard Edition* 23:271–278.

———— (1938b). An outline of psycho-analysis. *Standard Edition* 23:141–207.

———— (1939). Moses and monotheism: three essays. *Standard Edition* 23:3–137.

———— (1965). *A Psycho-Analytic Dialogue: the Letters of Sigmund Freud and Karl Abraham, 1907–1926*, ed. H. C. Abraham and E. L. Freud, trans. B. Marsh and H. C. Abraham. New York: Basic Books.

———— (1974). *The Freud/Jung Letters: the Correspondence between Sigmund Freud and C. G. Jung*, ed. W. McGuire, trans. R. Mannheim and R. F. C. Hull. Bollingen Series XCIV. Princeton: Princeton University Press.

Freud, S., and Breuer, J. (1893–1895). Studies on hysteria. *Standard Edition* 2:1–306.

Granoff, W. (1979). *La Pensée et le Féminin*. Paris: Éditions de Minuit.

Granoff, W., and Perrier, F. (1979). *Le Désir et le Féminin*. Paris: Aubier-Montaigne.

Groddeck, G. (1979). *Un Problème de Femme*. Paris: Mazarine.

Horney, K. (1924). On the genesis of the castration complex in women. *International Journal of Psycho-Analysis* 5:50–65.

Jones, E. (1935). Early female sexuality. *International Journal of Psycho-Analysis* 16:263–273.

Klein, M. (1968). *Contributions to Psycho-Analysis (1921–1945)*. London: Hogarth.

Kleist, H. von. (1959). Penthesilea. A. Tragedy. In *The Classic Theatre*, ed. E. Bentley, pp. 313–508. New York: Doubleday Anchor.

Klossowski, P. (1991). *Sade my Neighbor*, trans. A. Lingis. Evanston, IL: Northwestern University Press.

Lacan, J. (1949). The mirror stage as formative of the function of the I as revealed in psychoanalytic experience. In *Jacques Lacan. Ecrits. A Selection*, trans. A. Sheridan, pp. 8–29. New York: Norton, 1977.

———— (1951). Intervention on transference. In *Feminine Sexuality. Jacques Lacan and the École Freudienne*, ed. J. Mitchell and J. Rose, pp. 61–73. New York: Norton, 1985.

———— (1953). The function and field of speech and language in psychoanalysis. In *Jacques Lacan. Ecrits. A Selection*, trans. A. Sheridan, pp. 30–113. New York: Norton, 1977.

———— (1953–1954). *Seminar. Book I. Freud's Papers on Technique*, ed. J.-A. Miller, trans. J. Forrester. New York: Norton, 1977.

———— (1954–1955). *Seminar. Book II. The Ego in Freud's Theory and in the Technique of Psychoanalysis*, ed. J.-A. Miller, trans. S. Tomaselli. New York: Norton, 1991.

——— (1955–1956a). *Seminar. Book III. The Psychoses*, ed. J.-A. Miller, trans. R. Grigg. New York: Norton, 1993.

——— (1955–1956b). On a question preliminary to any possible treatment of psychosis. In *Jacques Lacan. Ecrits. A Selection*, trans. A. Sheridan, pp. 179–221. New York: Norton, 1977.

——— (1957–1958). Seminar V. Les Formations de l'Inconscient. Unpublished.

——— (1958a). The signification of the phallus. In *Jacques Lacan. Ecrits. A Selection*, trans. A. Sheridan, pp. 281–291. New York: Norton, 1977.

——— (1958b). The direction of the treatment and the principles of its power. In *Jacques Lacan. Ecrits. A Selection*, trans. A. Sheridan, pp. 226–280. New York: Norton, 1977.

——— (1958c). Guiding remarks for a congress on feminine sexuality. In *Feminine Sexuality. Jacques Lacan and the École Freudienne*, ed. J. Mitchell and J. Rose, pp. 86–98. New York: Norton, 1985.

——— (1959–1960). *Seminar. Book VII. The Ethics of Psychoanalysis*, ed. J-A. Miller, trans. D. Porter. New York: Norton, 1992.

——— (1960). The subversion of the subject and the dialectic of desire in the Freudian unconscious. In *Jacques Lacan. Ecrits. A Selection*, trans. A. Sheridan, pp. 647–684. New York: Norton, 1977.

——— (1960–1961). *Le Séminaire, VIII. Le transfert dans sa disparité subjective*. Paris: Seuil, 1991.

——— (1961–1962). Le Séminaire, IX. L'Identification. Unpublished.

——— (1964). *Seminar, Book XI. The Four Fundamental Concepts of Psychoanalysis*, ed. J.-A. Miller, trans. A. Sheridan. New York: Norton, 1981.

——— (1966). *Écrits*. Paris: Seuil.

——— (1966–1967). Le Séminaire, XIV. La logique du fantasme. Unpublished.

——— (1971–1972). Le Séminaire, XIX. . . . ou pire. Unpublished.

——— (1972–1973). *The Seminar of Jacques Lacan, Book XX. En-*

core. *On Feminine Sexuality, the Limits of Love, and Knowledge,* ed. J.-A. Miller, trans. B. Fink. New York: Norton.

———— (1973). L'Étourdit. *Scilicet* 4:5–52.

———— (1974). *Télévision.* Paris: Seuil.

———— (1976–1977). Le Séminaire, XXIV. L'Insu que sait de l'Une-bévue s'aile à mourre. *Ornicar?* 12–13:114–118.

———— (1977). *Jacques Lacan. Ecrits. A Selection,* trans. A. Sheridan. New York: Norton.

Lampl-de Groot, J. (1983). *Souffrance et jouisance.* Paris: Aubier-Montaigne.

Lemoine, E. (1976). *Partage des femmes.* Paris: Seuil.

Louÿs, P. (1959). *La femme et le Pantin.* Paris: Albin Michel.

Mannoni, O. (1969). *Clefs pour l'Imaginaire.* Paris: Seuil.

Miller, J.-A. (1982). Symptôme–fantasme. *Actes de l'École de la cause freudienne,* vol. 4, October.

Molière, J.-B. P. (1673). *The Hypochondriac,* trans. M. Sorrell. London: Nick Hern, 1994.

Perrier, F. (1978). Psychanalyse de l'hypochondriaque. *La Chaussée d'Antin,* vol. 1, 10/18.

Plato. *On Homosexuality. Lysias, Phaedrus, and Symposium,* trans. B. Jowett and E. O'Connor. Buffalo, NY: Prometheus, 1991.

Plutarch. *The Rise and Fall of Athens: Nine Greek Lives,* trans. I. Scott. Baltimore: Penguin, 1960.

Reynes, G. (1983). *L'abbé de Choisy ou l'ingénu libertin.* Paris: Presses de la Renaissance.

Rilke, R. M. (1972). La dormeuse. In *Poèmes en langue française. Oeuvres complètes,* tome 2, p. 498. Paris: Seuil.

Rivière, J. (1929). Womanliness as a masquerade. *International Journal of Psycho-Analysis* 10:303–313.

Safouan, M. (1974). *Études sur l'Oedipe.* Paris: Seuil.

Schreber, D. P. (1903). *Memoirs of my Nervous Illness,* ed. and trans. I. Macalpine and R. A. Hunter. London: Dawson, 1955.

Schur, M. (1972). *Freud: Living and Dying.* New York: International Universities Press.

Shakespeare, W. Romeo and Juliet. In *The Riverside Shakespeare*, vol. 5, pp. 241–318. Boston: Houghton Mifflin, 1934.

Sissa, G. (1990). *Greek Virginity*, trans. A. Goldhammer. Cambridge, MA: Harvard University Press.

Sollers, P. (1990). *Women*, trans. B. Bray. New York: Columbia University Press.

Teresa of Avila. *The Complete Works of St. Teresa of Jesus*, trans E. A. Peers. London: Sheed and Wood, 1975.

Index

Also of interest from Other Press . . .

OTHER